Developments in British Politics

Developments in British Politics

Revised and updated

Henry Drucker *General Editor*
Patrick Dunleavy, Andrew Gamble, Gillian Peele *Editors*

MACMILLAN

First edition 1983
Reprinted 1983
Revised edition 1984
Reprinted 1985

Published by
Higher and Further Education Division
MACMILLAN PUBLISHERS LTD
Houndmills, Basingstoke, Hampshire RG21 2XS
and London
Companies and representatives
throughout the world

Printed in Great Britain by
Camelot Press Ltd.,
Southampton

ISBN 0–333–38646–9 (paper cover)
ISBN 0–333–38645–0 (hard cover)

ACKNOWLEDGEMENTS

The authors and publishers wish to thank the following who have kindly given permission for the use of copyright material:

Edward Arnold (Publishers) Ltd for figures by V. Duke and P. Edgell from *International Journal of Urban and Regional Research*.

Cambridge University Press for extracts from tables in the *British Journal of Political Science*, vols 7 (1977) and 12 (1982).

The Economist Newspaper Ltd for data from charts published in *The Economist*, 14 May 1979.

Contents

PART THREE: THE POLITICAL SCIENCE OF BRITISH POLITICS

Preface

This book is the result of unusually thorough discussions among the editors and with Steven Kennedy of Macmillan. I am grateful to them all for their patience and hard work. I am also grateful to the authors, who put up with my stream of late-night telephone calls and cheerfully accepted redrafting suggestions – and deadlines. Rodney Barker, John Bochel, John Bennett (who compiled the index), Paul Crompton, Richard Parry, Patrick Seyd and Adrian Sinfield were immensely helpful. Kathie Brown and Helen Ramm typed and retyped several chapters at impossible speeds.

Comments on this book and suggestions for future editions would be welcome.

The book was revised in the winter of 1983–4 to take account of the 1983 election and other recent events.

Department of Politics
University of Edinburgh
April 1984

Henry Drucker

List of Contributors

Paul Arthur is Senior Lecturer in Politics at Ulster Polytechnic, and author of *Government and Politics of Northern Ireland*.

Nick Bosanquet is Lecturer in Economics at City University, and author of *After the New Right*.

Paul Byrne is Lecturer in Politics at Loughborough University, and author of articles on equal opportunities.

Henry Drucker is Senior Lecturer in Politics at Edinburgh University, and author of *Doctrine and Ethos in the Labour Party*.

Patrick Dunleavy is Lecturer in Government at the London School of Economics, and author of *Urban Political Analysis*.

Andrew Gamble is Reader in Politics at Sheffield University, and author of *Britain in Decline*.

Martin Holmes is Lecturer in Politics at Lady Margaret Hall, Oxford, and author of *Political Pressure and Economic Policy: British Government 1970–74*.

Martin Kettle writes for *The Sunday Times* and is co-author of *Uprising!*

Joni Lovenduski is Senior Lecturer in Politics at Loughborough University, and author of *Women in British Political Studies*.

Peter Nailor is Professor of History and Dean of the Royal Naval College, and author of 'Defence Policy and Foreign Policy' in *The Management of Britain's External Relations*.

Gillian Peele is Fellow and Tutor in Politics at Lady Margaret Hall, Oxford, and co-author of *The Government of the United Kingdom: Political Authority in a Changing Society*.

Raymond Plant is Professor of Politics at Southampton University, and author of *Political Philosophy and Social Welfare*.

R. A. W. Rhodes is Lecturer in Government at Essex University, and author of *Control and Power in Central/Local Relations*.

List of Abbreviations

AES	Alternative Economic Strategy
ASLEF	Associated Society of Locomotive Engineers and Firemen
AUEW	Associated Union of Engineering Workers
BNOC	British National Oil Corporation
CAP	Common Agricultural Policy
CBI	Confederation of British Industry
CLPD	Campaign for Labour Party Democracy
CLPs	Constituency Labour Parties
CLV	Campaign for Labour Victory
CND	Campaign for Nuclear Disarmament
CPRS	Central Policy Review Staff
CSD	Civil Service Department
DAC	Direct Action Committee
DES	Department of Education and Science
DHSS	Department of Health and Social Security
DoE	Department of the Environment
DTp	Department of Transport
EEC	European Economic Community
EMS	European Monetary System
ERA	Equal Rights Amendment
FCO	Foreign and Commonwealth Office
GATT	General Agreement on Tariffs and Trade
GDP	Gross Domestic Product
GLC	Greater London Council
GNP	Gross National Product
GREA	Grant Related Expenditure Assessment
IEA	Institute of Economic Affairs
ILEA	Inner London Education Authority

IMF	International Monetary Fund
INLA	Irish National Liberation Army
IRA	Irish Republican Army
LCC	Labour Co-ordinating Committee
MINIS	Management Information System for Ministers
MoD	Ministry of Defence
MORI	Market & Opinion Research International
MSC	Manpower Services Commission
MTFS	Medium Term Financial Strategy
NATO	North Atlantic Treaty Organisation
NEB	National Enterprise Board
NEC	National Executive Committee
NHS	National Health Service
NIO	Northern Ireland Office
NIRC	National Industrial Relations Court
NM	Nautical Miles (6,076 feet)
NUPE	National Union of Public Employees
NUR	National Union of Railwaymen
OECD	Organisation for Economic Co-operation and Development
OPEC	Organisation of Petroleum Exporting Countries
PAC	Public Accounts Committee
PC	Plaid Cymru
PESC	Public Expenditure Survey Committee
PLP	Parliamentary Labour Party
PSBR	Public Sector Borrowing Requirement
QGA	Quasi-Governmental Agency
QUANGO	Quasi Non-Governmental Organisation, or Quasi National Governmental Organisation
RSL	Revolutionary Socialist League
RUC	Royal Ulster Constabulary
SAS	Special Air Service
SDLP	Social and Democratic Labour Party
SDP	Social Democratic Party
SNP	Scottish National Party
T & GWU	Transport and General Workers' Union
TUC	Trades Union Congress
TULV	Trade Unions for a Labour Victory
UDA	Ulster Defence Association
UDR	Ulster Defence Regiment

UWC   Ulster Workers' Council
WLM   Women's Liberation Movement

Glossary of Terms

accountability Requirement for a public body, or a group of people who receive money from the public purse to account for how they behave. Conventionally many such groups, the police for example, have in effect been accountable to themselves. Many on the left now seek accountability to Parliament or local government.

adversary politics A version of two-party politics in which each party is extremist and each uses government to reverse wholesale the policies of its predecessors.

beer and sandwiches Description of Wilson government's (1964–70) attempts to solve industrial disputes by prolonged negotiations at No. 10 Downing Street involving 'beer and sandwiches' as refreshment.

block grant The unified central grant designed to equalise the resources and spending needs of individual local authorities (*see* GREA). It replaced the rate support grant, which had separate needs, resources and domestic elements. This last element was, in effect, a subsidy to householders and it continues as the 'domestic rate relief grant'.

Cabinet Secretariat The Prime Minister's office of about 100 civil servants, expanded under Wilson to include the Central Statistical Office and Heath to include the Central Policy Review Staff (the 'think tank').

capital expenditure expenditure on assets of some lasting value, usually more than one year. Most commonly it refers to money spent constructing schools, houses, roads, etc. Money for such projects is usually borrowed and the cost of repayment spread over a number of years.

cash limits System of public spending calculations used from 1976–82 in which cash limits are imposed on particular items of public expenditure programmes.

cash planning The post-1981 method of planning of public expenditure which includes the *whole* of a programme, not just some items.

child benefit Cash payment for all children under 16 (or older if at school) usually paid to the mother. Introduced in 1977.

Child Poverty Action Group (CPAG) Pressure group of academics formed in the late 1960s to call attention to the failure of family allowances to keep pace with inflation.

child tax allowances An income-tax relief in respect of each child. Abolished in three stages from 1977 to 1979.

class A major line of division in society. Liberals define class in terms of occupations. Occupations are ordered into a lengthy status hierarchy, and then occupational classes are a simplified version of this hierarchy. Marxists define class in term of positions in a system of production; especially central are labour, ownership of capital and ability to determine one's own work.

class de-alignment A major weakening of the association between occupational class positions and patterns of voting.

clawback Adjustments to the block grant settlement of individual local authorities to reduce the total monies paid by central government in the course of the year.

coalition A government consisting of members of more than one party supported in the House of Commons by MPs of most constituent parties.

Common Agricultural Policy (CAP) The system of intervention prices for agricultural products which prevent prices falling below an agreed level, thus ensuring the protection of high-cost producers and encouraging the production of surpluses that cannot be sold.

community policing Idea that police officers should be known to and identified with the area in which they work and live. Many differing policies claim to be CP (*see* fire-brigade policing).

contingency funds Income which is not allocated to any

specific purpose but reserved to cover unexpected calls on the funds of an authority.

core curriculum Proposal that central government should determine what teachers teach (the core) and examine. An attempt to return to 'basics'.

corporatism The view that government should seek agreement with the representatives of major interest groups over the management of the economy so as to secure their acquiescence in economic policy and to use the interest groups as instruments to carry out government policies.

current expenditure Constant, recurring expenditure on assets with a short life, usually less than one year. Most commonly it refers to money spent on salaries, goods and services and the interest on loans.

de-alignment Where one pattern of voter alignment (say, between class and a party) decays without being replaced by some new basis.

deterrence A doctrine about defence in a nuclear age which holds that safety and peace are best ensured by convincing the Soviet Union that any nuclear attack will be answered in kind – thus deterring it.

devolution Literally, the passing of power to subordinates. Usually, the creation of directly elected assemblies for one or more parts of the United Kingdom (e.g. Northern Ireland or Scotland) to control the domestic government of that part.

direct action Seeking to exert political influence directly, sometimes illegally, rather than through representative institutions.

dries and wets Terms derived from school-child slang commonly used (sometimes affectionately, often critically) to refer to the two factions of the Conservative Party. Dries are more concerned with the long-run effect of policy; wets with immediate pain and dislocation. 'Wet' is sometimes used derisively to refer to an MP who lacks courage or principle.

echelon advance An argument to the effect that if the rich become richer in a market economy, the poor, too, will become relatively richer. The increase in the standard of living will 'trickle down' to all sections of the community.

European Monetary System (EMS)   Established 13 March 1979. It comprises an exchange-rate structure which obliges members to keep their exchange rates within 2.25 per cent of agreed parities, an intervention mechanism and a system of credits. Britain declined to join in 1979.

factions   A part of a political party which, remaining loyal to the whole, tries to move the party close to some principle or other. Factions tend to be long-lasting.

feminism   Advocacy of women's rights in society on the basis of a belief in the equality of the sexes. May involve support for positive discrimination in favour of women in order to bring about equality more quickly.

fire-brigade policing   Idea that police officers should be rushed to actual or potential areas of difficulty to apprehend suspects. Based on an assumption that police cannot effectively prevent crime. The concept involves the use of technology (two-way radios, computers, fast cars) rather than the confidence of ordinary citizens.

free collective bargaining   Ability of unions and employers to bargain freely about wages and conditions of service without, or with minimal, government interference.

Grant Related Expenditure Assessment (GREA)   The demand or need for services varies between local government areas because each area has different numbers of schoolchildren, old people, etc. Taking account of these variations, the government calculates how much money each authority needs to spend for each service in order to provide a common standard of service. The assessments for each service are totalled to give the GREA.

Gross Domestic Product (GDP)   A standard measure of the value of all goods and services produced in a country (slightly narrower definition of wealth than GNP).

Gross National Product (GNP)   A standard measure of the total output of goods and services produced in a given year valued at factor cost (i.e. excluding indirect taxes and subsidies).

Keynesianism   A theory of economic management which dominated both main parties and the Treasury from the end of the Second World War to the mid-1970s. It bid government balance the economy, not the budget, and keep unemployment down by manipulating the level of effective demand by putting money in or taking it out of the economy.

International Monetary Fund (IMF)   Founded in 1945. Industrial nations lend the Fund money which it lends back to them and other governments. Strict controls over a borrower government's economic and social policies are often imposed.

income maintenance   Social security. An attempt to keep a person's or family's income above a certain level. It takes into account all state payments to an individual.

Manpower Services Commission (MSC)   Established in 1974 by Heath government to run employment centres. Is a fast-growing QGA (*which see*). Performs employment and education tasks.

means-tested benefits   State benefits to individuals paid out after taking account of the recipient's own income from all sources. The 'means' tested for many benefits varies with the 'benefit'.

Medium Term Financial Strategy (MTFS)   Introduced in the 1980 budget. It sets targets for the growth of £M_3 (*see* money supply) and published projections for the public sector borrowing requirement (PSBR) (*which also see*).

monetarism   Economic doctrine which asserts a clear relationship between the growth of the money stock and the rate of inflation in the medium term, and argues that the elimination of inflation by strict control of the money supply should be the major priority of policy.

money supply   According to monetarism the key to the control of inflation is the control of the supply of money. The principal definitions are:
1. M_1 – notes and coins in circulation with the public plus sterling current accounts held by the private sector.
2. £M_3 – notes and coins plus all sterling deposits held by UK residents in both public and private sectors.
3. M_3 – equal to £M_3 plus all deposits held by UK residents in other currencies.

National Enterprise Board (NEB)   Established in 1975 and is a QGA. Initial capital of £1 billion, it was intended as a state holding company which would establish state companies in the expanding sectors of the economy. It became part of the British Technology Group in 1980.

neo-liberalism The idea that the state has a very modest role to play in economic life. The state should concern itself with the institutional and procedural preconditions for successful production. It should not seek to direct investment in particular areas, or distort market decisions by inducing investment through tax concessions. The state should not be involved in questions of social justice and distribution.

1922 Committee Of back-bench Conservative MPs. First met in 1922, can exert considerable influence on the front bench.

North Atlantic Treaty Organisation (NATO) The chief Western alliance. Founded in 1949 at the peak of the Cold War it has fifteen member countries. Belgium, Canada, Denmark, France, Iceland, Italy, Luxembourg, the Netherlands, Norway, Portugal, the United Kingdom and the United States were members from the first. Greece and Turkey (both 1952) and the Federal German Republic (1955) were subsequently admitted. France and Iceland (which has no military forces) do not play a full role.

Organisation for Economic Co-operation and Development (OECD) The industrialised nations of the West: Australia, Austria, Belgium, Canada, Denmark, the German Federal Republic, Finland, France, Greece, Iceland, Ireland, Italy, Japan, Luxembourg, the Netherlands, New Zealand, Norway, Portugal, Spain, Sweden, Switzerland, Turkey, the United Kingdom and the United States. Acts to promote the economic and social well-being of the members and their citizens and to harmonise their relations with the developing countries.

Organisation of Petroleum Exporting Countries (OPEC) Founded in 1960 by countries largely dependent on the export of oil to earn foreign exchange. Tries to regulate the market for petroleum in their interest. Members: Algeria, Ecuador, Gabon, Indonesia, Iran, Iraq, Kuwait, Libya, Nigeria, Qatar, Saudi Arabia, the United Arab Emirates, Venezuela. Britain, though a net petroleum-exporting country, is not a member.

partisan de-alignment A weakening association between voters' choice of party and their views on major political issues.

party government As opposed to pressure group, civil service domination or direct government. The practice of parties, victorious at elections, trying to govern without support in the House of Commons from other parties, in line with their election promises.

peace movement A collection of mainly local groups, committed to unilateral disarmament, with the Campaign for Nuclear Disarmament (CND) acting as a national umbrella organisation.

permeation The view of political change held by leading members of the Fabian Society. Political change was to be introduced by the permeation of socialist ideas among the elite.

Polaris A submarine which carries sixteen nuclear weapon-carrying missiles; each missile has a range of 2,500 nautical miles and carries three warheads. Britain's Polaris submarines were commissioned in 1967–9.

privatisation (1) The sale of public assets, e.g. the share of public corporations like Amersham or British Telecom. (2) The contracting out of certain public services to private companies. (3) The setting up of private companies to compete with state corporations.

public sector borrowing requirement (PSBR) The difference between expenditure and revenue for the whole public sector. A main aim of monetarist (*which see*) policies was to reduce this figure.

quasi-governmental agency (QGA) A public body whose controlling board is appointed by the government to carry out a single function. Often known as a QUANGO (which name is confusing).

rates The local property tax levied on the value of a property and paid by the occupier of that property. Different classes of property (domestic and commercial) are valued differently, and some (agricultural land and buildings) not at all.

referendum A ballot of citizens on an issue of public policy. In Britain referendums are usually not binding. For example, one was held with respect to Britain's membership of the EEC in 1975.

revenue expenditure *See* current expenditure.

revisionism The term used for socialist and social democratic critiques of Marx. It was first used to describe Edmund Bernstein's critique of Marxism, *Evolutionary Socialism*. By the 1950s it had come to be used to identify the Gaitskellite wing of the Labour Party who were anxious to move the party away from class-based politics and from large-scale commitments to nationalisation.

Royal Commission on Criminal Procedure Inquiry set up by the Callaghan government under the chairmanship of Sir Cyril Philips to examine police powers in the criminal process up to the start of a trial. Reported in 1981. The basis of legislation in 1983.

Social Contract Agreement between unions and the Labour government of 1974–9 that in return for union wage restraint the government would legislate to extend trade-union powers.

social limits to growth The view associated with Fred Hirsch that certain kinds of goods are inherently scarce because the more widely they are distributed, the less value they have. Power and education are examples.

social protest movement A group which advocates fundamental changes in public policy and/or political institutions, but does not seek political office.

Special Air Service (SAS) Created during Second World War. Brought into Ulster by the government in 1976 to help defeat terrorists in the border areas. Its undercover operations raised tensions among Ulster Catholics.

Special Patrol Group Elite crime-busting squad set up by Scotland Yard in 1965 with its own separate structure answerable directly to the Commissioner. Much copied by other British forces and hugely demonologised. The SPG was involved in the killing of Blair Peach.

'special relationship' Between the United States and the United Kingdom. Supposed to link the two English-speaking powers closer to each other than to third parties. Unheard of in the United States!

statism The view that the state has a duty to intervene in and manage the economy with the intention of securing a particular set of social and economic priorities.

supplementary benefit   Payments by the state to heads of households who do not have full-time work and whose 'needs' exceed their income.

Think tank (CPRS) was a small body of advisors established in 1970 by the Heath Government to aid long-term planning and policy development. Its first head was Lord Rothschild and it consisted of individuals recruited from outside the civil service. After Lord Rothschild's departure its functions became unclear and it was abolished in 1983.

trading services   Those local authority services for which a charge is made to the consumer. They are expected to generate enough revenue to meet their outgoings and include passenger transport, cemeteries and crematoria, harbours, docks and piers, restaurants, markets and slaughter houses, airports. Council-house rents are the main source of such revenues but differ from the foregoing services in that the income can only be credited to the housing revenue account and not to the general rate fund.

Trident   Submarine system planned to replace Polaris. Each carries sixteen missiles and each missile carries up to fourteen warheads. The missiles have a range of 6,000 nautical miles.

tripartite talks   Discussions between the TUC, CBI and government aimed at finding agreement on a voluntary incomes policy. They were most fashionable under the Heath government.

two-party system   Electoral and parliamentary dominance by two large parties each of which reasonably expects to form a government without help from any minor party after each election. Apparent in the United Kingdom from 1945 to 1974 and important features of it are still present.

Ulster Defence Association   The largest Protestant paramilitary organisation. Formed in September 1971, at its peak it probably had 40,000 members. By 1982 it probably had no more than 12,000. In recent years its leadership has been moving towards Ulster independence.

Ulster Defence Regiment (UDR)   Locally raised, and a largely part-time force, it began operations in April 1970. It is under the control of the British army and is open to all religions, but perhaps no more than 3 per cent of its membership is Catholic. It serves as a back-up force for the British army.

unilateralism   Action, such as disposing of nuclear arms, which affects or is binding upon only one party or country.

volatility   The frequency and extent to which people change their votes or views on issues. Has been increasing in recent years.

volume targets   The desired level of public expenditure expressed in constant-price terms. For local authorities the base year for 1981–2 targets was the 1978–9 actual expenditure repriced at November 1980 prices.

'winter of discontent'   Wave of strikes in the public and private sectors in the winter of 1978–9 which destroyed the Callaghan government's 5 per cent pay policy.

Zimbabwe   Formerly Rhodesia. Country in southern Africa whose white rulers, led by Ian Smith, unilaterally declared independence from Britain in 1965. Granted formal independence after prolonged war in 1979.

Introduction

British politics in the 1980s differ from British politics in the 1960s and early 1970s in surprising and fundamental ways. We have seen the revival of ideological debate; the weakening of the two-party system; the assertion of strong political control over the machinery of central government; an attempt by central government to overrule local government while blaming many ills on autonomous local decisions; the re-emergence of defence policy at the centre of the political stage; political controversy about the role of the police; a dizzying increase, apparently without political cost, in the rate of unemployment; and the eclipse of the trade-union movement, with a consequent reversal of the movement to corporatism. Partly as a result of these developments, the study of British politics has become more dynamic and diverse.

This book seeks to chart, examine, and explain these changes. It is designed primarily as a text for first-year university and polytechnic students but should prove equally useful to second-and third-year students, to teachers of politics at 'A' level and even to interested general readers. We have tried, above all, to stimulate thought and discussion about recent events and ideas which might not be treated in conventional textbooks. In this way it is intended to supplement them. Each chapter is written by an authority on the subject. While the authors are diverse, all have shared an objective: to make important changes in their specialities accessible to students. For this reason the chapters have been more extensively edited than is normal in a book of this kind. The authors have written on the assumption that readers will have no previous knowledge of the material, and hence have striven for clear, non-technical English.

The book has three main parts. The first contains eight chapters on the topics which all students of British politics have long needed to consider. The second part consists of four, shorter, chapters on developments which have come more recently to demand attention. The third part is a single chapter that offers a student's guide to the political science of British politics.

Some senior members of all parties are debating the proper scope of the state. In Chapter 1, Raymond Plant traces the lineage of neo-liberalism and Marxism and shows how political leaders are seeking to transform these ideas into practice. In Chapter 2, Patrick Dunleavy examines the ways in which the ideas and ideologies of politicians are influencing the now volatile electorate, and how social factors, such as home ownership and trade-union membership, influence the way people vote. The flexibility of voters has been matched and even exceeded by the parties. In Chapter 3, Henry Drucker discusses the growth of factions within the parties which led, in the extreme case, to the breaking away from Labour of the Social Democrats, and argues that this has assisted a revival in the importance of Parliament. In Chapter 4, Gillian Peele places the centralising trends which might lead to the creation of something like presidential government, into the context of the wider changes in British government. Chapter 5, 'Beyond Whitehall', is about the conflict between central and local government. R.A.W. Rhodes and Patrick Dunleavy argue that, although central government needs local government to administer public services, it has changed the rules of the relationship between them so frequently and unilaterally that it is breaking down.

Thus the first five chapters of Part One review British political ideology, voting patterns, the parties and Parliament, and the machinery of government. Its final three chapters discuss the product of this machinery: the main policies of government. Economic policy has become the central concern of every government. Andrew Gamble shows how, since 1979, under the impact of recession and ideological polarisation, economic policy has become overwhelmingly concerned with controlling inflation and, secondarily, with 'privatising' large parts of the public sector. This is a tribute to the power of ideology. But can it last in the face of such high rates of unemployment? The consequences, intended or not, of economic strategies overflow into social policy as both the Labour government of 1974–79 and the succeeding Conservative government discovered. Nick Bosanquet shows that the efforts of professionals and pressure groups within the social services have been knocked sideways by the backwash of economic policies. This is not to argue that governments get the social policies they want or those their ideologies promise, or, even less likely, that services will improve. Foreign and defence policies, marginalised for much of the post-war era, have re-emerged to centre stage. Peter Nailor discusses the strain this has put on the Foreign and Commonwealth Office and the difficulties of adjusting to increased popular concern with nuclear weaponry, the Falklands conflict, and membership of the European Community.

A book about developments in British politics requires a section on changes which lie in areas outside the normal curriculum. Institutions and issues which are not part of that curriculum can rise suddenly to importance and then drop away. Devolution is a case in point. Part Two is designed to cope with this fluidity. Martin Kettle's summary of the recent rapid changes in the relationship between the police and governments is covered in Chapter 9. He points to the collapse of the consensus after the uprisings of the summer of 1981, and the uncertainty this collapse has caused. In Chapter 10, Martin Holmes carefully outlines how the Conservative government, elected in 1979, has pulled the teeth of the trade-union tiger and of tripartite economic policy-making at the same time; he argues that the lack of a formal incomes policy is the key. At the other end of the 'pressure-group' spectrum stand the protest movements. In Chapter 11, Paul Byrne and Joni Lovenduski explain how the informally structured peace and women's movements have tried to take advantage of the rising public protest for their causes. Finally, in Chapter 12, Paul Arthur places the recent hunger strikes and Assembly elections in Northern Ireland in the context of British and Irish government. Our choice of subjects in Part Two has been restricted. Given more space we would have happily included others. Some discussion of the recent and forthcoming changes in both the press and in broadcasting would have been helpful. Another reluctant omission is a paper dealing with politics and ethnic minorities. In future editions we would hope to rectify these omissions.

Textbooks can be coy about their own perspectives and we have tried, in two ways, to avoid this. First, we have deliberately gone out of our way to bring together authors of different political and academic persuasions. While we have worked to make the book a coherent collection of interlocking chapters, there has been no attempt to hide differences of emphasis and opinion. Second, we have, in Patrick Dunleavy's Chapter 13, made an express attempt to give a summarised view of the different theories about British politics. Each of the main areas of the discipline is discussed in turn and the major contending schools presented. Chapter 13 will provide students with accessible guidance to current disputes.

This book aims to fill a gap between the newspapers and the conventional textbook, but it lacks two of the newspaper's advantages. First, it cannot be precisely up to date. If Thatcher calls an election between the submission of the manuscript and publication, we will be sure that she has done so largely to embarrass us! Second, our authors, unlike the journalists in a newspaper, do not have a common starting-point. Today's newspaper covers events since yesterday's last edition, while the different issues and institutions discussed here have different time-scales. The chapters on economic, social and foreign policy compare the action of the Labour government between 1974 and 1979 with those of the subsequent Conservative administration. However, the chapter on the electorate needs to go further back to explain what has changed, while the chapter on the police is almost wholly concerned with events since the summer of 1981. These are the time-scales relevant to the subjects.

The book concludes with an annotated bibliography for each chapter a glossary and an index of names and subjects.

Henry Drucker, Patrick Dunleavy, Andrew Gamble,
Gillian Peele

PART ONE
The Constants

1

The Resurgence of Ideology

RAYMOND PLANT

End of Consensus

British politics have in the last ten years been marked by a considerable revival of ideological argument about fundamental political values and principles. While it is of course true that differences between political parties have been profound, nevertheless most commentators have tended to argue that from the late 1940s to the early 1970s there was a consensus about the fundamental parameters of the post-war political settlement: an acceptance of the welfare state, the mixed economy managed by Keynesian techniques, a duty on the government to secure 'full' employment, combined with low rates of inflation, and economic growth. Of course, within this broad 'Butskellite' consensus (a term of art combining the name of Hugh Gaitskell, Chancellor of the Exchequer in the Labour government of 1951 and R. A. Butler, Chancellor in the subsequent Conservative government) parties had different priorities: Labour seeking to extend the services of the welfare state and the boundaries of the public sector, the Conservatives placing more emphasis on private consumption rather than public expenditure and the 'social wage'. In specific fields of policy differences were very marked. The Conservatives, for example, in the sphere of education supported a meritocratic grammar-school system in pursuit of equality of opportunity, whereas the Labour Party when in power from 1964 sought to secure comprehensive, non-selective education as a road to a much more substantive view of equality. Nevertheless, the broad outlines of the post-war political settlement seem to have been accepted, so much so that academic commentators were tempted to refer to an 'end of ideology' not just in Britain but in the Western world generally. This consensus and its apparent success in the 1950s and 1960s rendered very marginal both Marxism and economic liberalism, which, in the harsh world of the 1970s and 1980s, have become more potent political forces. Political debate might still have been sharp but it was taking place within the basic commitments outlined above.

However, during the 1970s a marked change came over the political climate, the consequences of which are only now becoming fully apparent. Those changes tend to concentrate in the end on the role of the state in modern society. The Butskellite period tended to presuppose a statist view. The state had a duty to secure welfare, full employment and low rates of inflation and thus had an enduring role in economic management and social intervention within a mixed economy and a pluralist society. However, the preconditions that enabled this consensus to operate without too much strain seem to have broken down, though exactly why they have is a matter of sharp political controversy. Two things seem clear, nevertheless. In the first place the state's increasing role in welfare, seeking to promote equality and social justice, have meant an increasing public sector in the economy and an incrementally increasing level of public expenditure financed by taxation of the private sector and by government borrowing, *and* this type of state activity has now become part of the very process whereby state activity has been legitimated. The state is expected by citizens to play this kind of role. However, an increasing public sector within a mixed economy has caused problems for the privately incorporated sector of that economy. In that sector of the economy profitability and capital accumulation are necessary.

During the 1950s and 1960s governments seemed by and large to be able to satisfy the imperatives both to secure public welfare and greater social justice with the higher social spending which these entail, while at the same time securing, broadly speaking, the profitability of the private sector of the economy. Second, economic growth, although relatively very slow in the UK, was a central factor in maintaining the equilibrium between the private and the public sectors and meeting rising expenditure. Problems of achieving growth for anything like a sustained period has exacerbated social tensions. Growth acts as a solvent to distributional problems either by holding out the promise that what an affluent minority consume today will be available to all tomorrow – the 'echelon advance' view of growth endorsed by Hayek in *The Constitution of Liberty* (1957) – or more radically the claim that growth will act as an equalising force in society enabling the fiscal dividend of growth to secure the absolute living standards of the better off while increasing the relative position of the worst off – levelling up and not levelling down (the view endorsed by Crosland in *The Future of Socialism* (1956), and in 'A Social Democratic Britain' (1974).

The limits to growth, both natural and social (on which see Hirsch, 1976), have posed a central problem for any kind of government which seeks to improve social justice and to promote shares for all by non-coercive methods. A static or diminishing national cake exacerbates tensions over who is getting what and how. Growth secured profitability for private industry and provided a fiscal dividend to help finance the public sector. However, difficulties in securing sustained growth during the past decade have exacerbated the tension between the two imperatives on governments both to secure increasing welfare and social justice, critical to its legitimacy and the profitability of private industry in a mixed economy, crucial to financing the public sector without the inflationary effects of increasing public borrowing from banks and financial houses.

This growing tension has led to demands from the Right to begin to restrict, cut back and even to abolish altogether the state's role in welfare, a policy which has its intellectual roots in the work of Milton Friedman and F. A. Hayek, whose work was a major influence on the recasting of Conservative policy in the period 1974–9. Certainly the extrication of the state from this kind of activity is one possible, and radical, response to the problem described above and might be called the neo-liberal solution, the details of which will be discussed later in the chapter. The difficulty involved in pursuing this goal is equally obvious. Citizens have come to expect the state to play a role in this sphere, and it is very difficult to see after a generation and a half's activity in this field how governments can extricate themselves from the expectations which have been built up.

The response on the Left to the crisis is equally radical and would consist in greatly reducing the private sector of industry and thus the need to secure the condition for capital accumulation which increasing public-sector spending threatens. The two responses are opposites: the tension between private accumulation and public spending is to be reduced on the Right by radically reducing the state's role, and on the Left by reducing the role of private accumulation in the economy. The difficulty with the radical left-wing approach also mirrors the problem of the Right: is the reduction of the private part of the 'mix' that constitutes the mixed economy likely to secure consent given the consequences which it would have for pluralism and individual liberty in the British context? In addition, granted that the policy of the Left is to increase public spending, this would seem to require faster rates of economic growth irrespective of whether the productive sector is in private or public hands.

The political centre is faced with the question of how far the two imperatives of securing welfare and social justice with a mixed economy can be reconciled in a harsher international economic climate when the prospects for economic growth are poor and when the demands on public expenditure, in the context of high unemployment, an ageing population and general expectations in this field, seem likely to grow rather than diminish.

The role of the state in recent British politics has also come under attack by Left and Right for other reasons which have also led to the problem of the state being put more clearly at the centre of the political agenda. There has been strong criticism from both the Left and the Right, though for different reasons, of the supposed growing corporatism of British politics. The issue at stake here is the growing tendency of British governments, from the time of the Macmillan government's establishment of the National Economic Development Council, the National Plan period of the Wilson government, but carried much further during the Heath government of 1971–4 and the Social Contract period of the 1974–6 Wilson government, to seek to incorporate organised sections of industry and labour, particularly the TUC and CBI, in economic decision-making and for government to operate through Quangos in the economic and social fields. Government agreements with TUC and CBI over the direction of economic policy, prices, incomes, levels of investment, etc., are thought by the radical Right to be dangerous for a number of reasons, some political, some constitutional. The political reason is fairly obvious. Arrangements reached between interest groups in the field of economic management are thought to emphasise an overly collectivist view of the role of the state which in the view of the radical Right should have no role in attempting to reach a consensus about prices, incomes and investment which should be left to the market mechanism. Failure to do so is likely to distort the economy and the labour market, usurping the function of management in the sphere of investment and to be a threat to individual freedom and initiative.

The constitutional objection is also clear. In so far as agreements about the broad issues of economic management are agreed by tripartite arrangements between government, the CBI and the TUC, Parliament is bypassed and presented with a policy which becomes a *fait accompli*. The role of Parliament as the 'forum of the nation' is bypassed by arrangements which are made in a non-democratic way by corporate interest groups. Thatcher's government has certainly been persistent in keeping both the CBI and the TUC out of economic policy-making.

The disagreement with this kind of corporatism on the Left is fundamental. It is argued that, in so far as TUC leaders reach agreements with governments, particularly over incomes policy, as they did with the Wilson government in 1976, in the context of an economy which is *not* being planned on socialist lines, the leaders of the TUC betray the interests of their members. In a mixed economy in which market prices play an important if not dominant role unions should pursue free collective bargaining in order to secure their members' interests. Incomes policies which are agreed between union leaders and governments outside a socialist society betray, on this view, the objective interests of members.

In addition to the objection that the incremental statism of the post-war political settlement has accentuated corporatist tendencies in British politics, there is also the view that statism has displaced other important political and social values. On the Right these values are seen largely in terms of personal freedom and individual responsibility. Insofar as the state takes increasing responsibility for welfare and education, it decreases both the ranges of choice open to individuals to make their own arrangements in these spheres and also diminishes the proper range of personal responsibility. If the state continually acts as a safety-net in both the economic and social spheres, individuals become freed of responsibility and as a consequence act irresponsibly. For example, in the economic sphere, if the state rescues industries which have priced themselves out of markets, is there any incentive for workers and managements to take full responsibility for their actions whether in the sphere of wage claims or investment discussions? In the sphere of welfare, if the state provides, free at the point of delivery, a full range of personal social services, for example to the aged, this decreases the sense of responsibility which children have to care for and provide for aged and infirm people. In addition, recipients of state benefits become transformed from active citizens, freely choosing their way of life, into clients of state bureaucracies, their standard of living and well-being becoming a matter of discretion of the welfare bureaucracies and social workers. Expectations of state provision in these fields lead to a decline in personal responsibility and stifles individual initiative.

Resurgent Ideology

We have seen, therefore, that a central feature of modern British political life has been the extent of disenchantment – across the political spectrum – with the post-war political settlement and the role of the state within it. This is partly the result of intellectual change – the influence of neo-liberal ideas from Hayek, Friedman, Popper and others on the Right and various forms of updated Marxism on the Left – but it is also equally due to the fact that the settlement has become unstable for the reasons which I have tried to outline. Those who proclaimed the end of ideology in the late 1950s and 1960s were profoundly mistaken. The crisis of the modern state has led to a resurgence of ideological politics which makes it difficult to imagine that there could be any easy return to the efficient management of the mixed economy and the welfare state by a benevolent centralised state. Having tried to identify what I take to be the fundamental causes and features of the resurrection of ideological politics, I shall now turn to the intellectual changes which have occurred within political parties.

CONSERVATIVE IDEOLOGY

I am a minimalist. It is the function of government to remove specified causes of unhappiness. But government cannot create happiness and they cannot create wealth ... I am a nineteenth century Liberal. So is Mrs Thatcher. That's what this government is all about. (John Nott, *The Guardian*, 13 September 1982).

The thing that people do not recognise is that Margaret Thatcher is not in terms of belief a Tory. She is a nineteenth century Liberal. But her party consists largely of Tories. They don't really believe in free markets. They don't believe in free trade. They never have as a party. (Milton Friedman, *The Observer*, 26 September 1982).

Neo-liberalism. The Conservative government came to power in 1979 with the intention of pursuing a vigorous policy of restricting the role of the state in economic management, a commitment to increasing the role of market forces in the economy and as far as possible within the public sector, and too, economic liberalism and deregulation. A good many of these policies mirrored those developed nearly a decade earlier under

Heath's leadership; they were known as the Selsdon policies (after the name of the Surrey hotel where they were ratified by the then Conservative Shadow Cabinet). However, Heath effectively abandoned these policies with his famous 'U' turn after the collapse of Rolls-Royce, and the increasing unemployment of 1972. His policy then became much more interventionist and he sought to involve the CBI and TUC much more in economic decision-making. He also operated a detailed prices and incomes policy. Some of these policies were deeply unpopular among Conservatives on several grounds: the state assumed too large a role in economic activity, the attempt to incorporate the CBI and the TUC in the making of economic policy seemed to be both corporatist and anti-libertarian; and lowered the status of Parliament. Sir Keith Joseph was an early critic of these developments, and in a number of speeches after the 1974 defeat argued that the party had become corrupted by a kind of socialism. This critique obviously struck a deep chord within the party and the works of IEA economists, and of Hayek and Friedman, became very influential. The IEA – the Institute of Economic Affairs – has regularly published pamphlets on all aspects of social and public policy emphasising an economic liberal line; particularly important publications have been Seldon's *Charge* (1978) and S. Brittan's *Government and the Market Economy* (1971), together with the same author's *Participation without Politics* (1976). Many of these rather academic ideas have been popularised by the Centre for Policy Studies, funded by Joseph and Thatcher, which has sponsored the publication of *Why Britain Needs a Social Market Economy* (1975) and various papers by Joseph himself, particularly *Reversing the Trend* (1975) and *Stranded in the Middle Ground* (1976). Within the Conservative Party the chief pressure group for undiluted economic liberalism has been the Selsdon Group who take the view that economic liberalism and political freedom are indivisible. As they argue:

> The basic principle upon which Conservative policies should rest is that what the public wants should be provided by the market and paid for by the people as consumers rather than tax payers ... The function of government should not be to provide services, but to

maintain the framework within which markets operate. (*A Second Selsdon Group Manifesto*, 1977, p. 3)

Although the term 'monetarist' strictly speaking denotes someone who is convinced that the role of the money supply is the central determinant of inflation (and therefore the government, by printing money, has the major responsibility in the causation of inflation), the term has nevertheless come to encompass more or less the whole range of government policy: the running of the economy on a much more market-oriented basis, the privatisation as far as practicable of nationalised assets, a progressive reduction in the percentage of GNP consumed in the public sector, the abolition of exchange controls, the weakening of what is seen as the monopoly power of the unions in order to make market forces work more effectively, an attempt to encourage private activity in the sphere of health, education and welfare, the reinforcing of inequality through the tax system (a view which fits into Keith Joseph's rejection of equality: see Joseph, 1978), keeping the CBI and TUC out of economic policy-making, and a vigorous onslaught on Quangos.

Government policy, not very concerned with the politics of *distribution* but a great deal with the political conditions of *successful production*, has been seen as a form of neo-liberalism, and Professors Hayek and Friedman have been regarded as the neo-liberal mentors of the government. Patrick Cosgrave in *Margaret Thatcher* (1978) and Robert Behrens in *The Conservative Party from Heath to Thatcher* (1979) have both chronicled and emphasised the importance particularly of Hayek's general political philosophy on Thatcher, and if we are fully to understand the nature of the political debate in the Conservative Party it will be necessary to say a little about this perspective. Hayek's most influential political works are *The Road to Serfdom* (1944) the *Constitution of Liberty* (1957) and *Law, Legislation and Liberty* (1976).

Perhaps the basic principle lying behind these complex books is the view that it is not the duty of the government to seek to implement any particular conception of the good life, whether this is seen in terms of social justice, equality, or some specific conception of human happiness. We have no way of establishing or grounding particular conceptions of the good and a government does not treat its citizens equally, if it prefers one conception of the good over others, because individual citizens will differ in their view of the good. Individuals should as far as possible be allowed to pursue their own good in their own way. The only genuine public good is the framework of order and law which enables an individual to pursue his or her own good and not be coerced by others. This form of libertarianism applies also to the economic sphere. The government should not pursue substantive economic policies other than those which will secure the maximum freedom for individual economic actors to act on what they take to be their best economic interests. The preferences, desires, interests of individuals are basic and incorrigible. It is wrong for a government to seek a particular economic settlement which goes beyond the revealed desires, interests and preferences of individuals. Individuals, with their preferences, responding to market prices, undistorted by government action, are in the very best position to determine what is in their interest and to take responsibility for choices once made.

This view is combined with a theory about the particular nature of the complexity of society such that in Hayek's view it is logically impossible for a government to plan an economy because the kind of knowledge required of individual preferences and prices is just not available. Hayek's theory is strongly individualist and he rejects the view that social 'wholes' such as the state or the community have any genuine meaning or significance, certainly not any that would sanction the sacrifice of individual freedom. There are only individuals in indefinitely complex relations, and responses to market prices, to supply and demand, are the least coercive ways in which these relationships can be organised. It is certainly not the duty of the state to seek social justice, and any attempt to do so will require a form of bureaucratic planning which is likely to turn citizens into serfs, into clients of the state. We have no agreed criteria of social justice whether in terms of merit or need, or within these alternatives what sorts of merit or what types of need. A welfare system which seeks social justice is therefore a basic affront to individual freedom for Hayek and would require the imposition by the state of a substantive view of the good.

In pursuit of this theory Hayek seeks to weaken the hold of the idea that the poor, and the deprived, those groups in society which in his view preoccupy socialists and social democrats, are suffering from injustice. If they were, there would be a strict duty, a duty of justice for the state to rectify their condition. The poor and the deprived would in their turn have a right to have their condition remedied. Such is in fact the fundamental basis of the argument in favour of welfare rights of various sorts. However, in Hayek's view someone can be said to suffer an injustice only if the individual's position is the result of an intentional process. However, the differential rewards which are distributed through market transactions are not *intentional*:

> We do cry out against the injustice when a succession of calamaties befalls one family while another steadily prospers, when meritorious effort is frustrated by some unforeseeable accident and particularly if, of many people whose endeavours seem equally great, some succeed brilliantly while others utterly fail ... And we will protest against such a fate although we do not know anyone who is to blame for it or any ways in which such disappointments can be prevented ... It is no different with regard to the general feeling of injustice about the distribution of material goods in a society of freemen. Though we are in this case less ready to admit it, our complaints about the outcome of the market as unjust do not usually assert that somebody has been unjust; and there is no answer to the question of who has been unjust. Society has simply become the new deity to which we complain and clamour for redress if it does not fulfil the expectations it has created. (Hayek, 1976, p. 68)

The practical political consequences of this in Hayek's view is that the state becomes the focus of resentments and tension on the part of those who are less successful in the market. The state becomes the object of group and individual resentments. However, this is illegitimate, it is not the duty of the state to secure any particular socio-economic position of any particular individual. There is no moral basis for such claims and any attempt to secure social justice imposes a particular conception of morality and will lead to a freedom-threatening form of bureaucracy. The only possible solution is to remove the state as far as possible from the distributive arena and to endorse the quasi-naturalistic outcomes of the market as in principle unjustifiable. On this view the state may have a duty in humanity to relieve basic or absolute poverty and destitution but it does not have a duty to secure the social and economic position of any particular individual.

This is not to say that the Hayekian view is indifferent to poverty, rather it is a central aspect of the theory that markets unconstrained by regulations other than the general constraints of law and order, contract-keeping, etc., will in fact increase the standard of living of all more effectively than any form of socialist planning.

'One-nation' Conservatism. While of course it would be absurd to suggest that modern Conservative policy is concerned to implement this kind of doctrine as a complete ideological system, nevertheless it does provide the background of neo-liberal theory which has had an important effect on modern policy. However, there are many qualifications which have to be made to this story to provide a fuller account of modern Conservative politics. In the view of Conservative critics of the influence of neo-liberalism such as Sir Ian Gilmour the theory as it stands contains a number of defects. In the first place, and perhaps most fundamental, is the criticism that there is something profoundly unconservative about a Tory government pursuing a particular set of ideological commitments. Critics of this type tend to cite the importance within the Conservative position of the emphasis upon tradition, and politics as a tentative, sceptical attempt to modify a particular tradition of political life to changing circumstances. This sceptical, pragmatic, traditional view of the nature of politics is, on this view, a surer guide to political action rather than commitment to general theories of which neo-liberalism would be one.

In addition, Conservative critics of neo-liberalism, as Friedman acknowledges in the passage cited earlier, are not prepared to elevate market relationships above tradition and the morality embodied in such a tradition. Put rather abstractly the point is this: can a market order of the sort which Hayek and Friedman endorse secure the loyalty and commitment of citizens? Surely, the argument goes, a market order in which individual positions to a very large extent depend upon luck is not going to be able to inspire citizens, particularly in the light of the differences or large inequalities that are likely to result. The 'one-nation' conception of conservatism, which is often invoked by Conservative critics of neo-liberal monetarism, is very concerned about the effects which a rigorous market order would have on the maintenance of social solidarity and the basis of political community. This point has been made particularly vigorously by Ian Gilmour, perhaps the most fervent advocate of the one-nation approach to Tory policies now best represented in the Tory Party by the Tory Reform Group. In *Inside Right* Gilmour argues as follows:

> if people are not to be seduced by other attractions, they must at least feel loyalty to the State. This loyalty will not be deep unless they gain from the State protection and other benefits. Homilies to cherish competition and warnings against interference with market forces will not engender loyalty ... Complete economic freedom is not therefore an insurance of political freedom: indeed it can undermine political freedom. Economic liberalism because of its starkness and its failure to create a sense of community is likely to repel people from the rest of liberalism. (Gilmour, 1978, p. 118)

The neo-liberals try to remove as far as possible the task of social choice away from the sphere of parties and government and onto the market. By narrowing the sphere of government, to evade the problem of overload, the neo-liberals seek to enhance the legitimacy of the choices that the state, more narrowly conceived, does in fact make.

The older Tory tradition is far less critical of the modest collectivism, corporatism and elite management of the economy which was more characteristic of the Macmillan and Heath years. This tension between neo-liberal and high Tory views of the legitimate sphere of state activity has yet to be fully worked out, but the major difficulty of the neo-liberal view is to mobilise consent for the massive switch from social or public choice to market choice; the response engendered by the CPRS report on the proposed privatisation of the NHS and educational system seems to make it really rather unlikely that such consent can be mobilised. At the same time, it would be a mistake to regard the importance of neo-liberalism as being somehow imposed on an unwilling country. There does seem to be some empirical evidence for a popular reaction against some of the basic tenets of the social-democratic post-war political settlement – particularly the bureaucracy of the modern state, high taxation and increasing public expenditure (Crewe *et al.*, 1977, pp. 150–2). The modern Conservative Party is both responding to and adding stimulus to this public mood.

LABOUR IDEOLOGY

So far I have argued that underlying the ideological conflicts of modern British politics is a dispute about the nature of the state and its role in modern society and this is equally true of theories on the Left of the political spectrum. There are a number of strands to the left-wing critique of the role of the state and in a way they mirror the neo-liberal/Conservative critique. It is widely held on the Left as on the Right that the post-war political settlement has been decisively undermined and that the relationship between the public and private sector has become unstable. However, the solution is radically different: instead of reducing the role of the state in an effort to make its activities more legitimate and to make the private sector more profitable, the socialist view is to extend the role of the state into the private sector through proposals for large-scale nationalisation in order to harness industry to social priorities and social needs rather than private profit and private accumulation. However, the Labour Party and its current programme is not in any sense reverting to the kind of policies characteristic of the 1964–70 and 1974–9 Labour governments and it is worth explaining the reasons for this.

Marxism and revisionism. There has been a considerable growth in the influence of a Marxist, class-based analysis of British politics in the Labour Party over the past ten years. This analysis has developed out of a critique of what is seen as the rather timid repercussions of the Wilson and Callaghan governments and their failure to make sufficient impact upon the structure of inequality, relative poverty, the structures of power and the class system of British society and to pursue radical economic and foreign policies. On this view, the democratic socialism best summed up in Anthony Crosland's *The Future of Socialism* (1956), is dead. Croslandism, which is taken to provide much of the intellectual background to policy during the recent Labour administrations, was based upon over-optimistic assumptions about the levels of economic growth which could be sustained, a faulty analysis of capitalist society and the class relations found within it and the lack of an adequate understanding and theory of the state.

The Crosland position defines socialism in distributive terms, in terms of equality and social justice rather than in terms of the ownership of the means of production – the view which is characteristic of Marxism. Central to the strategy of securing what Crosland called, following the American philosopher John Rawls, 'democratic equality', meaning much more than equality of opportunity, was the attainment of consistent and high levels of economic growth. In Crosland's view economic growth pointed the way to the easiest, although not necessarily the only, way in which greater equality could be attained in a democratic society, because the fiscal dividend of growth could be used to improve the relative economic position of the worst off while at the same time maintaining the absolute standard of the better off. Without growth, an egalitarian strategy would have to be much more coercive and would be much more productive of social tensions. However, such rates of growth have not been sustained in the British economy and large-scale inequalities still persist.

It was also central to Crosland's thesis in *The Future of Socialism*, and this has a bearing on the previous point, that capitalism had changed fundamentally during the Second World War and during the 1940s and 1950s. The power of the unions had grown to countervail that of the owners of capital. Ownership had become diversified and in that respect management control was more important than ownership. On this view, managers were more socially responsible than owners and private industry was now more sensitive to social goals and priorities than had been the case. On the 'Crosland–Gaitskell' revisionist analysis, this made public ownership or nationalisation much less relevant to the achievement of socialism. Public ownership of the means of production was not an end in itself but rather one among a number of means to the achievement of social justice and equality which are genuine ends of socialist politics. Each proposal for nationalisation should be defended on its merits and no blanket endorsement should be allowed.

In the view of critics, this analysis of capitalism has been shown to be faulty on a number of levels. At a practical level the failure of the 1974–6 Wilson government to negotiate any planning agreements on a voluntary basis with the private sector demonstrates the unwillingness of British capitalism to co-operate with the objectives of a socialist government. Economic recession has forced capitalism much more on the defensive and has led to a decline in the sensitivity of capitalism to social objectives. In addition, as part of its defensive strategy, attempts have been made to cut back the power of unions in order to enable capitalist market economics to operate more effectively. The abolition of exchange controls has given new freedoms to the movement of capital, while at the same time the freedoms of unions on this analysis have been restricted, and are likely to be cut back even more. On this view we are not living in a Croslandite post-capitalist society, rather the period of the 1950s and 1960s was an exceptional and untypical period in capitalist society in which boom conditions had given the leeway for capitalism to be more socially responsible than in fact it is. The remedy, therefore, is to be seen in terms of a radical extension of public ownership to produce an irreversible shift in the balance of society towards 'working people and their families'.

There is, in addition, a more deep-seated issue here. Marxist and Marxisant socialists reject the view that socialism can be defined in distributive terms – in terms of equality, social justice, etc. Rather, the pattern of distribution in society reflects the pattern of *ownership of the means of production*. Distributional equality cannot be secured without a more equal distribution of the ownership of the means of production and this means further and more extensive forms of public ownership than the post-war Labour Party has been committed to. Also central to the revisionist case was the assumption that class antagonisms in modern society are likely to diminish as we enter more fully into the post-capitalist world, and the Labour Party should not present itself to the electorate as a predominantly class party. The Labour Party must appear as a national party – as the 'natural party of government', in Wilson's phrase – and not merely the political embodiment of a specific set of class interests. National community rather than class should be the basis of the appeal. As Crosland wrote: 'a Socialist Party should be and should be seen to be a national party and not simply a class party ... a Labour Party must have a genuinely national and classless appeal' (Crosland, 1963, p. 15). This has to be so for reasons of political principle – class politics were seen as destructive and divisive – but also for electoral reasons. The fundamental changes in capitalist society which revisionists had detected had led to a decline in the extent to which voters identified themselves as working class. A wholly class appeal was likely to secure the support of a minority of the electorate, and this perception lay behind Douglas Jay's proposal after the 1959 electoral defeat to change the Party's name from the Labour Party to something less class conscious – perhaps the Social Democratic Party.

The example of the German SPD was thought to be instructive here. At Bad Godesburg in 1959 the SPD abandoned its class-based, Marxist analysis of modern capitalism and subsequently went on to achieve both electoral and economic success. While proposals to change the name of the Party and to deny the importance of clause IV in the Labour Party constitution were both rejected, nevertheless the practice of the 1964–70 and the 1974–9 Labour governments were heavily influenced by revisionist strategy, and certainly Callaghan was the embodiment of a Baldwinesque appeal to nation rather than class. However, the Left argue that the recession has accentuated class antagonisms and the Labour Party should become much more class-oriented. Indeed, in *The Future of Socialism* Crosland wrote a prophetic paragraph which the Left could use to fault a revisionist approach to British politics in the late 1970s and 1980s:

Economic politics are characteristic of any country to which a Marxist analysis might be plausibly applied. Thus they are typical of periods of growing pauperisation, depression and mass unemployment, falling real wages, and a sharp polarisation of classes. It is at such times, when a direct clash of economic interests occurs between clear cut productive classes against a background of material scarcity, that economic issues are the main determinants of political attitudes. (Crosland, 1956, pp. 196–7)

In the view of critics of revisionism this specifies precisely the position of British society from the late 1970s, and the Labour Party should adopt a much more self-consciously class-based position. A very good example of this kind of argument is to be found in Eric Heffer's *The Class Struggle in Parliament* (1973).

The other central plank in the Left's critique of revisionism is the role of the state. In the classical Marxist view, in a society characterised by the private ownership of the means of production, the state is an instrument of class. The state embodies the interests of the dominant economic class in civil society, in a capitalist society the capitalist class. It is a standard criticism both on the Left and elsewhere (see, for example, Marquand, 1982) that revisionists did not have an adequate theory of the state. Insofar as they discussed state theory at all it was largely in terms of Fabian notions of permeation, the achievement of socialism being a matter of the permeation of socialist-collectivist ideas among the elite and having the political will when in power to implement socialist policies. The institutions of the state were seen to be neutral between substantive political values, and the achievement of socialism is largely a matter of a majority in the House of Commons and the political will to implement socialist objectives.

Tony Benn. The Left's critique of this view has been developed by Tony Benn, notably in *Arguments for Socialism* (1979) and *Arguments for Democracy* (1982). On this view, state institutions, particularly the House of Lords, the civil service, the legal system and the police, work *against* the implementation of socialist policies. They embody a systematic bias *against* socialist values and radical reforms will be necessary before socialism can be introduced (Benn, 1979, p. 162). In terms of formal state institutions, proposals include the abolition of the House of Lords, the reform of the civil service and greater political accountability of the police. At the same time it is also part of the Left's view that non-state institutions, particularly television, the press and the educational system, are pursuing, in more or less explicit ways, biases against socialist aims and values. Important in this context has been renewed interest in the theoretical work of the Italian socialist Gramsci, who described the way in which the legitimacy of ruling-class values is secured by their permeation through the population of such biases through these informal institutions. Central to the achievement of socialism, on this view, is the reform of the educational system and the media to make them more accountable and to extend democratic procedures to their activities.

This enthusiasm for greater democratic control of the agencies of state power, powerfully stated by Tony Benn, has also been applied by him to relations in industry, drawing particularly upon his experience as Secretary of State for Industry in 1974–5. Benn favours workers' co-operatives as an important component in extending the control of individuals over their working lives and in reducing the centralised power of the state. However, he recognises that a co-operative strategy probably has to be second best, because in the nature of the case co-operatives cannot be imposed from the top. The initiative has to come from workers and this is only likely to happen when things have gone badly wrong with an industry. As he argues, 'People will not turn their minds seriously to institutional change when everything is going all right. You wouldn't expect people in a successful company with a growing labour force and rising living standards to want to turn their factory upside down and run it differently' (Benn, 1979, p. 158). However, he advocates a co-operative development agency which would be able to facilitate the setting up of worker co-operatives. But, this cannot in any sense be the whole solution, so there has to be a role for central state activity through a national enterprise board operating within a framework of compulsory planning agreements in which the request by a company for government help is linked with the development of new structures under which unions are given a much bigger say in the investment and managerial objectives of companies. Benn's basic theme is a shift away from the balance of power within which capital hires labour to one in which labour hires capital.

ALLIANCE IDEOLOGY

Arguments about the nature of the state are also central to current Social Democratic and Liberal politics. In his book *Face the Future* (1982) David Owen expresses concern lest the critique of the state should be monopolised by neo-liberal conservatives:

> The argument that Britain has begun to move inexorably towards a corporate state is not new, and in recent years that critique has been vigorously mounted from the New Left as well as from the Hayek Right. The year 1979 saw the return of a Conservative Government which, for the first time, meant a government that was openly critical of the corporate state. The challenge for Social Democrats is not to allow this political critique to be mounted only from the viewpoint of the Right, but to ensure that the Social Democratic Party is seen to be reassessing the strength of the corporate state with conviction and coherence. (Owen, 1981, p. 31)

This same theme is discussed in Evan Luard's *Socialism without the State* (1979) and Shirley Williams's *Politics is for People* (1980). This argument develops an internal critique of both the theoretical centralism or statism of Labour Party theorists of the post-war period, particularly in the work of Anthony Crosland, and of the practical political arrangements of the 1964–70 and 1974–9 Labour governments. Crosland's socialism saw a major role for the state, as we have already seen, and this necessity for strong centralism is justified in terms of the pursuit of equality. Egalitarian redistribution of both income and power seems to require a strong centralist state in order to constrain these vested interests which would obstruct the push towards equality. This statist orientation was mirrored in political practice by the development of corporatism in British politics, which as we have already seen is an aspect of the Thatcher critique of the Wilson and Heath governments. The Social Democratic and Liberal view is that this tendency neglects an important number of defects in the role of the state which, these critics argue, have become part and parcel of ordinary political consciousness. This comes out in a number of ways: individuals become 'alienated' from large-scale government and quasi-governmental institutions; individuals are, in many areas of their lives, turned into clients of the state. Such a centralist tendency neglects the values of community and fraternity and, more abstractly, but of immense importance, the attempt to impose socialism in the revisionist understanding of it neglects the importance of changing individual attitudes. Socialism requires a change in consciousness, a remoralisation of society and not just the imposition of policies and proposals by a remote central government.

The problem could perhaps be put in another way. Egalitarianism is supposed to enhance individual freedom, to ensure that individuals have broadly similar resources in order to plan their own lives, greater equality in the possession of income, education and power makes citizenship a reality for all, while at the same time the institutions which have been devised to achieve this in themselves *constrain* the exercise of choice and active citizenship. The development of corporatism removes from democratic citizens the opportunities for the exercise of choice and citizenship.

The political results of this critique of centralism are manifold. At the institutional level there is a demand for *decentralisation of power* – as far as the SDP is concerned – to a set of regional assemblies with considerable powers of self-government. To make central government more responsive to the real structure of political interests in the community there is a proposal to seek a large measure of electoral reform. It is argued that recent election results show the extent to which individuals are alienated from modern politics. It is pointed out that only 76 per cent of the electorate voted in May 1979 and in 1974 only 55 per cent of those eligible to vote voted for the two main parties. At the same time, there is a need, in the view of Owen, Williams and Luard, to build up a strong sense of community at the local level. This has also been an important and central aspect of modern Liberal Party politics – the emphasis upon community politics, identifying local needs and interests and bringing these to bear with considerable success on national electoral politics.

The emphasis in both of these traditions is upon extending democratic and participatory focus to wider and wider spheres, in education, in the place of work, and in local government. However, the obvious intellectual difficulty here is clear: on the one hand, at least among the SDP there is a commitment to egalitarianism, on the other to decentralisation, but how is greater equality to be secured without a central state involved in continual redistribution? The answer to this seems to be in terms of moving the egalitarianism away from what Marquand has called 'obsessive material equality' and towards equalising power. It is assumed that the former requires a strong state whereas the latter does not. However, it is not clear that this is so. It might well be argued that a strong central state will be required to challenge the vested interests which would resist the redistribution of power just as much as it requires a centralised state to challenge vested interests in the spheres of income and wealth. Nevertheless, there is an important issue here. How far is the achievement of greater equality compatible with the issues for which equality is desired. If equality requires a suffocating level of state activity, can it be compatible with the greater freedom and citizenship which equality is supposed to underpin? This is a central problem for both the Social Democrats and the revisionist tradition in the Labour Party. At the time of writing, however, it might seem that the difficulty for the SDP is being resolved in favour of a move away from the commitment to equality in favour of a greater degree of liberty and decentralisation.

The nature of the state, the range of obligations and duties on government, the role of class, public *vs* private choice, are therefore at the centre of modern political debate in Britain, and at the moment the future is difficult to predict. One thing is certain, however, and that is that debate about *values* and not just *interests* is the stuff of democratic politics, and political philosophy, understood as the analysis of political values and the forms of political argument, is quite central to a democratic society. It is mistakenly seen as a narrow academic specialism; it is on the contrary central to informed citizenship.

2

Voting and the Electorate

PATRICK DUNLEAVY

Superficially the 1979 election produced a result very similar to that held almost exactly twenty-four years previously. The Conservatives won 334 seats in 1955 and three more in 1979, while Labour's MPs decreased from 277 to 269 across the two years. In May 1955, 76.7 per cent of voters went to the polls; twenty-four years later the figure was down very slightly, by 0.7 per cent. In both cases the Conservative government had a clear working majority in Parliament, and the House of Commons was dominated by the two major parties. Yet most commentators agree that 1955 was the heyday of the post-war two-party system, while 1979 was a key stage in its decline. This basic change showed up far more graphically in the 1983 election, when Labour's share of the poll collapsed to its lowest level since 1918, boosting the Liberal–SDP Alliance's vote to the highest achieved by any third party since the inter-war period. The electoral system ensured, however, that the primary change in Commons' representation was an 'artificial' Conservative landslide, giving them 397 seats. Labour was slightly protected from the full consequences of defeat, retaining 209 seats. The Alliance secured only 6 SDP and 17 Liberal MPs (around 140 seats short given their share of the vote).

But these surface differences remain fairly small scale, and provide little direct indication of the sweeping changes in party fortunes and electoral behaviour which have occurred since 1979. To understand the deeper-rooted causes and mechanisms of voting change we need to go beyond a consideration of election results and look at the evidence thrown up by the key research tools of political science in this area, survey data and opinion poll results. These sources of information allow us to know with some accuracy what kinds of people are voting for which party, and how their choice of party leaders or party labels relates to their attitudes on political issues. Two key trends can be identified in voters' behaviour over the last fifteen years. The first of these is 'class de-alignment' – a major weakening of the association between people's occupational class positions and their political alignments. The second is 'partisan de-alignment' – a significant reduction in the 'fit' between people's choice of party and their views on individual political issues.

Class De-alignment

The concept of 'class' is notoriously controversial, and means many different things to different people, both in everyday language and within social science. Marxists see 'class' as defined by positions in a system of production, and distinguish between employers ('the bourgeoisie'), the self-employed, wage-earners who control other workers (e.g. managers or foremen), and a working class who simply sell their labour for a wage and have little or no control over what work they do. Hence for them 'class' is basically about power in the work-place. Many liberal sociologists, on the other hand, see 'class' as about people's chances in life, their prospects of achieving particular kinds of income, education, well-being or life-style. The single best predictor or indicator of these life-chances is what kind of job someone does – what their occupation is. Different jobs have different kinds of prestige or status in society as a whole, and by ranking occupations in order from the most to the least highly valued it is possible to see where any given job stands in a hierarchy or ladder of positions. Naturally this ladder has many rungs, far too many in fact for it to be used easily. So sociologists have collapsed occupations with similar status rankings together in order to

create a manageable number of categories; usually between
five and eight 'occupational classes' are distinguished, ranging
from a 'professional and managerial' category at one end to
'unskilled manual workers' at the other end of the range. In all
the many permutations of occupational class schemes, one
distinction is always present, namely that between non-manual
or 'white-collar' jobs and manual or 'blue-collar' jobs. Despite
the many difficulties in making sense of this division in an age
where some notionally manual jobs may be more skilled (and
much more highly paid) than many routine non-manual
occupations, the manual/non-manual dichotomy has
remained a key factor influencing whether most people think of
themselves and others as 'working class' or 'middle class'.

Since 1945, occupational class has been widely seen as the
main social basis underlying electoral politics in Britain. A
pattern of 'class alignment' was clearly apparent in the 1950s
and 1960s. Non-manual people in the mid-1960s split their
support between the two major parties in the ratio of three
Conservative votes for every one Labour vote, while manual
workers were strongly Labour-inclined, with well over two
Labour votes for every one Conservative. Clearly, then,
knowing someone's occupational class in this period allowed
politicians and political scientists to do significantly better than
tossing a coin in predicting how they would vote. Of course,
there was never at any stage a situation where *all* non-manual
people or *all* manual workers voted for one party; in this sense
the pattern of class alignments was strictly a matter of
probabilities, not hard-and-fast rules. But by international
standards the influence of occupational class on voting
behaviour was quite high in Britain, well above the levels
detectable in North America, considerably more pronounced
than class voting elsewhere in Western Europe, but still slightly
below the levels found in Scandinavian countries.

There are two possible ways in which a major pattern of
alignment such as this can change. *Re*-alignment occurs where
a previously important social basis for voting is replaced by
some new line of division in society, by another social cleavage
which influences how people vote. If an existing pattern of
voting is not replaced, however, but simply decays, then we
may legitimately speak of the process as *de*-alignment. This is

what seems to have happened to 'class voting' in Britain during the 1970s; most commentators suggest that the association between occupational class and party support has simply faded away. It has consequently become much more difficult than formerly to predict how people will vote from knowing where their job stands in a status hierarchy of occupations in society. Indeed, by 1979, as we shall see, tossing a coin was almost as useful as knowing whether someone was middle or working class in guessing how they would vote. Fundamentally, different occupational classes have converged towards each other in terms of their political alignment, while at the same time the composition of the two major parties' support bases has become much more similar.

TABLE 2.1   *Manual and non-manual voting, 1964–74*

| Occupational class | Percentage Conservative lead over Labour | | | | |
	1964	1966	1970	Feb 1974	Oct 1974
Non-manual	50	44	40	36	30
Manual	−36	−44	−30	−40	−34

Note: The table shows the percentage Conservative support *minus* the percentage Labour support in each occupational class amongst people 'identifying' with the two major parties.

Source: Crewe *et al.* (1977).

But there seem to have been two distinct phases in this process of class de-alignment. Table 2.1 shows how middle- and working-class people voted between 1964 and 1974, by looking at the 'Conservative lead over Labour' among people supporting one or other of the two main parties. A large positive figure here indicates a solid Conservative majority in that occupational class at a given election, while a negative figure of course shows that a balance of voters supported Labour. The most surprising thing to notice is that the Conservative lead among non-manual voters consistently declined over this decade. In contrast, Labour's majority over the Conservatives among manual voters shows no consistent trend over time, and was much the same at the end of the period

TABLE 2.2   *The social basis of major party support, 1964–74*

| Party and occupational class | % of party's support base from each occupational class | | | | |
	1964	1966	1970	Feb 1974	Oct 1974
Conservative					
Non-manual	57	59	54	63	58
Manual	43	41	46	37	42
Labour					
Non-manual	17	19	22	25	27
Manual	83	81	78	75	73

Source: Crewe *et al.* (1977).

as at the beginning. This evidence suggests, therefore, that class de-alignment up to 1974 was mainly caused by the weakening Conservative leanings of the middle class rather than defections from Labour among manual workers. Some confirmation of this can be gained from Table 2.2, which shows the social make-up of each party's support base. It is clear that around four out of every ten Conservative voters were manual workers at every election in this period; there were fluctuations around this figure over time rather than any consistent trend in the importance of working-class voters for the party. By contrast, the minority of Labour voters from the middle class grew from one in six in the mid-1960s to over one in four a decade later, a change which was much more rapid and extensive than the gradual increase in the ratio of non-manual to manual jobs over the same period.

The second and accelerated phase of class de-alignment occurred in the late 1970s, when the way in which voting patterns converged across different occupational classes was significantly different from what had gone before. This change is worth considering in detail, as we do in Table 2.3, which splits up the middle class into a managerial/professional group and a routine non-manual group, and the working class into skilled workers and semi- or unskilled workers. In October 1974 there was still a sharp drop in Conservative voting at the

TABLE 2.3   *Class dealignment, 1974–83*

	Occupational class			
	Managerial (AB)	*Junior non-manual (C1)*	*Skilled manual (C2)*	*Other manual (D)*
Share of the three party vote *1974 October*				
Conservative	65	53	27	23
Labour	12	25	52	60
Liberal	23	22	21	17
1979				
Conservative	67	58	44	32
Labour	18	21	45	55
Liberal	15	20	10	13
1983				
Conservative	54	57	37	33
Labour	11	17	36	43
Alliance (Lib/SDP)	35	27	27	24
Conservative lead over Labour (Con vote — Lab vote)				
October 1974	53	28	−25	−37
1979	49	37	−1	−33
1983	43	40	1	−10
Swing to Conservatives *from Labour* (+ = to Con; − = to Lab)				
1974–79	−2.0	+4.5	+12.5	+7.0
1979–83	−3.0	+1.5	+1.0	+6.0
Swing to Liberals/Alliance *from other two major parties*				
1974–79	−8.0	−1.5	−10.5	−9.0
1979–83	−20.0	+6.0	+16.5	+11.0

Sources: *The Economist*, 14 May 1979; London School of Economics, Election Studies Unit, 1983 General Election Survey. Vote figures using 'Share of the three party vote' are calculated excluding votes going to minor parties. Full details of the LSE survey are given in Dunleavy and Husbands (1984).

non-manual/manual borderline, and the Conservative lead over Labour switched from a healthy positive score to a substantial negative figure. But in 1979 there was a remarkble growth of Conservative voting among manual workers, partly fuelled by a collapse of Liberal support from its 1974 peak. This switch largely survived the renewed Liberal–SDP surge in 1983, which took place largely at Labour's expense. Among routine non-manual staffs there was much less dramatic change, with Liberal support falling only slightly in 1979 and a more gradual ebbing of the Labour vote towards first Conservatives in 1979, and then the Alliance in 1983. Earlier trends for non-manual Conservative voting to decline were still present in 1979 and 1983, but only in the managerial/professional group. Here Labour voting actually increased at the Liberals' expense in 1979, while in 1983 the bulk of the new Alliance voters came from the Conservatives. The result was a reduced Conservative lead over Labour in this occupational class, contrary to the overall national trend for the electorate to move to the right.

If the evidence of class de-alignment was clearly apparent by the end of the 1970s, there were still a number of puzzling aspects to the changing social influences on voting. These involve the apparent continuing importance of variables widely seen as associated with occupational class. It seems odd, even paradoxical, that occupational class itself should be less and less useful in predicting or explaining voters' alignments, but that class corollaries (secondary variables mainly influenced by occupational class) should continue to prove as useful as ever in this respect. Three instances of this kind are particularly worth noting.

First, Table 2.4 demonstrates that in 1979 members of trade unions were much more likely to vote Labour than non-members, an effect virtually as strong then as it had ever been. Up to this point then, class dealignment seemed to have had little impact in blurring or softening the separate voting patterns of union members and non-members. But in 1983, while the Alliance recruited new voters among non-unionised people almost evenly from the Conservatives and Labour, among union members a 19 percentage points increase in Alliance support was made entirely at Labour's expense.

TABLE 2.4   *The influence of unionisation upon voting, 1979–83*

| Party | % of three party vote among: | | |
	Non-members	Union members	Difference made by union membership
1979			
Conservative	52	34	−18
Labour	33	53	+20
Liberal	15	13	− 2
Conservative lead over Labour	*+19*	*−19*	*−38*
1983			
Conservative	46	34	−12
Labour	27	34	+ 7
Alliance	27	32	+ 5
Conservative lead over Labour	*+19*	*0*	*−19*

Source: *The Economist*, 14 May 1979; LSE Election Studies Unit, 1983 Survey.

Second, over the whole period of the 1970s, people's housing tenure continued to be closely associated with voting. After occupational class influences have been controlled for, home owners in each class are more than twice as likely to vote Conservative as council tenants. As early as the 1970 election, some statistical techniques suggested that housing tenure alone was a greater influence on voting than occupational class (Rose, 1974b). If these results were at that time mainly freak products of the analytic methods used, by the early 1980s they were a central feature of voters' real behaviour.

Third, class dealignment is very much a phenomenon confined to the individual-level changes of voting behaviour investigated by survey research. But at the level of explaining why particular areas or constituencies vote the way they do, knowing the mix of occupational classes in the local area continues to be very valuable in explaining or predicting election results. Indeed Miller (1977, 1978) showed that variations in the mix of occupational classes across constituencies could statistically 'explain' up to 70 per cent of the variations in Conservative/Labour voting. The fact that people of different occupational classes tend to live in different areas – for example, non-manual people live in the suburbs, while inner-city areas have mainly manual worker residents – is of course one of the key foundations of the present two-party system. Over the post-war period and even in the 1970s this area-level influence of class has, if anything, slightly increased. What seems to happen is that all groups of voters in a constituency are influenced towards the characteristic alignment of the majority occupational class in the area. Thus in places like Cheltenham or Eastbourne the predominant Conservatism of the middle class is considerably strengthened, but so also is working-class support for the party. In places such as Tower Hamlets or inner Birmingham, working-class Labour loyalties are stronger than the national average and even the restricted number of middle-class residents are less Conservative in their leanings. The enduring influence of class mix in showing constituency voting patterns has meant that in terms of the seats they win the Conservative and Labour parties have become further polarised. Table 2.5 shows their respective seat distributions in 1955 and 1979, a particularly useful comparison because their relative totals of seats won were about the same in both years. The Conservatives clearly became more of a southern English party in this period, drawing support more from the suburbs, widening commuter belts and the countryside. Labour became more reliant on big city seats, losing ground dramatically elsewhere in southern England, but gaining more seats in 1979 in northern English regions and in Scotland. Labour's defeat in 1983 eliminated virtually all its seats outside the inner cities in southern England, while the Alliance surge and SDP defections produced some spectacular losses in previous safer Labour areas as well.

Partisan De-alignment

The changes in voting behaviour which have been brought together under the umbrella label of 'partisan de-alignment' are

TABLE 2.5   *Distribution of major party seats by region and type of area in 1955 and in 1979*

	Proportion (%) of seats drawn from			
	Southern shires	Northern shires	Southern cities	Northern cities
1955				
All seats	48	29	13	10
Conservative seats	58	25	9	9
Labour seats	35	33	19	12
1979				
All seats	50	28	12	10
Conservative seats	71	19	6	4
Labour seats	25	38	19	18

Source: computed from figures in *The Economist*, 14 May 1979.

both more complex and less widely agreed than class de-alignment. All the processes involved in 'partisan de-alignment' have in common a declining association between people's party loyalties and their views on particular issues. The political science orthodoxy of the 1960s suggested that most voters come to 'identify' with political parties, mainly via family socialisation in early life and imitating the views of others with whom they come in contact in their daily lives, at work or in local neighbourhoods. Voters' loyalties were on the whole affective or emotional in character, rather than based on any closely rationalised philosophy or calculation of where their interests lay. Once formed, these party identifications tended to endure over successive elections, producing stable blocks of voters with almost habitual tendencies to choose one party. Voters had relatively little information or interest in politics, and tended to adjust their views on individual issues to fit in with their party loyalties, rather than vice versa, or even to adopt positions on issues in an almost random, unstable and unstructured way.

Those reasearchers who claim to have discovered a process of partisan de-alignment going on in British politics (notably Ivor Crewe, Bo Sarlvik and their colleagues at the University of Essex) cite three developments which have weakened the earlier association between party identification with the major parties and attitudes on specific policy questions or issues. These are: the growth of third-party voting; changes in the issue basis of British politics; and an increase in electoral volatility.

GROWTH OF THIRD-PARTY VOTING

In 1955 the Conservatives and Labour between them received a remarkable 97 per cent of all votes cast. By 1964 this figure drifted down to under nine-tenths of the poll, a level where it remained until in 1974 increased Liberal voting pushed it sharply down to 77 per cent. The switch from Liberal to Tory voting in 1979 raised the two major parties' combined share again to 83 per cent, before the Alliance success in 1983 reduced it to an unprecedented post-war low, just 72 per cent. More direct evidence of voters' feelings towards the two major parties can be gained from their responses to a question asking which party they 'feel closest to', or whether they normally think of themselves as a supporter of any party. Figure 2.1 shows that while the number of people who 'identify' with one of the major parties remained fairly high (over three-quarters of all voters) in the 1970s, the proportion of people with strong attachments have halved over the decade to just one voter in every five. It seems, then, that people's party loyalties are becoming more conditional.

The timing of increases in third-party support adds a further interesting dimension to the weakening grip of the two-party system. Figure 2.2 shows that since 1960 there have been three major upward 'blips' in support for the Liberals or the new SDP/Liberal Alliance, in 1962, 1973 and 1981. Each of these came towards the mid-term of a Conservative government perceived at the time by many of the electorate to be failing. Obviously also the blips in the opinion poll ratings show a general upward drift, especially towards the end of the period where the creation of the Alliance produced a base level of third-party support running fairly consistently above 20 per cent. But notice that under Labour governments, third-party opinion poll ratings and end-of-term election results were much lower, largely (as we note below) because opposition to unpopular Labour governments seems to switch directly into

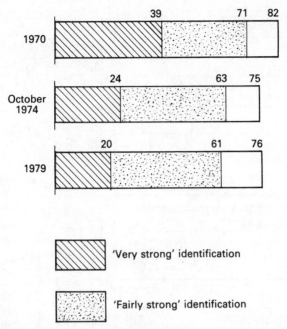

FIGURE 2.1 *Percentage voters identifying with one of the two main parties,*
1970–79
Source: Crewe *et al.* (1977)

increased Conservative support rather than stopping at a
'half-way house'. In contrast, under an unpopular Conservative government there seems to be an increasing resistance
among a large block of dissatisfied voters to switching directly
to Labour, producing a search for an intermediate party to
serve as a home for protest votes. This asymmetry in two-party
performance in opposition is mirrored in their relative success
in adapting to changes in voters' feelings about specific policy
questions.

CHANGES IN POLITICAL ISSUES

Three changes in the character of political issues at the
forefront of public attention have been involved in the process
of partisan de-alignment. In the first place, some issues have
declined in importance or changed form quite substantially in

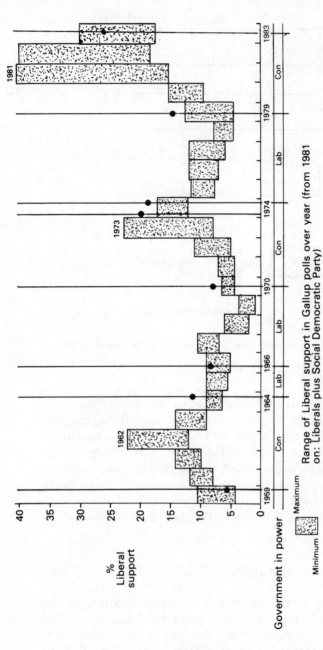

FIGURE 2.2 *Indications of support for the Liberals, and Liberal–Social Democrat Alliance, 1959–83*

Sources: computed from figures in Butler and Sloman (1979) and Gallup Political Index, March 1979 – January 1984.

Note: Until March 1982 the question posed was 'If there were a general election tomorrow which party would you vote for?' After March 1982 the question posed was: 'If an election took place tomorrow and the following candidates were standing in your constituency, how would you vote? Would you vote for: the Conservative Party/ the Labour Party/ the Alliance between the Liberals and Social Democratic Party/another the period since 1960. Crewe *et al.* (1977) suggest that issue decay has particularly affected Labour Party support on questions of basic principle for the Party such as further nationalisation, the extension of the welfare state, and its close links with the trade-union movement. They show that between the mid-1960s and the mid-1970s support for these policies decayed significantly among Labour supporters, and link this to the seepage away of working-class voters towards the Liberals or the Conservatives and their partial replacement in Labour's ranks by newer middle-class supporters with views not necessarily encompassing these traditional 'articles of faith'. This would be less problematic for Labour if it had succeeded in finding new issues with major appeal; but in their absence Crewe *et al.* feel justified in talking of a 'haemorrhaging' of 'core Labour support'.

Second, both the major parties were plagued in the 1970s by issues which obstinately failed to fit into the pre-existing framework of two-party debate. These were issues on which the parties were deeply divided internally, or where they tended to shift their positions from one election to another. The most important has been the question of an incomes policy, which governments of both parties have introduced after election campaigns pledging their opposition to it. Attitudes towards the EEC have been another problem area for Labour, though the Conservatives have taken a more consistent pro-European stance. It is possible that the growth of these poorly integrated issues (outside a simple Left/Right dimension as it is conventionally recognised) may have been influential, not so much in changing people's voting solely on that issue, but because dissatisfactions over party stances here helped to prise voters out of traditional and stable loyalties into more third-party voting.

Third, a number of new issues have grown in salience since the mid-1970s. Perhaps surprisingly there has not yet been any major partisan involvement in so-called 'post-industrial' issues – such as environmentalism or opposition to civilian nuclear energy. Although the founders of the SDP floated such concerns as a possible basis for their new party, their salience for the electorate as a whole remains low key. Instead the big issue breakthroughs of the last decade have been in areas already structured on two-party lines, fitting quite closely into a left/right political framework, and hence leaving the Alliance with no very clear-cut intermediate position.

Traditionally, of course, economic issues have been among the major concerns of British voters, with inflation and unemployment hardy perennials in survey rankings of the top issues. In 1979 prices were the most frequently mentioned issue influence on voters' decisions, with rising unemployment second. Table 2.6 shows that by 1983 levels of unemployment were voters' chief concern, with prices displaced to third place, perhaps a natural response to the first Thatcher government's record (see Chapter 6). But more interesting than this apparent reversal of economic priorities, is the arrival of two new concerns clearly in the category of major issues, namely 'crime rates and policing' and 'defence and disarmament'. Both of these are issue areas where Conservative and Labour policies diverged sharply in the 1979–83 period. The Conservatives promoted 'law and order' issues into national prominence in 1979, when they were mentioned by one in ten voters as a factor influencing their decision, overwhelmingly to the Tories' advantage. By 1983, with crime rates still rising, and new controversy about the political accountability of police forces, the issue was firmly established in voters' consciousness (see Chapter 9).

But defence and disarmament concerns are undoubtedly the most spectacular growth issue of the 1980s, following Labour's commitment to unilateral nuclear disarmament in 1982, breaching the previous two-party consensus on the UK deterrent. The 'new cold war' in international relations and the scheduled arrival of Cruise missiles kept controversy at a peak up to and past the 1983 campaign, during which the Conservatives successfully attacked Labour's defence policies. Twice as many voters (40 per cent) favoured Conservative defence policies in 1983 as felt close to Labour's stance (only 20 per cent). But it is possible that this situation will change, given continuing East/West tensions and greater voter familiarity with non-nuclear options and positions. Certainly attitudes on nuclear weapons may contain a considerable potential for changing people's alignment, simply because they are so deeply felt (see Chapters 8, 11).

TABLE 2.6   *Voters' ranking of issues in the 1983 election campaign*

Issue	% seeing issue as 'extremely important' (1)	% seeing issue as 'not very' or not at all important' (2)	Majority for 'extreme importance' (1)–(2)
The level of unemployment	74	6	68
Crime rates and policing	58	10	48
Rising prices	54	12	42
Defence and nuclear weapons	52	13	39
The standard of public services	33	22	11
The government's handling of the Falklands war	37	32	5
Britain and the Common Market	31	25	6
Trades unions and industrial relations	24	39	−15

Source: LSE Election Studies unit, 1983 Survey. These are pre-defined responses to the question: 'I am going to read out some issues which were raised during the campaign. Can you tell me from this card how important or unimportant each one was to you personally during the campaign. I do not want to know whether you approve or disapprove, just how important they were.' Options on the card were: 'Extremely important/fairly important/not very important/not at all important/don't know.' 'Don't knows' were excluded in calculating percentages for this table.

One central feature of British politics in the mid-1980s remains the assymetrical ability of the major parties to exploit issues. The Conservatives differ from all other parties in the extent to which they have established a predominance on a range of mostly secondary or latent issues – such as defence-cum-patriotism (newly renewed by 'the Falklands spirit'), opposition to taxes and rates, criticism of the trade unions, a commitment to 'efficiency' in the public services, etc. – which can be exploited when the time seems ripe. Labour, by contrast, has some definite minority-appeal commitments, of which only opposition to nuclear weapons may in time become an active vote-winner. Labour's most bankable electoral asset remains its association with popular aspects of the welfare state, such as the NHS. But this is threatened with erosion by the privatising policies of the two Thatcher governments. Finally the Liberal/SDP position is rather different. They offend far fewer voters by their policy commitments than either of the other two parties. But this is because there are almost no major issues where they are seen by voters as having very distinctive policy solutions of their own.

INCREASE IN ELECTORAL VOLATILITY

The growth of third-party voting has obvious implications for electoral volatility; as more people vote for a new party, so the overall amount of vote changing in the electorate will increase. Table 2.7 shows that in the 1974–9 period (when around a quarter of people changed their votes) the two major parties held onto a much larger share of their support than did the Liberals, even though Labour as the losing party clearly fell somewhat below the Conservatives in retaining voters. The Alliance surge in 1983 pulled all the parties into much the same configuration, but this time with Labour having most difficulty in holding their 1979 voters. Critics of the two-party system claim that there has been a quantum jump in electoral volatility, reflecting voters' fundamental disillusionment with a Conservative/Labour choice, and hence constituing a further dimension of partisan dealignment. But most people still 'identify' at some level with one of the two major parties (see Figure 2.1). And half of Alliance supporters in 1983 'identify' with the Conservatives or Labour, or else with no party at all (Dunleavy and Husbands, 1984. ch. 7). So greater electoral voltility has by no means eliminated a pattern of long-run loyalties favouring the Conservatives and Labour.

Volatility also embraces voters' behaviour between elections. From the late 1960s on, when the Wilson government experienced a deep trough of unpopularity following the 1967 devaluation of the pound, every government has at some stage reached a similar mid-term slump point. Figure 2.3 demonstrates that the extent of government popularity *vis-à-vis* the opposition has been much the same, and the yearly range of opinion poll ratings – the extent to which government popularity has fluctuated within each year – has not shown a marked tendency to increase over time, as some writers implied in the mid-1970s. Volatility, like electoral turnout, seems for the moment to have stabilised at its current level.

Explaining De-alignment

There are two rather different approaches to explaining electoral trends over the 1970s, depending on whether class de-alignment or partisan de-alignment is seen as the more important or critical change in voter behaviour.

TABLE 2.7   *How people changed their votes, 1974–83*

Vote in October 1974

	Con %	Lab %	Lib %	Didn't vote %	Too young %
Vote in 1979					
Conservative	90	12	34	46	43
Labour	4	78	11	43	41
Liberal	6	10	55	11	16

Vote in 1979

	Con %	Lab %	Lib %	Didn't vote %	Too young %
Vote in 1983					
Conservative	80	8	17	37	41
Labour	4	67	6	33	27
Alliance	16	25	77	30	32

Sources: *The Economist*, 14 May 1979; LSE Election Studies Unit, 1983 Survey. Votes for 'other' parties and non-voters in the second year of each comparison are excluded. The column variables thus show the distribution of the three-party vote at the 1979 and 1983 elections respectively.

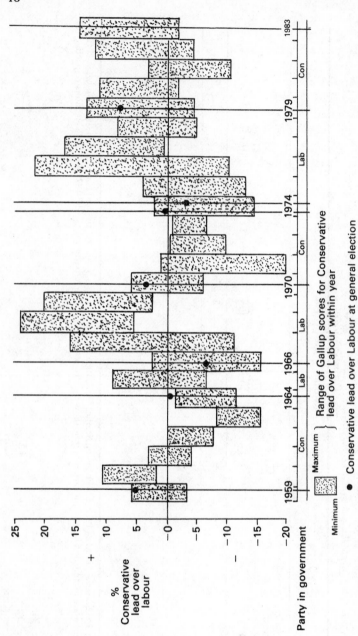

FIGURE 2.3 *Range of Gallup Poll scores for Conservative lead over Labour 1959–83*

Sources: computed from figures in Butler and Sloman (1979) and Gallup Political Index, March 1979 to January 1984.

SOCIAL-BASE EXPLANATIONS

Social-base explanations concentrate on changes in the character of British society which may account for some of the evidence of class de-alignment. It is important to note that some earlier approaches to this topic have seemed less appropriate as a result of recent trends. For example, attempts to explain why a large minority of manual workers voted Conservative in the 1950s and 1960s often resorted to the concept of 'deference' – a tendency to ascribe exceptional qualities to traditional, aristocratic leadership cadres. However accurate or otherwise these approaches may have been at the time, they cannot help explain why middle-class Conservative voting has decreased or why working-class Labour loyalties should have weakened over time. If anything, deference is seen as a residual influence from an earlier period of aristocratic political dominance, and hence should presumably decline over the modern period. Equally suspect with hindsight seem the one-sided explanations of working-class Conservatism stressing rising post-war affluence as a factor undermining traditional Labour loyalties. In practice, Labour's problems have accelerated simultaneously with the disappearance of any substantial economic growth in the economy and the re-emergence of mass unemployment on a scale and of a duration unprecedented in the post-war period. Changes in the income-tax system and worsening employment prospects mean that inequalities of life-chances between the top and the bottom of the occupational class hierarhy were probably more marked in 1983 than for much of the previous decade, yet working-class Labour support has never been weaker in the post-war period.

Some similar problems confront explanations of class de-alignment in terms of social and geographical mobility. In the period up to the early 1970s a large number of children from manual worker families moved into lower middle-class jobs, and a substantial proportion penetrated even further into the professional and managerial categories. This upward social mobility might help explain class de-alignment in two ways. First, it might suggest the decreased middle-class Conservative voting is a simple consequence of the growth in the numbers of

middle-class people from working-class backgrounds who are
ore likely to have been exposed to pro-Labour socialisation
processes in their early family life. Second, the number of
households where both husband and wife fall into the routine
non-manual or manual worker categories has diminished.
Where, for example, a car worker is married to a secretary, or a
clerical supervisor's wife works part-time as a shop assistant,
then their households have a 'mixed' class background. Some
sociological studies claim that this greater cross-class contact
within families helps account for some part of class de-
alignment among skilled manual and lower-status white-collar
employees. But note that again the tempo of upward social
mobility has slowed dramatically since the mid-1970s, because
the number of middle-class jobs is no longer expanding at its
previous rate.

Social and geographical mobility are sometimes closely
associated. Young people leaving the education system often
take up new jobs in quite different parts of the country from
their parents, and people often have to move house for career
reasons. But most of these would tend to affect more
middle-class people, and some would offset the effects claimed
for social mobility. For example, someone from a working-class
Labour family who takes up a middle-class job in a uniformly
middle-class neighbourhood might be expected to have a
reduced chance of retaining a Labour alignment than an
equivalent person starting the same job in the town where they
were brought up. More local geographical shifts (for example,
a move out of the inner city into the suburbs) might have a
greater role to play in explaining class de-alignment among
manual workers. But such shifts are often linked to other
changes which are not purely geographical, such as changes in
housing tenure.

Some writers have tried to explain away class de-alignment
by redefining occupational classes in order to regain a better fit
between 'class' positions and voting behaviour. Rose (1974b),
for example, has suggested that there are 'core classes' where
people's alignment remains much more clearly defined, but
which now include only a minority of the electorate. His 'core
working class' are not only manual workers but also must be
trade-union members and live in council housing, while his

'core middle class' not only have non-manual jobs but also are not union members and own their own homes. He then demonstrates that these 'core classes' have much higher rates of Labour and Conservative voting respectively, and argues that the rest of the electorate, with a much more mixed background, tend to take their voting behaviour from which-ever 'core class' they most come in contact with. Critics of this approach suggest that it rests on a misunderstanding of the concept of class. The point of the original idea of class alignment was to be able to predict voting chances from job status – it was not to include anything which influences voting in the concept of class. In this direction lies a logical circle: we can make core classes 'explain' voting better than occupa-tional class proper, but only because we have worked back-wards from people's votes to define 'core classes' in the first place.

A much more genuine problem about occupational class cate-gories is whether simply knowing where a job fits into a prestige ranking table is a good enough index of people's position in society. We noted above that Marxists, for example, focus their concept of class on power in the work-place. In their terms self-employed plumbers may be put in a different social class from plumbers working in a large factory, because they have that much more control over their own work-loads and conditions. Such considerations may be important in consider-ing, for example, the well-established strong Conservatism of self-employed people. Similarly, sociologists from liberal and Marxist traditions have pointed to the 'status strain' which other groups around the non-manual/manual boundary may well experience. For example, unskilled non-manual employ-ees who are not supervisors may well go to work in a neat pinstripe suit, but then be as doomed to boredom and 'bossed' about as any worker on an assembly line, often for a much lower salary. Conversely, foremen may go to work in a boiler suit and think of themselves as working class, while the essential content of their work involves exerting authority and control over their work-mates. Forcing these different groups to fit into a straight middle/working-class division may be inappropriate to the underlying realities of social divisions in contemporary Britain. Hence a genuine recasting of our class categories to take account of people's position in a system of production as well as the prestige of their job might enable us to achieve a better class-based explanation of attitudes and alignments. But to what extent it can help explain the trend for class positions to be less associated with support for particular parties remains unclear at present.

The final social-base explanation, by contrast, tackles the trend towards class de-alignment head on, by arguing that a new line of cleavage has grown up which crosscuts occupational class divisions. This new cleavage is a sectoral one, with public/private-sector conflicts of interest at its core (Dunleavy, 1979, 1980a). In employment terms, which sector you work for has a major impact upon whether or not you are likely to join a trade union – the public sector now has far and away the highest unionisation rates in Britain, among non-manual employees as much as manual workers. Public and private employees are likely to have different interests on a range of other issues, including attitudes to incomes policy, and towards the extension or rolling back of state intervention. At its simplest, one group's pay increase may be another group's tax increase. The evidence is now quite compelling to suggest that sectoral effects have played a major part in blurring previous class–party associations. Figure 2.4 shows that in 1974 sectoral and union effects already blurred the appearance of sharp differences in alignment between non-manual and manual voters, with unionisation particularly important in this respect. By 1983 direct public/private sector differences were more influential in structuring voting than unionisation, due to a big loss of Labour support among private-sector union members in both the non-manual and manual groups. Since trade-union influence is anyway a product of sectoral locations, these two effects can be cumulated into a single production sector influence, quite comparable to, but cross-cutting, that of occupational class (Dunleavy and Husbands, 1984, ch. 6).

Sectoral divisions occur also in consumption processes, in how people gain access to goods and services, such as housing, transport, health care and education. In the past each of these has tended to be considered separately. But it now seems likely that whether or not people are more involved in public or private consumption overall may be important in shaping their

53

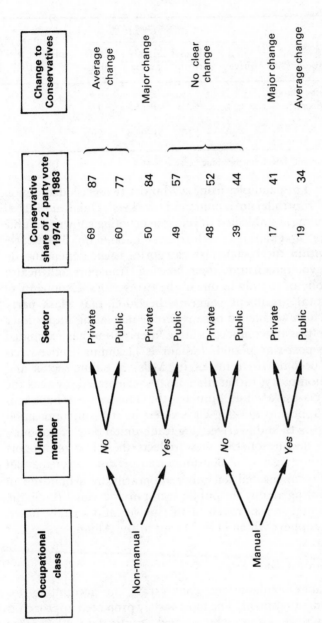

FIGURE 2.4 *Conservative share of the two-party vote, October 1974 and 1983*
Note: The percentage figures here show the Conservatives' share of the combined Tory/Labour vote.
Sources: Alt and Turner (1982); LSE Election Studies Unit, 1983 Survey.

TABLE 2.8   *Consumption sectors and voting, 1979*

Conservative lead over Labour (%)	Consumption sector				Percentage of sample ($N = 1,108$)
	Wholly private	Mainly private	Mainly public	Wholly public	
Controllers of labour (supervisors, managers, etc.)	+71	+23	+ 3	−44	26
Workers	+40	+10	−24	−29	74

Source: Duke and Edgell (forthcoming).

attitudes. For example, using a Marxist two-class distinction between 'controllers of labour' and 'workers', Duke and Edgell (forthcoming) established the pattern of voting shown in Table 2.8. Here the Conservative lead over Labour in 1979 clearly varies within the social-class categories used, depending on whether voters consume their housing, transport and health care wholly or mainly in one of the two sectors. Exponents of the sectoral argument suggest, therefore, that class–party linkages have weakened because of the increasing importance of public/private conflicts as state intervention has expanded over the post-war period. Labour is becoming (indeed has already become in terms of its MPs) a public-sector and trade-union party, rather than a party orientated towards the working class as a whole. Similarly the Conservatives have kept up their appeal to working-class voters by stressing opposition to state growth and overweaning trade-union power. Labour's apparent decline on this view reflects their loss of support among a large group of non-unionised private-sector manual workers, compensated for only temporarily by a build-up in Labour voting among the public-sector middle class. But in the 1983 election it was much of this newer and weakly based political support which ebbed away to the Alliance.

ISSUE-CHANGE EXPLANATIONS

Issue-change explanations concentrate on accounting for partisan de-alignment. The most widely promoted approach is that of Crewe *et al.*, who argued in the late 1970s that working-class defections from Labour were the primary lasting trend and that they could be directly linked with tensions between official party policy and the views of large numbers of Labour voters. For example, a majority of Labour voters disapprove of the close links between trade unions and the party, but it is hard to imagine the party being able to continue operating without those links, given the financial and personnel resources bound up in its trade-union membership. Supporters who held views out of tune with party policy were those most likely to switch their support by the mid–1970s, a trend that has only accentuated since. The Crewe *et al.* analysis of the May 1979 result suggests that Labour suffered then from a much more generalised shift by the electorate as a whole to the right. In 1983, however, Labour's problems were largely created by its own policy shifts, far to the left of what most voters could accept, and by the poor leadership image of Michael Foot (Crewe, 1983).

A similar emphasis on the rise of issue-voting characterises other approaches which place less stress on Labour's problems, preferring to emphasise the overall decline in the electorate's willingness to see separate policy issues through the lens of two-party competition. Voters are presented as moving towards a progressively more critical stance, as deciding issues on their merits, and hence as acting more 'rationally' than formerly. Voters' dissatisfaction with a worsening background of British economic performance, better levels of education, and more extensive and sophisticated mass-media coverage of politics, are all cited as possible factors explaining this change. Voters now make up their own minds, rather than relying on cues from family, workmates or neighbours, and their views on issues are decreasingly structured by adherence to a 'party line'. This is not to deny that large groups of voters continue to show 'brand loyalty' to one of the major parties, because to date their interests have been well represented by its policy positions. But these loyalties can always be reconsidered if conditions change, unlike the habitual or emotive commitments to the major parties emphasised by political scientists in the 1960s.

The New Three-Party System and Politics in the 1980s

Where does recent electoral change leave the political parties in the mid-1980s? Clearly the parties live in troubled times, a turbulent electoral environment marked by some sharp changes of fortune since the last general election alone. But some basic features seem to stand confirmed by the events of 1979–84, as well as by the longer-run trends discussed above. First, the Conservative Party has clearly succeeded in consolidating some of the gains made in May 1979 into lasting features of its appeal. Despite the current recession and the enormous growth in unemployment since Thatcher took office, working-class voters turned out and voted Conservative at the 1983 election in sufficient numbers to sustain their share of Tory support at well over the 40 per cent level characteristic of the 1960s and 1970s. In this sense of maintaining a cross-class appeal as vigorous as ever, the Conservatives remain a 'one-nation' party, even if the geographical basis of their 'nation' is focused more than ever on the relatively more prosperous regions of the country.

Second, Labour's support has apparently suffered a quantum reduction since the launch of the SDP in 1981, reducing its ability ever since to pull back enough opinion-poll support to achieve a positive lead over the government, or even to run it close (Figure 2.3). Labour's disastrous 1983 election result can to some extent be attributed to special factors – an electorally unappealing leader, a recent history of internal party conflicts, the problems caused by MPs defecting to the SDP, some newly adopted radical policy commitments unfamiliar to voters, and a seriously mismanaged election campaign. But even after Neil Kinnock's election as the new Labour leader, and a succession of government blunders in the autumn of 1983, Labour only regained poll ratings of the kind it had held before the campaign, mainly at the Alliance's expense. Labour may hope in future to shift ground on some unpopular policies (such as the EEC) and to win new converts on others (especially its nuclear disarmament stance). But rebuilding a Labour electoral majority still looks a long-term task.

Third, the new Alliance between the Social Democratic Party and the Liberals, seemed by 1984 to have stabilised its support at around 20–25 per cent. This is a dramatic fall from the peak levels of more than twice this size recorded in the immediate aftermath of the SDP launch in 1981–2, and places the new grouping rather below the two major parties still. The Alliance in 1983, like the Liberals previously, suffered additionally from the handicap of drawing support fairly evenly from all occupational classes. Under Britain's plurality rule ('first past the post') electoral system, this failure to attract support from one well-defined group, heavily concentrated in particular areas of the country, meant that the Alliance's ratio of seats won to votes received was much worse than that of the two major parties. Only a major sustained rise in support to levels over 30 per cent of the poll offers the Alliance any real chance of 'breaking the mould' of the two-party system sufficiently to win seats in rough proportion to its share of the national vote. Still, the Alliance can draw comfort from two facts. Its support base is now consistently higher than that the Liberals achieved on their own in the late 1970s, and higher than any third party has registered consistently before in the post-war period. And, since as the Liberals alone and the Alliance in 1983 have always garnered more votes at the end of a general-election campaign than opinion-poll results would suggest (see Figure 2.2 for confirmation of this), so the Alliance may hope to achieve a future campaign increment to their current vote base.

Some recent changes in party fortunes are clearly linked to some specific events of potentially limited significance. The Falklands campaign, for example, dramatically boosted the flagging fortunes of the government even before it was successfully concluded, an effect that also accelerated the decline in the Alliance's initially very high poll rating. But the parties' performance since 1979 also raises longer-term questions about possibly fundamental changes in voters' attitudes and orientations. At least three explanations of the Conservative's apparent strength despite Britain's poor economic performance have been suggested. First, the electorate could simply be moving to the right, retreating into Conservative attitudes as economic growth disappears and 'market disciplines' are once more seen as of paramount importance. Voters remain unhappy about rising unemployment, but pessimistic about any party's ability to provide a solution. Second, the electorate could be polarising into two groups. The majority group of voters, perhaps 35 per cent, still in work, living in prosperous regions and areas, working in jobs or occupations relatively safe from redundancies, and still enjoying rising living standards, may be moving to the right following the new market liberalism of Thatcherite Conservatism. A smaller group, perhaps 25 per cent, badly affected by the recession, living in depressed regions or inner-city areas, working in vulnerable jobs and industries, may be shifting left, following the Labour party's increasingly radical ideas on the need for economic restructuring. The rest of the electorate on this interpretation remains dispersed between these positions. Third, the electorate could be moving to the right in their views of economic policy (and also in endorsing the government's nationalistic line on the Falklands), while moving left on nuclear disarmament, and remaining committed to central elements of the previous consensus such as support for the welfare state.

There is at present no decisive evidence which could allow us to choose between these different interpretations. Nor are comparisons with other countries' recent experience particularly illuminating. In the early 1970s comparisons were made between 'de-alignment' in Britain and the USA. But although voters' support for the major US parties has declined, and issue-voting has increased, the result of these trends has not been rising third-party support (as in Britain) but a tendency for people to drop out of voting altogether. In the late 1970s, it was equally fashionable to detect a general swing to the right in liberal democracies due to the impact of the recession, and to locate the Conservative 1979 victory within this trend. But since then, socialist or social-democratic victories in Australia, France, Spain, Greece and Sweden have if anything suggested a counter-trend – but one that finds little apparent echo in the UK.

British electoral politics seem to be on the threshold of moving into a new era of permanent three-party competition, which may or may not be accompanied by a radical change in the voting system. But the exclusion of Alliance candidates from the Commons in numbers proportional to their votes continues to pose a fundamental question mark about whether the transformation of electoral politics apparently indicated by voting behaviour in 1983 will continue – and if so, with what final results and over what timescale.

3

The Parties and Parliament

HENRY DRUCKER

In recent years two of the long-immobile building blocks of
British politics, the party system and Parliament, have begun
to shift. From 1945 to the early 1970s, Britain had a stable
two-party system of government and electoral competition.
Two large parties, Labour and Conservative, took the reins of
office in turn, depending on which of them was the more
popular. No other party mattered. All the major interests
sympathised with one or other party and all accepted the
authority of the party that had won the most recent election.
The mechanism that translated victory at the polls into
government power was Parliament. The party that won the
majority of seats in the House of Commons formed the
government. Its MPs could be depended on to do as the party
bade. The party leaders, therefore, had unchallenged authority.

Yet there was always a paradox at the heart of this cosy
world. Parliament had great authority, but it did little. It did
not legislate. Bills were, to be sure, transformed into Acts by
their progress through Parliament. But to think of this as
legislation is to confuse the show with the reality. Parliament
had little say over the content of legislation. It could make only

such amendments as the government wished to accept. Backbench MPs could initiate legislation only on matters that the government's leaders did not want to touch – for example, on such matters of morality as divorce, homosexuality and capital punishment. Even Parliament's control over the government's money was limited. Much of the money the government raised, through loans, for example, was not subject to parliamentary scrutiny. Much of what it spent was nodded through the House with only ritual opposition. Since the government was the group of MPs who had a majority in the House, they could outvote the opposition anytime the opposition tried to be inconvenient. Hailsham's phrase 'elective dictatorship' was not far wrong.

The domination of the House of Commons – 'Westminster' for short – by the government was a feature of party government. It was made possible by the discipline of the MPs of the governing party and by the fact that, in this period, one or other party could always depend on having a majority of MPs. Had the MPs of the governing party, or coalition of parties, been less cohesive it might have been necessary for the government to bargain with them to preserve their control. So long as the two-party system lasted executive domination of the House of Commons was assured. This reliable world is passing. The party system is changing. We have more major parties and each of the parties suffers dissent within it. Simultaneously the executive domination of the House is loosening. These are the developments that I shall trace in this chapter.

Westminster

Dissent in the House

For all that they had been germinating for some time, these developments first made themselves felt in Westminster during the premiership of Edward Heath (1970–74). The government was defeated six times during Heath's premiership (Norton, 1981, p. 228). Each of these defeats required at least thirty-one Conservative MPs to dissent from their leaders. Since until the Heath Government it had been assumed that a government defeated on an important matter in the House would have to resign and ask the Queen for an election, fear that dissent would have this consequence held some MPs in check. Others were restrained by the fear of displeasing their leaders – from whom all preferment comes. What was striking about the successful rebellions against the Heath government was that no general election ensued. The government was forced to withdraw the measures it had lost, but it did not lose office.

The Labour governments elected in February and October 1974 were defeated twenty-three times by rebellions of their own MPs, and a further nineteen times by the united strength of the opposition parties. Again the government did not resign as a result (Norton, 1981, pp. 229–30). But the government elected in February 1974 had no overall majority; it could always be outvoted by the united opposition, and the government elected in October 1974 had a slim majority which it soon lost.

Once a government realises that MPs are not afraid to vote against it on important issues, it needs to pay much more attention to the voices of its backbenchers. This opens up the House to the kind of bargaining that was unknown when there was a strong two-party system. But this has not yet – quite – happened. The MPs who have rebelled have not done so consistently; their factions are not lasting, they lack formal leaders, they do not have openly organised support in the country. This being so, they do not carry enough weight to bargain with the party leaders on major issues – but they are getting closer all the time.

The return of a Conservative government in 1979 with an overall majority of forty-three seats restored some of the old party system, but not all. In the Parliament that followed, the government lost several proposals of consequence. Two local-government bills were withdrawn (see Chapter 5). Pressure from backbenchers and from within the Cabinet to increase public expenditure on unemployment benefit, for example, was successful (see Chapter 7). And the Government suffered rebellions over the regulations governing immigration to Britain from both 'wets' and 'dries' – the two major factional groupings within it (see below).

There were ways, too, that the Conservative government

suffered from indiscipline in its ranks which Labour had not known. It had difficulty with the House of Lords. Labour expects this. But for the Conservatives it points to the weakening of party loyalty. Over proposed cuts in rural school transport, BBC external services and the size of the navy, the Lords rebelled and the government obeyed.

NEW COMMITTEE SYSTEM

But the shifts in the party system within the House of Commons can no longer be understood simply as revolts against the government. The process has reached the point where governnments anticipate the change. This was shown clearly under the Conservative government's attitude to the committee system of the House. In 1978, the House of Commons Select Committee on Procedure (on which all parties are represented) recommended a number of reforms to select committees. It urged the replacement of the existing patchwork of select committees, some shadowing a department, some concentrating on particular policies (such as race relations) and some on parts of government (such as the nationalised industries), with a new system of committees – one for each of the major government departments. The 1978 Report also recommended giving the new committees more flexibility and more administrative support. The Labour government had resisted these proposals. The Leader of the House, Michael Foot, wanted to do nothing that would detract from the importance of the floor of the House. The Conservative government fulfilled its election pledge to implement the Procedure Committee's proposals after backbench rumblings on both sides of the House.

Compared with most legislatures, the House of Commons had had a weak committee system. Legislation is examined line-by-line in committee to be sure, but the committees (called misleadingly Standing Committees although a different committee is set up for each bill) consist of members in proportion to the party's strength in the House. Accordingly, unless there is a rebellion in a committee, the government normally gets its way. More commonly, Standing Committee sessions consist of repetitions of positions already staked out in the House –

though governments do sometimes accept minor amendments put forward by opposition MPs (often at the suggestion of pressure groups) on non-party issues.

The House also lacks a committee procedure for examining the government's proposed budget. But here again, there has been recent change. Days for opposition business, long known as 'Supply Days', are to be renamed Opposition Days. Three days a year are to be set aside for the consideration of estimates for particular departments. This will give the whole House some opportunity to discuss particular estimates – but there is no question of the House being allowed to raise any of them. Proposal of expenditure remains a Crown prerogative (i.e. a power possessed by the government as Her Majesty's Government, not by virtue of its control of the House of Commons).

The exercise by government of the Crown prerogative still precludes the House from considering some aspects of defence and foreign policy, the structure of government, or of the government's considerable patronage. There is nothing in Britain to compare with the examination by the American Senate of people nominated by the President to senior posts. And these things are little changed by the increase in powers for Select Committees.

After the Conservative government's reforms, select committees take evidence, consider and report on matters of public policy. There is a select committee for each of the major ministries. The most successful of the new committees is the Treasury and Civil Service Committee. Chaired by Edward Du Cann, who is also Chairman of the Conservative Party's backbenchers' '1922 Committee', it includes a number of Labour members who were formerly Treasury ministers. The reports of the Treasury and Civil Service Committee have criticised the government's effectiveness. But the impact of these reports depends much more on the reception given to them by the press and broadcasters than on the debate which follows on the floor of the House. This is just as well, as most select committee reports are not debated in the House. The impact of a report depends, too, on the select committee reporting unanimously. A divided report carries little weight. Such unanimity is not easily achieved. The less successful committees rarely achieve it. But unanimity does seem to be more frequent and its achievement reinforces other changes in the House. Moreover, there is now a system of select committees, not just (as before 1979) an *ad hoc* collection, within which to work.

In January 1983 St John-Stevas moved a private members' bill which was designed to strengthen considerably Parliamentary control over the executive. With support from senior backbenchers from both sides of the House he proposed to widen the remit of the Comptroller and Auditor General. At present, the Comptroller, who is appointed by the Government, will draw the attention of the Public Accounts Committee to any programme within the ambit of a Ministry which he thinks needs to be looked at. This excludes money spent by the public corporations (nationalised industries), as they are outside their ambit; St John Stevas's bill would include these.

OTHER CHANGES IN PARLIAMENT

Public assistance to parliamentary parties was radically increased. Public assistance to the parties began in 1975. The amount was raised in 1978 by 10 per cent and then by the Conservative government by a further 75 per cent in November 1980. The increase was the more remarkable for the fact that the government was in the midst of cutting public expenditure wherever it could. The amount the parties obtain is calculated on a formula that takes account of the number of parliamentary seats they hold as well as the number of votes they obtained at the previous election. As a result of the 1980 changes Labour received £300,000 p.a.: the Liberals just over £50,000. The sums involved are still tiny. It is absurd to think that an Opposition with £300,000 per year is an even match for a government with the resources of the civil service at its command: but it ought to improve the Opposition's performance in the House. It is a step towards the professionalisation of politics. Since the money is paid to the parliamentary group within the party it ought, too, to strengthen the hands of MPs within their parties (Shell, 1981, p. 144).

Other trends in British society, having little or nothing to do with changes in the parties, have come to a head and reinforced the party changes. One of the most important of these is the development of politics as a profession. When the party system was strong, service in the House of Commons was often seen as an honour or a duty to one's party or country. While this ethos prevailed it was hardly necessary to worry about dissent in the House. But there are signs that this is now a disappearing motive. MPs are younger when they first enter the House (Rush, 1979, p. 90). One consequence of this is that fewer MPs than in the past have experience of another occupation at a senior level before they enter the House. On the other hand, they want to do something once they arrive at Westminster. Their confidence may be raised too as new MPs tend to be better, or at any rate, more formally, educated than previously (Kavanagh, 1982, p. 99).

Both parliamentary groups are more homogeneous than they were just after the war. On the Conservative side there has been a decline in the numbers of new MPs who were born into the aristocracy and a rise in the MPs from professions in the private sector. On the Labour side there has been a rise in the number of MPs who have had middle-class occupations and a drop in the number of MPs who have worked with their hands. As a result of these changes Westminster is more homogeneous as a whole, but there are still differences between the parties. Labour MPs are more likely to have worked in the public sector (mostly as teachers or lecturers) than Conservatives. In 1974 the two parties were 39 per cent (Labour) and 8 per cent (Conservative) previously state-employed (Kavanagh, 1982, p. 109). Younger, better educated, often from the professions and often full-time politicians – not for them the habitual or deferential loyalty of their predecessors.

The Parties

The changes in the party system and in Westminster have affected all the parties, but not equally. The traditional notion (McKenzie, 1963) that the parties are similar in that both are dominated by their parliamentary leaders, is no longer accurate. Labour is more changed and more weakened than the Conservative Party, but neither of them nor the new Social Democratic Party nor its Liberal Alliance partner is the monolithic block of the traditional picture. All the parties are complicated coalitions. They are factional coalitions, divided right and left or dry and wet; horizontal coalitions, in which the troops are no longer willing to march into gunfire without good reason; and they are geographical coalitions in which the local interest of the northern regions of England, or Scotland or Wales pull in somewhat different directions. Managing these complicated organisations is nothing like as simple as it was and it is particularly difficult for the parties out of power.

LABOUR

With its elaborate federal structure (of affiliated trades unions, local constituency parties and MPs) and ideology, Labour has been the most changed recently. Personalities aside, Labour's internal differences centre around a debate over the proper place of Parliament and parliamentary ideas in the party. The debate is between those who want the party to be ruled, as are the other parties, by its MPs, and to be dominated by the procedures that suit the House, and, on the other hand, those who want the party's MPs – the Parliamentary Labour Party (PLP) – faithfully to reflect the views of party members.

Until 1979 Labour was arguably more parliamentary in its outlook and procedures than most other social-democratic parties. The leader of the PLP, in effect of the party, was elected solely by the MPs. This is unusual among social-democratic parties, most of whom allow some element of wider democracy, and was less democratic than the procedures of the British Liberal Party. In addition, MPs selected by constituency labour parties (CLPs) were virtually untouchable. They were all but automatically reselected by their party for each subsequent general election. The writing of the party manifesto for each election was in theory the chore of the Labour cabinet or shadow cabinet, but in fact the leader and his assistants presented the draft document to their colleagues too late for major changes to be incorporated. These three practices flew in the face of the Party's formal commitment to wider intra-party democracy. Formally Labour was committed to the notions that the supreme body in the party was the Annual Conference and that its executive arm was the NEC. In fact the leadership could and, particularly under Wilson, did repeatedly ignore the decisions of Annual Conference (Minkin, 1980, p. 327).

The division within the party was not merely about who made party policy. It was also about who was listened to. Labour's MPs had a dual mandate: they had obligations to their electors and to their party. This caused little difficulty until the late 1970s when differences between the ideas of the average elector and the party workers who controlled the CLPs opened up. The electorate had been moving away from the socialist ideas which Labour implemented in 1945–51, while the party workers moved on to more socialist positions. Most MPs were ill at ease with their constituency activists' new-found radicalism and tried to keep in touch with their images of their electors.

The difficulty was exacerbated by an apparent drop in the number of individual members. Official figures are of little help here. No party's central office really knows what its individual membership is, and most take steps to hide what they do know. From 1963 to 1979 Labour used an artificial method of calculating which, in 1978, credited them with 675,000 members: the real number was probably nearer 250,000 of whom about 55,000 were active. On the other hand, Labour can also count on the energy of very large numbers of the four million trade unionists who are affiliated members of whom perhaps one million help at elections. The best available estimates of the numbers of individual members in the British parties are shown in Table 3.1. There is some reason to think that the drop in Labour Party membership results from a disproportionate loss of working-class members. In other words, constituency parties, like the PLP, have become increasingly middle class (Whiteley, 1982, p. 115). This is confirmed by other research which shows that Annual Conference delegates in the late 1970s were disproportionately male, middle class and militant (Whiteley and Gordon, 1980).

These changes, and the tensions they have caused, have been articulated in ideological form. The preponderance of senti-ment within the PLP remains attached to a revised form of Keynesianism. Leaders like Callaghan, Healey, Hattersley and Shore have attempted to limit support for the Alternative Economic Strategy (AES). The AES has many variations, but

TABLE 3.1   *Individual party membership*

Party	Estimated members	Date
Conservative	1,495,000	1974
Labour	250,000	1978
Liberal	197,000	1974
Social Democratic Party	67,000	1982
Plaid Cymru	30,000	1982
Scottish National Party	15,000	1982

Sources: Lord Houghton, *Report of the Committee on Financial Aid to Political Parties* (HMSO, 1976) for Conservative and Liberal; Whiteley (1982, p. 115) for Labour. (SNP, SDP and Plaid Cymru – our estimate.)

basically requires selected import controls, large increases in public spending, strengthened direction over the flow of private capital and, perhaps, incomes policies. They have distanced themselves from the party's move toward unilateral disarmament, and wondered nervously what to do about the commitment to withdraw from the EEC.

For its part the cry from the left has come for a 'socialist government, not another labour government', and the cry reveals the bitterness of betrayal by the Wilson government and again in the last months of the Callaghan administration. The leaders Healey and Callaghan were warned clearly and publicly in the summer of 1978 that the party and the unions would not stand for a 5 per cent pay norm. These warnings were ignored by an exhausted leadership (see Chapter 7 and 10). Much of the passion for reform of the party's institutions comes from this experience and the determination not to let it happen again.

Tony Benn has been the main propagandist of the left within the PLP. He has championed all the policies that have swept Annual Conference since the 1979 election: the AES, withdrawal from the EEC, and unilateral disarmament. He has gone further and urged British withdrawal from Northern Ireland. But most of the fear Benn inspired in his parliamentary colleagues and the enmity he aroused in the press, came from his support for changes in Labour's own constitution. They are mistaken to think him opposed to parliamentary sovereignty, for he has repeatedly argued for greater accountability of government to Parliament and has been particularly keen to tie down the Prime Minister (Benn, 1980). For most of this period Benn has been a central figure in British politics: more controversial by far than his party's leaders. The left loved him and the right loved to hate him. There was something about his calm humourlessness under questioning that frightened his opponents.

For most of the period during which the Labour Party was dominated by its PLP (i.e. until the 1979 election) the PLP leadership had the ear and votes of the largest trade unions. This too has changed. The largest of all, the Transport and General Workers' Union (T & GWU) has been dependably on the 'left' of the Labour Party in the 1970s and the 1980s. The Engineers' union, the AUEW, was on the left in the early 1970s but moved right later. Other large and powerful unions such as the Miners' (NUM) and the National Union of Public Employees (NUPE) were normally on the left. The shift of union votes to the left was, however, not decisive or reliable. It meant simply that no one side could count on winning debates, and factions counted for more (Taylor, 1982).

Labour has developed a genius for creating factions. This is particularly true on the left. Among the most successful of the factions of the left was the Campaign for Labour Party Democracy (CLPD). Formed in 1973, the campaign involves some MPs, CLPs, unions and individual members. It was instrumental in pushing for changes to the Party constitution in the wake of Thatcher's 1979 victory (Kogan and Kogan, 1982). The Labour Co-ordinating Committee (LCC) was another powerful group which differed from CLPD in working on issues of public policy – withdrawal from the Common Market for example – and in not having individual members, but in co-ordinating the efforts of existing groups. There were groups on the right too. The Campaign for Labour Victory (CLV) was the most prominent until most of its leaders gave up and formed the SDP. And there were other groups not dependably right or left, such as the Trade Unions for a Labour Victory (TULV).

Groups like CLPD and the LCC were instrumental in orchestrating the energy of the left. On occasion their work was skilled and sophisticated. They were capable of quickly appreciating the importance of events and responding to them. In the debates on the party constitution in particular they had some success. But on a larger scale they lost. The reforms of the party constitution did not so much democratise it, as federalise it. The PLP was deprived of much of its autonomy in favour of the party as a whole, not in favour of its members – or voters. The leader, for instance, is now chosen by an elaborate college in which the unions, the PLP and the CLPs each have a say. The procedure is so comprehensive and lengthy that leaders, once elected, are strengthened. Michael Foot might well have been challenged in 1982: he was unpopular enough, but the new procedure would follow from any challenge. The leader is not chosen by the members or the voters. Similarly, MPs now have to gain renomination from their CLPs and the process is no mere formality. But individual members have no entry to the process. The decision is made, in Labour's traditional way, by branch and union delegates.

Confirmation that defeats for the PLP were not simply victories for the left came during the 1982 Annual Conference. The Party elected a right-wing dominated National Executive Committee (partly with the contested votes of the NUR, whose leader Sid Weighell was forced to stand down following a controversy over the way he had cast the union's block vote). Conference also accepted the recommendation of the NEC that it establish a register of affiliated organisations. This was designed to exclude Trotskyist groups from the party and was opposed by most of the left. *Militant* is the best known of these groups and it was the main target of the register. But, strictly, *Militant* is not an organisation, it is a newspaper. Its opponents claim that this is a ruse: that *Militant* is a newspaper run by a secret organisation, the Revolutionary Socialist League (RSL), to win recruits, provide cash for the RSL and give its members up-to-date information and guidance (Baker, 1981, pp. 31–55).

In June 1983 Labour suffered a crushing defeat winning only 27.6% of the vote and 209 seats. Michael Foot resigned as Leader and was replaced by his favourite Neil Kinnock. Kinnock's first job was to restore the morale of his party and end its internal feuding.

SOCIAL DEMOCRATIC

In March 1981 four former Labour Cabinet Ministers, Roy Jenkins, Shirley Williams, David Owen and William Rodgers and twelve other MPs formed the Social Democratic Party (SDP). Theirs was the largest breakaway of MPs from a parliamentary party since the beginning of the Conservative–Labour *pas de deux* in the 1920s. With the singular exception of Christopher Brocklebank-Fowler (Conservative MP for Norfolk North-West) all the new party's MPs were ex-Labour Party members. The SDP concluded an alliance with the Liberal Party almost immediately.

The most important thing about the new party is that it was created by a group of senior politicians who are young enough to dream of holding office again. They, and many others, thought there were enough people in Britain fed up with the apparently extremist main parties (and not yet attracted to the Liberal Party) to make a new party a serious contender for power. For most of 1981 it was possible to think they had guessed correctly. Polls conducted before the party was launched showed that 30 per cent of the electorate would support it. About 17,000 people joined the party in its first year and it performed handsomely in its first three by-elections at Warrington in July, at Crosby in November and in Hillhead in March 1982. But even while they won Hillhead, their peak had passed. In November 1981 they were the most popular party in the country; by the Summer of 1982 they had fallen to third behind Conservative and Labour.

Initially the party enjoyed a flattering press and was frequently in the news (Seymour-Ure, 1982). For many of the more serious papers the creation of the new party and its Alliance with the Liberals was not just a good story – the break-up of the Labour Party, a kick in the teeth to the Bennites, and a major outmanoeuvring of the Conservative government – it was at the same time an event to be welcomed in its own right. Most of the serious papers and television programmes about politics are dominated by people for whom the norm is still the Keynesian consensus. The Alliance promised a return to that norm and a way out of the Bennite/Monetarist choice now apparently offered by the two major parties. The initial by-election successes of the Alliance in 1981 kept press interest alive by providing more favourable news. It was 'David versus Goliath' – an irresistible story. So long as the Alliance could make itself the main political story they did well. In December 1980 the Liberal Party had 14.5 per cent of support; a year later the Alliance was tops at 46 per cent (Seymour-Ure, 1982).

But the story couldn't continue, for it was impossible for the Alliance to maintain such a high level of interest (Seymour-Ure, 1982). In the event the next running story the Alliance provided for the press – the fight between the two allies over the seats each would fight in the coming election – did the new grouping no good at all. But much more important, the Alliance could not long continue to make its own progress the main item of political news. The invasion of the Falklands in April 1982 was simply the event that confirmed the fact. During the battle to recapture British territory all domestic political opposition was temporarily forgotten (Stephenson, 1982).

By common consent the Liberal Party got the better of the division of seats. It is hard, in retrospect, to see how this could have been avoided. The SDP insisted on fighting the seats held by their MPs. But most of these were safe Labour seats where the Liberals had little strength. In return, however, the Liberals demanded and were given their 'Golden Fifty', the fifty seats where they thought they had the best chance of winning. When the SDP leaders conceded this exchange the Alliance was so popular that it hardly seemed to matter who fought which seat, and as the Liberals gave the SDP two-thirds of the next 100 'silver' seats the terms seemed equal. The problem for the SDP was that the Liberal Party knew what it wanted and they did not. The Liberals knew what they wanted because they are an activist-dominated party with a network of experienced constituency parties across the land. The SDP on the other hand were new. They were also strong in the centre and weak on the periphery. Arguably, strength in constituency parties counts for little when elections are fought – the SDP's leaders certainly thought so – but when it comes to dividing seats with another party the SDP's weakness in the constituencies was damaging.

The new party's policy-making process evolved quickly and acquired what was hoped would be its final form in November 1982. Policy is initiated by any one of the twenty-five policy groups whose membership and remit are decided by the Policy Committee. The Policy Committee consists of twenty members, ten MPs and ten others, all of them members of the National Committee of which the Policy Committee is a subordinate. The Policy Committee and its groups first publish their proposals as Green Papers, and then, having considered responses from local (area) parties and outside groups they reformulate the proposals as White Papers. The representations from the outside groups and the party members are taken seriously for they have considerable influence with the body that formally accepts policy. This is the Council for Social Democracy. The Council is a four hundred member body which meets three or four times a year and is chaired by the Party's President.

The Council cannot amend policy in a way that the Policy Committee does not approve; nor can the Policy Committee make policy that the Council does not approve. Formally the Council cannot amend the White Papers. It can send them back to the Policy Committee for further work. The first White Paper sent to the Council, on Industrial Strategy, was accepted. The second, on Economic Strategy, was accepted save for an objection to the Policy Committee's hope for a short-term statutory incomes policy. The Council wanted a more flexible incomes policy from the outset.

Half the membership of the policy committee is more than enough to ensure MP domination. Deference to Parliament, the MPs' long habit of working together, their greater access to publicity, all keep authority with the MPs. This domination is also reflected in the SDP's joint policy commissions with the Liberal Party. There is no mention of such commissions in the SDP's constitution. Nonetheless, there are two such commissions, one on Employment and Industrial Recovery and the other on Constitutional Reform. Half the members of both commissions are MPs. These commissions are finding few differences between the parties and coming to joint agreements rapidly. The Constitutional Reform Commission, for example, agreed to back a system of proportional representation on 'single transferable vote' lines, with little difficulty. The joint commission could easily lead to a joint manifesto.

CONSERVATIVE

Since the accession of Heath to the leadership of the Conservative Party in August 1965, the Party has changed considerably. These changes have been consolidated under the regime of Margaret Thatcher which began in February 1975. Before Heath became Leader of his Party, it was agreed that divisions within the Party tended to be temporary disputes on individual issues. Generally the divisions did not have doctrinal purchase and usually they were between changing groups of people (Rose, 1969). This was taken to mean that the Conservative Party did not have factions. It is much more difficult to argue that now (Russel, 1978; and Seyd, 1980).

One can discern two broad tendencies within the Conservative Party. These have been given the soubriquets 'wet' and 'dry'. The original meaning of these terms in schoolboy chatter matters less than the fact, no longer anywhere denied, that these terms refer to two doctrinally informed, more or less permanently opposed groups of MPs. Thatcher has when possible surrounded herself with dries and has promoted them: Sir Geoffrey Howe, Sir Keith Joseph, Norman Tebbit and John Nott are among the most prominent of those appointed in 1979. Dries are more concerned with control of the money supply, which they see as the key to the rate of inflation, than they are with the rate of unemployment. They argue that it is necessary to cut back on the state's intervention in the lives of citizens, but this does not extend to people's private lives where the dries tend to be anything but libertarians – and neither do they worry (as does the American Right, for instance) about the autonomy of local government.

Their opponents are known as 'wets'. When Thatcher formed her first Cabinet in 1979 it was not at all clear that the dries had a majority. Prominent Cabinet wets included Norman St John-Stevas (dropped from the Cabinet in January

1981) and Sir Ian Gilmour, Lord Soames and Mark Carlisle (all dropped in September 1981). In an unusual move ex-Labour Minister Reg Prentice, who had defected to the Tory Party, was also appointed but he too was dropped in January 1981. Remaining wets such as Peter Walker (once a protégé of Heath's) and Jim Prior have been isolated. Wets like to think that they have a greater social conscience than dries. They don't become terribly excited about the extent of the state's powers: but they wish to use them gently to heal the nation's rifts (Gilmour, 1978 pp. 109ff.).

Factionalism in the Conservative Party used to be less public than in the Labour Party, in part because Conservatives had the sense to conduct their disputes in private or in obscure places. More recently some of these places such as Conservative Backbenchers Committees and Select Committees have been attracting more attention from the press. When the leadership of the Conservative Party fears trouble from within the ranks, they go to backbench committees to listen. An illuminating case occurred in December 1982. The Government, under pressure from the European Courts, wanted to change regulations governing immigration to Britain. The initial proposals from the Home Office (whose Minister, William Whitelaw, was generally regarded as a wet) came before the House of Commons as a White Paper in November. Fifty-four 'dry' MPs abstained. The government tightened the proposals to meet this factional pressure. The water for the new proposals was tested in the Conservative backbenchers' Home Affairs Committee two days before the crucial vote in the House. All seemed well. Wets spoke in favour and only two dries spoke against. Yet the proposals were defeated two days later in the House when twenty-three Conservative MPs voted against the government and a further twenty abstained. The wets immediately took the field and made it clear that any further concessions to the dries would force them to vote against the government. This is factional politics.

But the complexity of the current divisions are disguised by the rough and ready terms 'dry' and 'wet'. Both groups are subdivided: there are three kinds of dry and two species of wet. There is an aristocratic anti-egalitarian dry section, including John Biffen, Winston Churchill, and Julian Amery who believe the government's job is to preserve and protect the organic fabric of society. They are quite different in style from the populist dries, many of whom are new MPs (i.e. they sit for former Labour seats) like Harvey Proctor, Tony Marlow and Ivor Stanbrook. Both of these groups are firmly opposed to further immigration, keenly interested in law and order (see Chapter 9) and fee-paying schools, and it is this (rather than any economic issue) which distinguishes them from the third group of dries, the market liberals. Geoffrey Howe and Nigel Lawson are in this group. Most of the new thinking coming into the government via the Conservative Party, especially on economic and social policy issues, comes in through this group.

Neither are the wets united. There is a group around Edward Heath and Peter Walker who are avid modernisers. Their intellectual position is not so very different from that staked out for the Labour Party in the mid-1960s by Harold Wilson (save, of course, that they don't think Labour is a possible instrument of the modernisation of Britain). They want to make Britain an efficient modern society and have no time for the rituals and constraints of the past. Membership of the European Community (and a passion for information technology) is a cause that unites this group as it divides them from the aristocratic, and to some extent from the populist, dries. These technocratic wets differ from the market liberals primarily on their attitude to the trade unions. The former would like to incorporate the union leaders in their modern Britain: the latter want to undercut the condition that give the union leaders power. Ian Gilmour and William Whitelaw are a different kind of wet altogether. They are humanitarians. They want a caring society, rather than one that places all its hope on up-to-date technology. They do not want to exploit the racial issue and are willing to conciliate trade-union leaders.

But these divisions were shallow as compared to Labour's, and Mrs Thatcher had no difficulty making divisions in the Labour Party, a key talking point in the 1983 election. Her party were rewarded with a small reduction in votes – from 43.9 per cent in 1979 to 42.4 per cent in 1983 – and a handsome increase in seats – from 339 to 397.

LIBERAL

Superficially nothing ever changes for the Liberal Party. At every general election since the Second World War they have won between six and fourteen seats. Never since the war have they formed a government or part of a government. Yet the superficialities are very misleading. Having touched bottom in 1951 with 2.6 per cent of the UK vote the party has been moving up since, rather dramatically so in the 1970s. The party won 19.3 per cent and 18.3 per cent of the UK vote in the two 1974 elections and 13.8 per cent in 1979. It has benefited considerably from the movement away from the major parties, and yet is not able to translate its new popularity into sufficient seats to command power in Westminster.

The main reason the party has not been able to translate votes into seats is the electoral system. The first-past-the-post system now in use ensures that parties with a lowish vote fairly evenly across the country win very few seats. The 19.3 per cent of the vote the Liberal Party won in February 1974 earned it a paltry 2 per cent of the seats in the House of Commons. But as the Liberal Party's popularity rises it has come tantalisingly close to the point at which large numbers of seats could begin to fall to it. In fact that party has been particularly, if predictably, unfortunate in the timing of elections. During each of the last few parliaments there has come a peak of support for the 'third' party(ies). In the parliament elected in 1979 the 'third' parties were well in front of Labour and Conservative toward the end of 1981. But elections tend not to coincide with these peaks – only in 1974's first election did the Liberals capitalise well on the unpopularity of the major parties.

A party that is long out of power can afford the luxury of criticising its opponents and contrasting their actual records with its ideals. The Liberal Party has more than its share of activists who indulge this freedom. The achievement of the Party under its leader David Steel, has been to form connections with two other parties as it has moved nearer and nearer the centre of the stage. In 1977 when the Labour Government had lost its overall majority in the House of Commons, it made a pact with the Liberals. No Liberal joined the Cabinet, but the government agreed to consult them regularly on major issues, and the two parties agreed to back certain common items of policy such as devolution to Scotland and Wales. The Pact lasted until May 1978. It accomplished little save that it made the Liberals look more like a party of government (Michie and Hoggart, 1978).

The Alliance concluded in 1981 with the leaders of the breakaway SDP was a more formidable affair. Steel was in on the formation of the new party from the first. There is even a suggestion that he discouraged Roy Jenkins from leaving Labour for the Liberals, on the suspicion that a new breakaway party would carry more weight into the political centre than any resignations from Labour to join the Liberals might do (Bradley, 1981, p. 79). In any event Steel encouraged the formation of the new party publicly and moved quickly to ally with it once it was created. As with the Pact, the Alliance was formed by the Liberal Party leader and then sold to his Party. In the 1983 general election Steel and Jenkins led the Alliance to win 26 per cent of the vote, only slightly less than Labour, and yet they held only 23 seats in parliament.

Scottish National

In the 1970s the Scottish National Party (SNP) emerged from the fringes of politics to become one of the major Scottish parties. From February 1974 when it won seven seats, to October 1974 when it won eleven seats, until May 1979 when it fell back to two, the SNP forced the Scottish question onto the agenda of British politics. Though committed ultimately to independence for Scotland, the SNP's policy through most of the 1970s was to work for devolution as the first step. When the Labour governments of 1974–9 proposed a form of directly elected assembly which would be able to make laws and which would have power over the Scottish Office, the SNP grudgingly voted for the proposals.

The party's problem was to mobilise its supporters. In October 1974 it had come second in Scotland with 30 per cent of the vote (much better than the Liberal performance in England), and its peak came in the May 1977 local elections when it swept the council estates (two-thirds of Scots live in publicly-owned housing). But the reasons for the advance and subsequent retreat of the nationalist tide are obscure. In a rough and ready way, it is clear that the party won votes from people who had been torn from their moorings in the old class alignment. It performed best among young males who lived in New Towns (Miller, 1981 and Drucker and Brown, 1980).

At its peak the SNP crystallised an exuberant enthusiasm for politics and an optimism about the possibility of political change which it is now almost painful to recall. The prospect of being oil-rich and independent may have had something to do with it. But whatever the reason, the euphoria had quite gone by May 1979 when the SNP's share of the Scottish vote dropped to (a still respectable) 17.3 per cent.

The bigger blow to morale and purpose had come in March 1979 when Scots only barely endorsed devolution in a referendum. Asked if the Scotland Act should be put into effect, slightly less than a third (32.5 per cent) said 'Yes', rather fewer (30.4 per cent) said 'No', and another third (37.1 per cent) didn't vote. The massive support for their proposals which its proponents had claimed did not exist. The new Conservative government did not implement the Act. From that point the SNP's difficulty was to find a new issue around which to regroup. Some left-wing members of the SNP thought the party should commit itself to the creation of an independent, socialist republican country. In the lee of the May 1979 election they formed a faction, the 79 Group, to forward this aim. The party spent much of the next parliament outlawing the Group and – almost – expelling, its leaders. In June 1983 the SNP's poll fell to 12 per cent of Scotland's vote and two seats.

PLAID CYMRU

The successes and difficulties of the Welsh party, Plaid Cymru (PC), were quite different. By winning the Caermarthen by-election in July 1966 they made their initial breakthrough first. But after the 1970 general election the SNP made the running. In February and October 1974 the Plaid vote fell back from its 11.5 per cent 1970 peak, while the SNP were setting the heather alight. Further, when the devolution referendum was held in Wales, the proposal was overwhelmingly thrown out. Only 11.8 per cent voted 'Yes', 46.5 per cent voted 'No', and 41.7 per cent stayed at home.

Recovery from such a defeat is not easy. Yet it is arguable that the PC – and the Welsh national movement generally – have had more influence in Wales since the referendum than the national movement in Scotland. The Welsh have rallied to the protection of their culture and language. The Conservative Party had promised during the 1979 election to allow the new 'fourth' television channel for Wales to be in Welsh. After the election the Home Secretary backed away from the promise. A nationwide campaign led by PC President Gwynfor Evans, in which Evans threatened a fast to death unless the government fulfilled its election promise, changed the government's mind again. The campaign reminded Welshmen that the failure of the devolution campaign did not end the role of Plaid. In its first months the Welsh-language Channel was substantially more popular in Wales than Channel 4 was in the rest of Britain. In June 1983, Plaid won 8 per cent of Wales' votes and two seats.

The Party System

If Britain once had a two-party system in which monolithic blocks exchanged supreme power after general elections, this system no longer works. The electorate no longer vote that way (see Chapter 2). Partly as a result, there are three large national party coalitions: Conservative, Labour and Alliance. The votes of the seventeen Northern Ireland MPs are not in the pockets of any of the British parties and the Scottish and Welsh nationalists can challenge the British parties for a scattering of seats in their nations.

Before the 1970s, the two-party system was not only secure, it was also much praised (Epstein, 1980). As the two great parties have lost support, so the system of their alternation in power has been increasingly criticised. One powerful school of critics, forcefully led by S.E. Finer (Finer, 1975) has argued that in place of two responsible parties, each led toward the centre by leaders who sought the votes of the middle-ground 'floaters', Britain now has two adversarial parties, each controlled by ideologically intense local activists, each cynically uncaring about the wishes of the electorate, each waiting only for the next turn of the wheel of electoral fortune so they can return to power, and having uprooted the policies of their predecessors, dig in their own. Finer argued that the British electoral system – popularly known as 'first past the post' – discourages the other parties and protects the major parties against the consequences of their loss of popular support.

There has been a revival of ideological thinking. There is also some evidence that the two major parties have lost popular support. It is arguable, too, that there has been a shift within the parties to greater member control, but the adversarial thesis overstates the extent of this shift. The final leg of the adversarial stool, that the parties change policies radically in office, is also open to challenge. Sometimes important changes of policy occur without reference to elections. The Labour government in 1976 adopted some of the tenets of monetarism when pressed to do so by the International Monetary Fund (see Chapter 6), and there are powerful constraints on party manifestos (see Chapters 6–8). Yet there are some areas of public policy that have seen rapid changes in the wake of successive elections: tax law, trade-union law and the extent of state intervention in the economy have all changed in this way. All these areas of policy closely affect the major interests of the most powerful groups associated with the major parties. It is hardly surprising that newly elected governments act swiftly here, and as there is general agreement that we can no longer assume sustained growth in the economy and hence in public expenditure, there is reason to think that successive governments now have to redistribute existing resources in order to placate their friends.

Finer and his colleagues hoped that a change in the electoral system to a form of proportional representation would make party politics less adversarial. Under proportional representation coalitions would be more common and stability of policy a likely consequence. It is unlikely that a Conservative–Alliance government formed after one election would be radically different from, say, the Labour–Alliance government that had preceded it. But we may not need to change the electoral system to have more coalition governments. Continuation of existing trends makes them more likely (Curtice, and Steed, 1982). The present electoral system may over-reward the major parties but even this advantage failed to provide the country with a single-party majority government in 1974 and the trend in that direction is clear. The sizeable Conservative majority elected in 1983 is simply a grotesque example of the peculiarities of the electoral system. The Conservative vote fell in the 1983 election.

4

Government at the Centre

GILLIAN PEELE

The prospect of a change of government in the United Kingdom inevitably leads to speculation about the extent to which the incoming administration will attempt to alter the structure of departments or rearrange the pattern of central government responsibilities. The results of the 1979 general election gave more reason than most transfers of power for such speculation and for a certain nervousness in Whitehall. Margaret Thatcher came to office as a radical prime minister committed *inter alia* to a reduction in the size of the civil service and to a new search for efficiency in government – a theme which, as one senior civil servant was later to comment, has come to dominate current political debate about the bureaucracy (Wass, 1982). Thatcher also brought with her a reputation for . challenging departmental assumptions and was expected to display an inherent distrust of the civil service at the abstract level, though her personal relationships with departmental advisers appear to have been warm. Since 1964 at least, all governments have come to power expecting their policies to conflict with the preferences of the civil service; but the economic and political climate in 1979 was such as to maximise the suspicion between the political and the permanent elements of the administration. The Conservative Party for its part had become convinced of the need for retrenchment in the public sector and felt that its natural ideological preferences and the trend of informed opinion were at one on this issue. Quite understandably the civil service feared the consequences of extensive cuts both in terms of jobs and in terms of professional morale. In short, as one civil servant expressed it in retrospect, May 1979 was seen as more than a change of government because in terms of political and economic philosophy 'it was a revolution' (Pliatzky, 1982).

Thatcher's Ambiguous Record

The actual experience of the Conservative government elected in 1979 and re-elected in 1983 has, however, proved curiously ambiguous. Many of the changes that occurred at the centre represented trends that had begun long before Thatcher entered Downing Street and many had been foreshadowed in the Labour administration of James Callaghan. On the other hand, the latter part of Thatcher's first government saw a flurry of press speculation about the likelihood of major alterations to the organisation of central government – most notably about the possible creation of a prime minister's department to strengthen the instruments for controlling the overall strategy of the government. The highly unusual crisis produced by the 1982 Argentine invasion of the Falklands focused attention on the machinery of government as well as on the quality of advice available to the government on foreign policy and security matters (see Chapter 8). The successful conclusion of the war, while it did not directly lead to the creation of anything akin to the American Executive Office, perhaps enabled Thatcher to adopt a more 'presidential' style of leadership and certainly strengthened her personal position within the cabinet and the party. Moreover, while constraints on public expenditure were hardly novel, they did add to the environment of uncertainty by giving rise to extensive discussions of alternative approaches to public provision of welfare services. Much controversy was generated by a leaked 'think-tank' report which suggested the privatisation of parts of the health services as a way of coping with financial pressures, and, within the sphere of local government, the various authorities found themselves having to adapt to increasingly intrusive demands for economy.

The purpose of this chapter is to set some of these post-1979 developments into wider perspective by relating them to the general framework of the British political and administrative system. Although it concentrates on the central institutions of the state, it would be a mistake to believe that what happens in Whitehall can really be viewed in isolation from developments at other levels of the system. The distinction between central and local government under the Tories has become frailer than ever as Whitehall has assumed responsibility for controlling local government expenditures (see Chapter 5). And behind the more visible aspects of policy-making there is a complex plethora of personal and institutional interactions which must be taken into account if the evolution of health policy, for example, is to be properly understood (Haywood and Hunter, 1982). Nevertheless it is at the centre that the guiding principles of an administration – and its contradictions – can most readily be studied, and it is this level of government that therefore forms a convenient starting-point for any more comprehensive examination of the contemporary political scene.

Several features of the political environment in which Thatcher had to operate when she acquired power in 1979 must be borne in mind when attempting to assess the specific developments in British central government since that time. Some of these are examined in greater detail elsewhere in this book but here four general points should be made.

Difficulties in Rolling Back the Public Sector

First, Thatcher and the Conservative Party were acutely aware of the difficulties of rolling back the frontiers of the public sector and conscious that previous efforts by Conservative governments had failed to make much impact on the size of public expenditure. Edward Heath had come to power promising a 'quiet revolution' and espousing a philosophy of revived capitalism and free enterprise; but his policies indicated that the philosophy had been equally quietly abandoned in response to the concrete pressures of office. In fact the Heath government saw no real shedding of functions and the revival of 'tri-partism'; observers were increasingly tempted to describe British politics in those years by reference to theories of corporatism rather than theories of *laissez-faire* capitalism or traditional notions of parliamentary democracy (Smith, 1979; Middlemas, 1979; Beer, 1982). The five and a half years in which Britain enjoyed minority or near-minority government (from March 1974 to May 1979) saw little change in the scale of government activity, and no major reduction in the range of services for which the state had direct or indirect responsibility, despite an increasing awareness on the part of some Labour politicians that there was a need to curtail public expenditure and some desire even among their own voters for a different balance between high taxation and extensive provision of services. Indeed, the period between 1974 and 1979 saw the establishment of a National Enterprise Board in 1975 as an experiment in new ways of organising government influence in the economy; and it also saw a rapid growth in the number of non-departmental government agencies to exercise all manner of functions of an advisory, executive and policy-making kind. These so-called 'Quangos' (see Chapter 5) had increased with the Heath government, and it seemed likely that another Conservative administration would swiftly abolish large numbers of them. In fact the Conservatives, once in power, again made only a limited assault on the number and budgets of non-departmental public bodies (Hood and Wright, 1981). The general review by Sir Leo Pliatzky in 1980 did, it is true, force departments to consider the purpose of a number of bodies that might have become superfluous, and resulted in recommendations to axe some 30 executive bodies and a further 211 advisory councils. However, the spirit of caution and consolidation – not radical deregulation – suffused the report, and few proponents of rolling back the frontiers of the state believed that much had been done to promote that goal by such moves as the merger of the White Fish Authority with the Herring Industry Board.

The development of alternative forms of state activity to the orthodox pattern of direct departmental control makes it difficult both to present a tidy picture of government operations and to assess the true scale of public sector involvement in

British society. The multi-faceted growth of the machinery of state according to some Conservatives, and the fact that previous administrations had failed to cut it, demanded vigorous action, but by the end of 1982 it was doubtful how much had actually been achieved in the effort to cut the size of the public sector. One measure that might be used is the ratio of public expenditure to Gross Domestic Product which rose from 33.4 per cent in 1959 to 45.6 per cent in 1975–6. For 1979–80 it was 41.4 per cent and the provisional figures offered by Pliatzky were 43.6 per cent for 1980–1 (Pliatzky, 1982). Another measure of the scale of the public sector which might be employed is the number of civil servants. Here the Tories claim to have made a qualitative and quantitative impact. It must be remembered, of course, that while the figures given for the number of public sector employees appear very large, many of them will be employed in an industrial capacity, so that the number of people employed in what is customarily thought of as the civil service is much smaller. A parliamentary answer given in November 1982 showed that the Thatcher government's efforts to cut the numbers of state employees had resulted in a fall of 77,300 or 10.6 per cent of the numbers of industrial and non-industrial staff in post in central government between May 1979 and October 1982. What this meant, according to the same source, was that as at 1 October 1982 central government employed 521,000 non-industrial staff and 133,900 industrial staff. It is worth noting, however, that the cuts have been particularly severe at the highest levels, so that the numbers of deputy secretaries and assistant secretaries within the administrative ranks have been sharply reduced. Although these numbers are perhaps small *in toto*, such a reduction does have implications for the career structure of the service and, together with other developments, could reduce its attractiveness to new recruits.

Piecemeal Changes

The scale of government operations would not have occasioned such political criticism had it not been for the second feature of the British political scene which needs bearing in mind in any discussion of central government under Margaret Thatcher: continued dissatisfaction with the policy outputs of government. The starkest failure, of course, was the stubborn resistance of the economy to all attempts to improve it and the poor performance of British industry. The extent of the state's involvement in the economy, including the numbers employed by government rather than by productive industry, became a natural target for academic and political criticism (Eltis and Bacon, 1976). When Thatcher became leader of the opposition in 1975 she made a number of moves that suggested that constitutional and institutional reform might be high on her order of priorities. In office, however, she has made the overriding concern of her administration the correction of the British economy. Moreover she has defined her economic goals in very clear terms – the reduction of inflation and the improvement of manufacturing output (see Chapter 6). Unlike Edward Heath, whose early period in office was marked by a major attempt to reorganise central government and introduce managerial innovations into the departments – attempts that themselves reflected a substantial interest in the problems of government organisation – Thatcher has avoided such experimenting with the machinery of government. Individual ministers have been relied upon to monitor waste in their own departments and have been scrutinised individually for their contributions to the exercise of reducing public expenditure (Lee, 1981). Certainly she had a desire to introduce sound business methods into Whitehall and appointed two key advisers from the business world – Sir John Hoskyns and Sir Derek Rayner. However, with the possible exception of the MINIS experiment at the Department of the Environment (see p. 99), there were few promotions of managerial techniques on a grand scale, and certainly no announcement of an intention to introduce a 'new style of government' along the lines heralded by the Heath government's white paper on central government reorganisation.

Dissatisfaction with the general position of the United Kingdom and the operations of the country's political system was reflected in many of the academic studies written during the 1970s. These works highlighted the national decline and stagnation and singled out two features of the political system for special criticism. The first object of criticism was the civil service, which was seen by many as being too narrow in its outlook, too general in its philosophy and too 'elitist' in its composition as a result of a perceived predominance of Oxford and Cambridge graduates in its upper ranks. The second target of attack was the electoral system, which was credited with the production of the two-party system and a syndrome labelled 'adversary politics'. (Finer, 1975). It is possible that the volume of criticism levelled at the civil service over the past decade and a half has undermined its morale but provided a useful questioning of some of the assumptions about its position in the political system. Recent moves towards a greater politicisation of the bureaucracy and towards public discussion of the contribution made by civil servants to the policy process, indicate that the constitutional position of the civil service is not a static one and memoirs of civil servants suggest that change is not wholly unwelcome (Pliatzky, 1982). Little evidence exists, though, to suggest that the two major parties have in any sense been affected either by academic criticism or by the electorate's disenchantment with both Labour and Conservatives. PM Heath's flirtation with the idea of a government of national unity in 1974 raised little enthusiasm in his own party, and once Thatcher became the Tory leader it became plain that what others might see as an unfortunate polarisation of British politics she welcomed as a clear choice between competing views. The formation and subsequent development of the Social Democratic Party and that party's alliance with the Liberal Party represented an attempt to recolonise the centre ground of British politics; but after an initial wave of publicity, it seemed that the impact of the new party was limited (see Chapter 3). The British political system thus seemed to many observers extremely gloomy, since it was marked by a combination of alienation from two parties which nevertheless retained a stranglehold on the polity because of apathy and the system's own inbuilt barriers to change.

Parliamentary Control of the Civil Service

The third aspect of British government that must be borne in mind in a sense lightens this picture. For while the two major parties have been resistant to change, there have been developments in other parts of the constitutional system and those developments have at the very least prevented the structure of British central government from becoming fossilised. Constitutional change in the United Kingdom tends to be unacknowledged and slow, although recent commentators have noticed the extent to which a great number of traditional assumptions about the British constitution are in need of revision (Peele, 1978; Norton, 1982). The introduction of new institutions such as the Parliamentary Commissioner for Administration, and the revision of old ones such as the comprehensive reorganisation of select committees in the House of Commons, may be adopted as isolated remedies for limited problems. Frequently, however, these changes have consequences that were unanticipated both in relation to their impact on other aspects of government and on political values. For example, the creation of a new select committee system in 1979–80 reflected an increased independence of mind on the part of individual backbenchers; but the structural change also *contributed* to that change by offering opportunities for legislative scrutiny of the executive and assertion of parliamentary interests. Critics of the idea of a Parliamentary Commissioner and of any extension of the select committee scheme often used the argument that additional work for the departments would be caused by these bodies. There is undoubtedly some truth in the view that more time has now to be spent within the departments to prepare for such investigations as the select committees or PCA may undertake, but it is perhaps indicative of the route which these institutions have taken that few would seriously now consider abolishing them on the grounds of economy or administrative convenience.

Equally important from the point of view of the routine workings of Whitehall has been the impact of the British membership of the European Communities where an additional burden has been placed on civil servants and ministers alike; and in the case of ministerial 'overload' it has been suggested that the frequent travelling involved may have compounded the problems associated with controlling large departments.

More Leaks but no Open Government

At the same time as these institutional changes have affected
the routine operations of central government, the political
environment has altered in somewhat less tangible ways.
Whitehall now has to operate in an atmosphere of greater
openness and iconoclasm than in the past. Although Thatcher's government has done little to reform the Official Secrets
Act, much less to promote any legislation on freedom of
information, it has had to tolerate greater exposure of the
working of government, including cabinet committees. Thus
when Thatcher in 1979 refused to admit more than the fact
that her cabinet possessed committees on economic strategy,
defence and overseas policy, home and social affairs and
legislation, she was resisting the general demand among
academic and media commentators for the relaxation of a rule
of secrecy more honoured in the breach than the observance.
The extent to which the environment had changed was marked
by *The Times*'s publication in February 1981 of an article which
not merely gave a tabular list of cabinet committees, but
invited any 'public spirited minister or civil servant' to make
corrections by supplying further details to *The Times* in an
'unsigned, typed message, slipped in the traditional brown
envelope favoured by "moles"' (Hennessy, 1981). At the same
time the relationships between ministers and civil servants,
which were formerly so sacrosanct, have received a great deal
more scrutiny both in Parliament and in the press than
hitherto, and certainly there is now much more comment on
the individual personalities and policy preferences of such
figures as Sir Robert Armstrong and Peter Middleton than
would have been customary even ten years ago. The *cause
célèbre* of cabinet secrecy in the 1970s – the so-called
Crossman diaries case – thus both highlighted a world that was
already passing and helped to hasten its demise (Young, 1976).

These developments on the wider stage of British government affect the discussion of specific problems at the centre of
British government in a variety of ways. At the most practical
level, constitutional changes have caused *ad hoc* adjustments
and improvisations which, while they bear witness to the
flexibility of Britain's governmental arrangements, also under-

line the reluctance of most administrations to think systematically about governmental organisation. On a more abstract level, the breakdown of consensus, coupled with the alienation from the two-party system which lies at the heart of the British constitution, has meant that there is now a gap between the way the system actually works and the way its practitioners will seek to explain and justify such doctrines as collective responsibility. American authors have pointed to the imbalance between the way the United States government operates and the values inherent in the constitution and approved by the public, and some have explained the problems of the United States in terms of idealistic efforts to bring the reality of government back into line with the goals of equality, liberty and democracy (Huntington, 1982). In Britain it could be argued that the imbalance between the traditional language of the constitution and political reality is more likely to lead to cynicism than to widespread demands for greater congruence between constitutional theory and political practice.

Gradual Erosion of the 'Super-Departments'

It is doubtful whether Thatcher was greatly troubled by the problems of organisational theory (much less of cognitive dissonance) when she came to form her cabinet in May 1979. Indeed the striking thing about the pattern of departments that she established and the style of her administration was the lack of major innovations in the central government structure. In the past, incoming prime ministers have changed the names of departments, invented separate ones for functions that required political limelight, and have generally sought to convey an element of freshness in the construction of both the cabinet portfolios and the junior appointments. It is possible that there is some merit in the argument also that any prime minister who wants to make radical changes in Whitehall would be well advised to introduce them immediately, and not wait until mid-way through a Parliament when resistance to change from ministers and civil servants alike may be overpowering. In any event Thatcher's first cabinet revealed little desire for departmental tinkering. She abolished the

Department of Prices and Consumer Protection and integrated it into the Department of Trade – somewhat to the chagrin of the Permanent Secretary, Sir Leo Pliatzky, who was offered early retirement as a result (Pliatzky, 1982). And Thatcher kept the Ministry of Transport as an independent department, which it had been under Labour between 1974 and 1979. Although it could be argued that this decision was the result of a failure to devote extensive attention to machinery-of-government questions rather than to a conscious rejection of Heath's ideas about departmental organisation, the move suggested that she was not greatly impressed by the idea of super-departments.

Very large departments – bringing together two or three formerly independent ministries – had become popular in the 1970s with respect to both domestic and overseas policy. The need to integrate the service ministries had prompted the creation of a single Ministry of Defence in 1964, and in 1968 the Foreign Office was merged with the old Commonwealth Office. Under Edward Heath, however, the model was used much more systematically as a way of bringing together related governmental functions. The idea owed much to Sir Richard Clarke and it was hoped that these larger departments would obviate the need for so much liaison between individual ministries. The forum for much of this liaison had been the interdepartmental committee which had multiplied in Whitehall, and it was thought that the construction of larger departments might produce a more comprehensive issue-oriented approach than was possible when representatives of departments came together. Apart from transforming the handling of issues where a number of different interests were involved, it was further imagined that the organisation of the cabinet might be improved by the existence of super-departments because less would have to be settled there. The cabinet could be reduced in size and, with ministers responsible for substantial areas of government work, business would be expedited, because disputes that might otherwise have to be settled in full cabinet could be settled earlier within a department. Heath added two new super-departments to the three (Defence, the Foreign and Commonwealth Office and the Department of Health and Social Security) that already qualified for that title. These departments were the Department of Trade and Industry and the Department of the Environment.

Yet even before the end of the Heath government, doubts about the experiment were beginning to be expressed and the Department of Trade and Industry in particular appeared unwieldy. The degree of functional integration that occurred was rather less than had been anticipated; and instead of strengthening the ministers *vis-à-vis* the civil servants, some observers suggested that the massive expansion of responsibility and work that such a large department entailed contributed further to the erosion of political control (Crowther-Hunt and Kellner, 1980). There was also the perennial problem of all such experiments – that it was difficult to reconcile with the way many MPs understood ministerial responsibility to work. As Winston Churchill's 'overlord' experiment had done, the concentration of responsibility in the hands of just a few ministers put additional strains on the doctrine of ministerial responsibility to Parliament even if the ministers were in the House of Commons. Ministers could hardly be expected to familiarise themselves with more than the outlines of the work of the whole department, and would understand in detail only a fraction of it. At the same time, in cases where it was a junior (i.e. non-cabinet) minister who did have first-hand knowledge of a given segment of the departmental empire, the House of Commons might prove unwilling to accept an answer from anyone but the cabinet minister. While it is true that MPs have adapted themselves to a new environment in which, for example, the Parliamentary Commissioner can supplement their own probing of ministers, the existence of super-departments subjected the doctrine to further strain and proved unsatisfactory for backbenchers (Beloff and Peele, 1980).

The first signs of the break-up of the super-departments under the Heath administration came not so much as a response to inherent administrative difficulties, however, but rather as a response to the energy crisis of 1973. Energy was accordingly made a separate department and this was retained both by the Labour administrations of 1974–9 and by Thatcher when she took office. Further break-ups of super-departments may be anticipated. The giant Department of Health and

Social Security has proved especially unwieldy since it combines two functions, one of which is direct and the other largely indirect in operation, and it may be that separate departments will be created from the single one in the near future.

Abolition of the Civil Service Department

In one area, however, Mrs Thatcher did effect a major change of government organisation, although in a sense this development highlighted her concern for economy and efficiency and her general scepticism about the results that might be achieved from extensive restructuring of departments. The abolition of the independent Civil Service Department and the transfer of its functions to the Treasury and the Management and Personnel Office in 1981 represented the culmination of nearly fifteen years of debate, both about the role of the Treasury in British government and about how best to acquire for the United Kingdom a civil service appropriate to the needs of the late twentieth century. The Management and Personnel Office was a new department under the Cabinet Secretary but with a separate minister; and the fact that the Prime Minister initially appointed a close colleague, Lady Young, to the post suggested that she intended to use this department as an instrument of central direction rather than, as with the Civil Service Department, to allow it to develop a role as defender of the sectional interest of the civil service.

The abolition of the Civil Service Department had become predictable as the political climate of the 1970s and the concern for controlling expenditure replaced that of the 1960s. No longer was there the assumption that a civil service was needed to cope with the ever-expanding functions of the state; rather there was a desire to reduce those functions and civil service numbers with them. The civil service itself became more militant with respect to pay and conditions and, as Sir Douglas Wass has pointed out, the 'first service-wide industrial action in 1973 was a watershed' (Wass, 1982). The disputes that followed in 1979 and 1981 had the effect of politicising parts of the civil service and diminishing the sympathy for it among

politicians. Under the discipline of cash limits, administration
was again conceived primarily in narrow financial terms, and
supervision by the Treasury, which the Fulton Report on the
reform of the civil service (1968) had seen as inimical to
creative administration, once more seemed preferable to the
continuation of a separate Civil Service Department. The
Expenditure Committee of the House of Commons in 1977–8,
when it came to review the success of the Fulton reforms, was
critical of the extent to which government itself had contributed
towards an escalation of public expenditure.

The 11th Report of the Expenditure Committee expressed
the view that the concentration of a range of responsibilities
relating to the civil service in a separate department had quite
simply been a mistake. In particular it regretted the fact that in
1968 the function of determining staffing levels had been split
off from the Treasury because this meant that, while responsibility for manning was concentrated in the Civil Service
Department, it was not properly co-ordinated with monitoring
the efficiency of the civil service, since that function had been
kept by the Treasury's public expenditure divisions. The
Expenditure Committee therefore wanted to see the personnel
functions of the Civil Service Department returned to the
Treasury – a suggestion that obviously implied a somewhat
emasculated Civil Service Department that would retain only
limited functions such as recruitment, training and pensions.
At the time of the Expenditure Committee's Report there was a
Labour government which may have been still wedded to the
thinking behind the original Fulton proposals. When it did
respond to the Committee's recommendations in March 1978
it indicated that it wanted no action taken.

It was noticeable that when Thatcher came to power she did
not regard the Civil Service Department as the natural centre
of her attempts to eliminate waste from Whitehall. On the
contrary, she seems almost to have avoided using it in her
efficiency and expenditure-reduction campaigns. It has been
noted that Sir Derek Rayner was initially placed in the prime
minister's private office and not in the Civil Service Department (Stephenson, 1980), and, although he did not remain
there throughout the Thatcher administration, this move

signalled the Prime Minister's personal interest in Whitehall efficiency. Sir Derek Rayner's teams of *ad hoc* scrutineers undertook 135 internal departmental scrutinies and 6 general inter-departmental reviews between 1979 and 1982 (Riddell, 1983). Thus, from a position in the early 1970s when the Civil Service Department might conceivably have been a rival to the Treasury and Cabinet Office as a central strategic instrument in the government's armoury, from 1979 onwards the Department was relegated to a backwater in Whitehall. This position was of course compounded by the suspicion which the Department incurred during the civil service industrial action of 1981, so that it became easy to cast the Department as a body whose survival might not altogether be in the public interest.

Reform of the Management and Personnel Office

The actual abolition of the Civil Service Department (CSD) necessitated some rearrangement at the Cabinet Secretariat and in the Treasury, in part because the years that had intervened between the creation of the CSD in 1968 and its eventual abolition had seen major alterations in the functions of both the Cabinet Secretariat and the Treasury. (Since 1972, for example, a substantial amount of diplomatic business related to the European Communities has been handled by the home civil service, with the result that there is now a much greater co-ordinating role for the Cabinet Secretariat.) Basically, in 1981, the Treasury acquired responsibility for the expenditure-related aspects of the defunct Civil Service Department – manpower (both numbers and levels of pay, which in 1982 was the subject of an independent report), the general supervision of conditions of employment, and responsibility for the conduct of negotiations with the civil service unions. The Cabinet Secretariat, on the other hand, acquired what had been seen as the machinery of government functions of the Civil Service Department; and the Management and Personnel Office – attached to, but increasingly independent within, the Cabinet Office – acquired responsibility for recruitment and personnel (including relationships with the Civil Service Commission), and a general watching brief on management and efficiency. Under the general supervision of Lady Young, the MPO thus absorbed some of the duties that until that time had been discharged by Derek Rayner's teams.

It is perhaps too early to say what effects these changes will have on the conduct of British administration; but as a reform it was unusual in coming mid-way through the administration. It owed more at the time to Thatcher's personal distrust of the Civil Service Department and confidence in Lady Young than to any long-term thinking about where the functions of manpower and personnel could most usefully be situated. And, rather confusingly, it was reported that Lady Young, although in theory in charge of a departmental unit that might facilitate greater control over the Whitehall machine and that might institute efficiency drives within the departments, was against the importation of political appointees and outsiders. The whole episode will probably result in a *de facto* strengthening of the Cabinet Office and nicely reveals the extent to which, even while making important changes in the pattern of government and experimenting with outside advisers, the Thatcher government purported to be doing nothing that was constitutionaly novel.

Management Information for Ministers (MINIS)

One internal reform, which has already been mentioned briefly and deserves further attention in the context of the drive for efficiency and greater control over the machinery of government, is the system known as MINIS, or Management Information for Ministers. It could have important long-term effects on other departments and reflects a willingness on the part of some ministers to adapt managerial techniques from the private sector. However, the mode of its introduction again underlines the strangely unstructured approach of the Thatcher government towards administrative reform. Ministers were clearly expected to do something about improving efficiency within their departments, but precisely what they did was left to them. The MINIS system has been introduced into two departments, the Department of Environment and Ministry of Defence as a result of Michael Heseltine's enthusiasm for the idea. The idea of MINIS is to enable ministers to exercise greater control over their departments than has been possible in the past, and to identify with greater precision than hitherto the objectives of departmental policy, the order of priority among competing objectives, and the efficiency with which they are being pursued. It also facilitates appraisal of the impact of cuts - a major achievement, given the Department of the Environment's responsibilities for local government. MINIS thus joins a long succession of allegedly powerful new techniques drawn from the private sector and, like its predecessors, it has had mixed reviews.

The doubts that surround MINIS derive in part from the extent to which it was employed as a tool to aid a minister whose policies involved expenditure cuts, so that civil servants may associate it with the policies rather than see it as a neutral tool – a fate that has to some extent befallen the use of cash limits. There is very little literature available on Britain to compare with that which deals with what has come to be called 'cut-back management' in the United States (Behn, 1983). However, it is clear that a rational and efficient approach to reduced resources should involve a search for the sharpest tools for discriminating between expenditures. But the MINIS experiment, it has been suggested, has acquired a bad reception in some quarters because part of the plan as developed by Michael Heseltine entailed the publication of a large amount of raw material – some of it material that neither civil servants nor other ministers wished to see published. Much of it was *so* raw, however, that only the sophisticated analyst would be able to unravel it, and very little of it was of general interest. Nevertheless the doubts about MINIS point to another contradiction in the Conservative approach to government: while wanting to see the encroachment of government on the wider society reduced, the Conservative government is not anxious to assist the process by making the operations of government more open. Cost may be a factor, but there is also an inherent suspicion of exposing the mysteries of Whitehall to the public gaze.

Specialist Advisers and 'Presidential' Government

One weapon which Labour ministers have found especially helpful in attempting to establish control over their departments has been the policy expert or specialist adviser brought into government on a temporary basis. At the start of her administration, Thatcher found herself in the paradoxical position of wanting to reduce the number of political advisers and of wanting to assert greater control over the policies of the government departments. The criticism generated by Harold Wilson's use of such advisers in the 1964–70 period had gradually abated, so that when Edward Heath formed a government in 1970 he too introduced political appointees into the departments. These appointments varied from policy experts such as Brendon Sewell and Michael Wolff, to more junior persons such as Robert Jackson, who became a personal assistant to William Whitelaw. The Callaghan administration, according to Sir Douglas Wass, had between twenty and thirty such advisers, and as a senior civil servant he was naturally concerned at the suggestion from the Labour Party that such appointees should in future exercise an even greater role than before in the formulation and execution of policy (Wass, 1982). But if one looks at the list of policy advisers appointed by Thatcher and her cabinet, there are at least twenty-two, if members of her policy unit and advisers to ministers within departments are counted. Not all ministers have political appointees as special assistance: at the time of writing, the Secretary of State for the Environment, the Secretary of State for Employment, the Secretary of State for Education and Science, the Secretary of State for Northern Ireland, the Chancellor of the Exchequer, the Secretary of State for Health and Social Security, and both the Chief Whip and Paymaster General, appeared to have special advisers, and indeed there seemed to be three people (Adam Ridley, Douglas French and Robin Harris) attached to the Treasury in a political capacity. Clearly not all the political appointments are at the same level. For instance, in the policy unit that was established in 10 Downing Street after the 1979 election, were two advisers – Ferdinand Mount and Christopher Monckton – whose skills might be thought to relate rather more to public relations than to policy. On the other hand, in a move that was seen as highly unusual, Thatcher appointed two very senior civil servants to her policy unit as a method of obtaining advice on foreign policy independently of the Foreign and Commonwealth Office. In the light of the Falklands invasion such a move was understandable, but the appointment of Sir Anthony Parsons in particular seemed to many to foreshadow a more presidential style of government.

Initially Thatcher had relied on businessmen for additional advice to that offered by the civil service. Mention has already been made of the work done by Sir John Hoskyns, but David Wolfson also acted as a kind of 'chief of staff' at No. 10. Precisely what this role entailed and how it was integrated with other appointments was not entirely clear and there has been doubt about the success of the idea. The major outside policy appointment which Thatcher made was perhaps of Professor Alan Walters, an academic economist who was well able to counter civil service arguments and in terms of offering an alternative source of advice to that of officials was at the same level as Sir Anthony Parsons.

The degree of control which a cabinet or an individual minister exercises over the policy-making process is crucially dependent on the clarity of the government's policies and the care with which they have been worked out in opposition. The style of the policies of the government as a whole will reflect the relationships within the cabinet and of course the style of chairmanship and leadership adopted by the prime minister. This is not the place to rehearse the varied arguments about prime ministerial power, though it is worth bearing in mind that even Richard Crossman, perhaps the most ebullient proponent of the demise of cabinet government theory, modified his views as a result of being a member of the Labour cabinets of 1964–70. In the Thatcher administration the experience of cabinet government has been affected by the need to conduct a war – albeit a brief one – and by the changing political position of the prime minister *vis-à-vis* her colleagues.

Thatcher's premiership appears to divide into two parts. The first part, which lasted from May 1979 until the reshuffle of September 1981, saw Thatcher as an assertive premier but one whose cabinet was in many ways not her own. She had felt the need in forming her government to bring in men such as Peter Walker, a close associate of Edward Heath's, had tried to balance the cabinet between 'wets' and 'dries' and had few really close supporters among the most senior figures in the cabinet. Thus, although prime minister, she often seemed to be in a minority position within her own cabinet. Together with the proliferation of leaks both from political and from civil service sources this early period was one in which cabinet disagreements both occurred regularly and were reported regularly.

From the autumn reshuffle of 1981 onwards, however, she appeared much more in control. The removal of Lord Soames, Sir Ian Gilmour and Norman St John-Stevas and the promotion of Lady Young made the cabinet more reflective of her views; and the Falklands campaign enabled her to rebuild her national popularity (which had slumped) and to acquire a massive dominance over the cabinet. Economic policy had produced bitter divisions within the cabinet and there had been a move inside the cabinet in 1981 to have a full discussion of the details of the budget and not, as is normal, to allow the budget to be presented to Parliament before the cabinet as a whole had considered it. The move to depart from traditional secrecy perhaps underlines the difficulty of holding the cabinet to a collective economic strategy in conditions where there are deep divisions about the conduct of economic policy. In this matter, however, Thatcher adhered to the traditional practice, and it may be that the demand for full prior discussion of the budget will not be renewed.

Such other features of Thatcher's style of cabinet government as can be discerned from the evidence point to an emphasis on efficiency rather than prolonged debate. She seems to favour a more streamlined cabinet committee structure than her predecessors and is unsympathetic to extensive debate in full cabinet. In the management of the Falklands crisis she took the unusual step of adding to the Defence Committee – quickly dubbed the 'war cabinet' by the press – the then Chairman of the Conservative Party, Cecil Parkinson. It could be argued that such a move enabled her to keep in touch with party and public opinion more easily; but it can equally be argued that, at the beginning of the war at least, she felt threatened by the voices of the rest of the committee and needed a loyal lieutenant to support her own political instincts. On a more general level, the ability of the cabinet to adapt to the exigencies of war perhaps underlines the flexibility of the system. The 'war cabinet' met regularly, and only when there was substantial disagreement were issues referred to the whole cabinet. As an instrument of military direction it proved at least as efficient as any American counterpart.

The Falklands episode did, however, lead to disquiet about the quality of advice coming from the Foreign Office and the way the security and intelligence services had operated. There developed a general feeling that in some senses the British official machine was almost too efficient and reconciled differences of opinion long before they reached the cabinet or the prime minister so that, as the jargon had it, much of the 'creative tension' was removed from the policy dialogue. The dissatisfaction with the security services had been compounded by a long series of revelations about breaches of national security, and the House of Commons heard calls for an independent body akin to the American Central Intelligence Agency and for greater parliamentary control over the work of the intelligence staff. Thatcher had up to early 1984 resisted such demands.

The steps which Thatcher took to improve the sources of her personal advice on foreign and defence policy – the appointment of Sir Anthony Parsons to her private staff at No. 10 being the most obvious example – reinforced speculation that she was seriously contemplating the establishment of a prime minister's department to bring together the variety of personal staff and advisers and provide an alternative view of policy to that offered by the departments.

The arguments for such a move can be simply stated. Sir Kenneth Berrill (1981) has pointed out the need for greater centralisation of the policy-making process and for strengthening the support for the departments charged with the co-ordination of government strategy. The many *ad hoc* attempts thus far to provide greater resources at the centre have, it could be argued, failed because they have not been institutionalised in a single department. Policy advisers and specialists come and go, but their impact is patchy; the Central

Policy Review Staff had lost its original purpose and influence and it was abolished in 1983; the private office is too small and the policy unit at No. 10, while it can be useful, if men of high quality are attached to it, needs to be integrated into the machinery of government as a whole.

The case against such a development echoes that made earlier when the now defunct CPRS was established by Edward Heath, and indeed in some instances reflects some of the nervousness displayed when Lloyd George's entrenchment of the cabinet secretariat was opposed by many Conservatives because it was thought to buttress the premier's personal rule. The arguments fundamentally depend upon an assumption that the prime minister has an interest which is distinct from that of the cabinet and the party and that to build up the resources available to a premier would be constitutionally improper because it would institutionalise what is in fact an informal position. Regardless of the strength of the arguments, the prime minister has stated that the development of a single powerful prime minister's office is not contemplated and she is herself perhaps sufficiently lacking in interest in the machinery of government *per se* not to want to fight for such a radical course. However, it is quite likely that, by adding incrementally to the Management and Personnel Office, by complementing her private office with advisers of a high calibre and – formal protestations to the contrary – encouraging a politically sensitive selection of the senior civil service advisers, she will in effect have achieved some of the same objectives. Thus it may be found that at the end of the Thatcher administration government centralisation will indeed have been reinforced and there may be a prime minister's department in all but name. Names will be retained to protect a few innocent myths but the reality will be a much starker concentration of power in Downing Street and a new degree of politicisation of the civil service. The machinery of government became a subject of wider debate as a result of public criticisms offered by insiders such as Sir John Hoskyns and Sir Douglas Wass (who gave the 1983 Reith Lectures).

However it was unclear what echo that debate found among politicians. If at the end of two Conservative administrations a leaner and more efficient state sector has emerged – along with a more centralised and politicised civil service – that will be as much the result of policy and personality as of any conscious theories held by politicians about the proper manner of organising central government.

5
Beyond Whitehall

PATRICK DUNLEAVY AND R. A. W. RHODES

Who Administers Britain in the 1980s?

Most textbook discussions of British politics restrict their analysis of administrative matters to the civil service, and make much briefer references to the role of local authorities and the public corporations. Anyone observing the relative coverage of Whitehall departments and other agencies might feel justified in concluding that the civil service is an overwhelmingly important influence on national policy-making, far more so than any other group of administrators. But, in practice, civil servants rather rarely administer things directly. And so to know what goes on within Whitehall is to know only part of the story. To get a broader picture of how the entire public sector operates in Britain (a public sector currently consuming some £115,000 million a year or 45 per cent of gross national product), we need to go beyond Whitehall to look at the full range of organisational settings within which national policy is shaped.

It is important to note that the central government includes a relatively small number of agencies, accounting for only one in ten of all public sector employees (Table 5.1). Furthermore, the significance of the civil service within overall public-sector manpower has remained very much the same over the last

	Number of agencies	Percentage of all public sector employment
Central government		
Major Cabinet departments	18	
Other Cabinet departments (e.g. law officers)	5	
Ministerial departments outside Cabinet	6	10.5
Major non-ministerial departments	20	
Major departmental agencies	3	
Armed forces	3	4.2
Quasi-governmental agencies		
Public corporations	48	
Water authorities (England and Wales)	15	27..7
New town and urban development corporations	30	
National health service: regional authorities	14	16.5
district authorities	194	
Local government		
Top tier local authorities (counties, regions, metro authorities)	66	38.6
Bottom tier local authorities (districts)	454	
Police authorities	52	2.5

Notes: All figures refer to Great Britain for agencies, but to UK for employment. The agency figures are not comprehensive, in particular omitting mention of:

—military and security sub-agencies (central government)

—companies with state equity holdings – such as Rolls-Royce or BL; 'fringe' executive and advisory bodies, of which there are several hundred; regional agencies; systems of tribunals s(all of which should be included in the quasi-governmental sector)

—local public corporations and consortia of local authorities (local government).

Police authorities are half-way between being quasi-governmental agencies and local authorities, because a third of their members are appointed magistrates, and in many areas several counties have been amalgamated to form a police authority with only a few councillor representatives from different council areas.

TABLE 5.2   *Changes in public-sector manpower, 1961–81*

Numbers of employees (000s)	1961	1971	1981
Public corporations	2,150	1,860	1,740
Local government	1,760	2,500	2,770
National health service	580	790	1,260
Central government	730	790	760
Armed forces and police	580	520	530

Source: *Economic Trends*, November 1981. (Figures for public corporations are for 1980 in the last column.)

twenty years, after allowances are made for the transfers of civil service responsibilities to other organisations. Indeed the crude civil-service total (unadjusted for transfers) shows a decline from 1961, when Whitehall departments absorbed one in every eight state employees (Table 5.2). Whitehall has not been a major growth area expanding its responsibilities *vis-à-vis* other parts of government. Instead it has barely held its share of public-sector employment at a time when most other forms of public-service administration (excluding the declining public corporations) were expanding rapidly.

Most civil servants, anyway, work in just three areas of government operations, which are of special sensitivity and importance for the national interest, and where there are good reasons for ministers to want personnel under their direct control carrying out policy implementation. These are:

(1) running the Ministry of Defence (excluding the armed forces proper) which accounts for 126,000 staff;
(2) collecting income tax and VAT, which requires some 113,000 people;
(3) paying out transfer payments to individuals (pensioners, the unemployed or people on supplementary benefits), which involves around 120,000 staff (Butler and Sloman, 1979, pp. 264–5). [Our estimate of staff who administer transfer payments may be an underestimate.]

Outside these three areas, the typical Whitehall department ranges in size from around 2,000 staff in small departments with few 'line' responsibilities (i.e. services that are directly administered), to around 14,000 staff in large departments.

Larger ministries than this invariably have rather separate or discrete functions counted in their totals – for example, the Home Office total (29,000 staff) includes the entire Prison Service, and the Department of the Environment figure (32,000 staff) includes the agency responsible for providing office accommodation and furnishings to the rest of the civil service. But this sort of function is always a 'sideline' and only a fairly small proportion of administration in such areas relates to the central policy-making role of the department concerned.

Clearly the amount of direct service provision that can be effectively carried out by Whitehall departments in most areas of domestic policy is fairly restricted. In most departments the number of core policy-making staff (leaving aside those concerned with clerical work, routine administration or separate 'line' responsibilities) varies between two or three hundred people and around two or three thousand. Their preoccupations are usually twofold. On the one hand they are concerned with the traditional 'political' functions stressed in textbook discussions – drawing up new legislation, organising consultation with interested parties, advising ministers on policy decisions, answering Parliamentary questions, and responding to new developments within their area of responsibility. But on the other hand, a great deal of their activity typically involves allocating finance to other parts of the public sector and supervising service provision by other government agencies, agencies that account for 85 per cent of state employees and which finally spend the vast bulk of the public sector budget in the UK.

There are two basic types of other agency involved, quasi-governmental agencies (or QGAs) and local authorities. We use the term 'quasi-governmental agencies' and the acronym QGA deliberately to avoid the confusion of meaning that has grown up around the more common label 'Quango'. Sometimes this means 'quasi-autonomous *national* government organisation', which is much the same as our use of QGA, except that many QGAs are regionally or sub-nationally organised. At other times Quango means 'quasi-autonomous *non*-governmental organisation' (which refers to *private*-sector bodies carrying out functions for government, and hence is quite distinct from our use of QGA). The differences between these organisations are well known but are worth re-emphasising briefly:

Quasi-governmental agencies	*Local authorities*
● Non-elected bodies with controlling boards appointed by ministers to carry out an executive or administrative function for government.	● Elected councils with powers to define their own policies within a framework of current legislation.
● Funded either mainly from commercial operations backed up with Exchequer investment funds (e.g. most public corporations); or wholly by the Exchequer (e.g. the National Health Service).	● Funded by a combination of central government grant (45 per cent), local property taxes or rates (24 per cent) and charges for some services (31 per cent).
● Single issue agencies with control only over one policy area (such as health care, or the supply of water, or the production of coal).	● Multi-issue agencies covering a wide range of local public services.
● Organised at various levels – either at a national level alone (e.g. the Housing Corporation); or at national and regional level (e.g. the electricity industry); or at regional and local levels (e.g. the National Health Service).	● Organised at a local level in two tiers (top tier counties, bottom tier districts over most of the UK).

Roughly speaking there are two possible reasons for creating quasi-governmental agencies. The first is organisational deconcentration, to ensure that a function is carried out separately from a government department. The reasons why such separation is useful vary quite widely. It may be that a new organisation is needed which can operate freely in a day-to-day manner (for example, in commercial areas) while remaining ultimately answerable to ministers. Or the issue concerned may be a sensitive one where the government does not wish to be seen as having a direct role: for example, in funding artistic activity, the government uses the intermediary of the Arts Council to avoid charges that it is creating a 'state culture'. Or the policy task of the QGA may simply be one for which standard civil service management or personnel are not appropriate (as in the case of the Atomic Energy Authority). Indeed the list of reasons under this heading may be almost as long as the list of different types of QGA. Second, QGAs may be used where the central government makes key decisions in a policy area directly, but where the scale of the administrative task is so large that it must be subdivided between many organisations if each is to remain of manageable size. The clearest example is public-sector health care, where the one and a quarter million employees and hundreds of facilities involved could only be run as a central department at a cost of creating the largest and most unwieldy single agency in any Western democracy. In practice the NHS is administered by a spatially organised system of QGAs which breaks up the administrative task into manageable chunks and allows local and regional management a considerable area of discretion to innovate and respond to their particular circumstances, within an overall framework of financial accountability.

It is a little difficult, however, to say more about relations between Whitehall and its quasi-governmental agencies, for three reasons. Perhaps the most basic is the lack of any authoritative knowledge about how many QGAs exist, and about their diverse organisational arrangements (Barker, 1982). Estimates of the numbers of quasi-governmental agencies vary widely. Depending on the criteria used for classification, the total ranges from a few hundred to a few thousand or more. Second, because QGAs are single-issue agencies, each of them tends to be distinctive to some degree. Even within a general sub-category, such as the public corporations, there will be little continuity in the internal organisation of different QGAs. In practice the detailed character of any one agency's relations with Whitehall will depart in many ways from any standardised or generalised model we would have to use. For example, the gas industry is organised as a single, nationwide corporation; but the electricity industry is split between three different types of organisation – a single power-generating board for England and Wales, fourteen separate regional boards distributing and marketing the electricity produced, and combined power generation and distribution boards in Scotland and Northern Ireland. Although both gas and electricity are nationalised fuel industries, their mode of operation is radically different. Once we move away from well-mapped areas such as the public corporations, into the field of one-off fringe agencies, these severe difficulties of generalisation become intolerable barriers to analysis.

Third, even in those areas of QGA operation that have been studied, there has been rapid change in the character of relations between agencies and government. For example, the Thatcher government has embarked on an ambitious pro-gramme of 'privatising' numerous public corporations (includ-ing British Telecom, British Airways and Britoil). Although these initiatives are at present widely seen as examples of the power of the central executive to override public corporations' opposition to privatisation, in the longer term they may imply a major reduction in Whitehall's influence. Privatised corpora-tions will still be involved in areas of key public policy significance. But the government will no longer be able to appoint their key personnel, vet their operational policies, determine their capital purchasing, regulate their pricing decisions, or use them as means of achieving other policy objectives. For example, in his 1983 autumn mini-budget the Chancellor, Nigel Lawson, announced an 'artificial' rise in electricity prices in order to generate more public expenditure without visibly increasing taxes. Clearly this kind of 'hidden taxation' could not be implemented via privatised firms. Similarly it may be much harder for Whitehall to push a privatised British Airways into buying British or European planes than if it remained a conventional public corporation. But just how significant privatisation will be for the scope of ministerial or civil service influence remains a matter of speculation at present.

For these reasons we want to explore the importance of

administration beyond Whitehall by looking at the relations between Whitehall and local government. We return to the more general picture only in conclusions. Focusing on central–local relations is easier because the structures of local authorities are relatively uniform, the mechanisms by which they interact with central departments are better documented. Local politics are not examined directly. Rather, attention is firmly fixed at a national level – on how Whitehall departments, ministers and local government as a whole get on with each other, and to what extent the overall reactions of several hundred local councils influence or shape *national* policy-making and politics.

The Framework of Central–Local Relations

Recent work on central-local relations argues that they can be described as 'power/dependence' situations in which both Whitehall departments and local authorities have some resources for independent action or exerting influence, but are also limited because of their dependence on the other tier for resources outside their own control (Rhodes, 1981). Central government has resources which councils rely on to carry out their tasks; but, conversely, Whitehall departments depend on local authorities to go on producing outputs on the ground. The balance of key resources can be summarised as follows:

Central government	*Local authorities*
● control over legislation and delegated powers	● employ all personnel in local services
	● local knowledge and expertise

- provide a large part of local service finance under block grant

- control of capital expenditure
- sets standards for and inspects some services

- party control in House of Commons
- national electoral mandate

- control policy implementation and have key knowledge about how to administer policy

- independent powers to raise taxes (rates) to finance services

- local electoral mandate

Central government's powers are considerable. Ministers can usually change the law to require councils to do what they want. They can acquire extensive powers to regulate what local authorities do under legislation, set service standards, and maintain an overall 'quality control' over councils' outputs. And, of course, central grants provide much of the money for local services. But the limits on what Whitehall can do are also considerable. Most obviously, central departments do not have the staff or the operational knowledge to run local services themselves (nor do they want to). Indeed, central departments do not have enough staff to police the full range of controls they formally have over local government. Consequently they have to be selective, concentrating only on the most serious departures in local-authority policies from the goals they would like to see met. Nor can central governmet easily manipulate much of its funding to control local authorities. Over four-fifths of central finance is paid over in a general or block grant which is not directly linked to particular services. Within their grant total, local authorities may distribute money between services as they wish, even in a way that will frustrate central objectives. For example, councils may protect one service from centrally imposed cuts by reducing spending elsewhere in their budgets and using these savings to preserve the threatened service's funding.

Local authorities' powers are less decisive but equally real. Most important, they have the power either to do nothing, or to delay implementing government policies for a considerable period, or simply to be half-hearted about doing something they dislike. Even when a government builds into new laws draconian powers to compel councils to do things (for example, to force sales of council houses, as the Conservative government did in a 1980 act), it can only use these powers very sparingly; and threatening their use cannot force councils who drag their feet without obviously breaking the law, to change their ways. Council-house sales in the period 1979–81 were considerably reduced because large numbers of Labour councils claimed that they had not the staff to process sales quickly, and generally made it as difficult and slow as they could within the law for tenants to buy property. Above all, central government cannot force local councils to do something *well*. They need to encourage them to behave as they wish, and this encouragement can only be very successful if local authorities feel free to take the initiative and guide their own affairs.

All these points tend to mean that central-local relations take on the aspects of a 'game' in which both sides manoeuvre for advantage, deploying the resources they control to maximise their influence over outcomes, and trying to avoid (where they can) becoming dependent on the other 'player'. This is not, of course, to suggest that central and local government are always in conflict, merely that their interests are by no means identical and that both sides are vigilant in defence of their interests. There are three special features of this 'game' that define the framework of central–local relations: differences within central government in Ministers' and departments' interest in local service provision; divisions within local government between councils in different tiers, in different regions or controlled by different parties; and the roles played by organisations representing local authorities on a national level.

THE INTERESTS OF CENTRAL DEPARTMENTS

Differences in central ministries' attitudes to and involvement with local authorities can be summarised between four types of department:

(i) *The Department of the Environment* is the 'lead' Whitehall agency for local authorities in England and Wales. It plays a key part in negotiating the annual block grant settlement with the

Treasury, which it then allocates between local authorities, after negotiations with their national organisations, and using a complex computer formula designed to accommodate different areas' needs and resources. Since 1980 the department has also operated a radically new and restrictive system of financial controls over all day-to-day (current) council spending, whether it is financed out of central grants or from local rates. When he was Secretary of State, Heseltine made no less than four separate efforts between 1979 and 1982 to get a power that no previous minister in his position has ever possessed, namely to set an upper limit to day-to-day spending by *each* local authority. The DoE again allocates these targets to councils via alternative formulae, one based on inflation increases plus government policy cuts applied to 1978–9 spending levels, and the other on civil service computations of how much different local authorities 'need' to spend to achieve a common level of services at the same cost to local taxpayers. These two controls, known as 'volume targets' and 'grant-related expenditure assessments', are, of course, completely incompatible with each other. Volume targets are set by the DoE in splendid isolation, though it negotiates grant-related expenditure assessments with the associations of local authorities. Volume targets are always lower. It is rarely clear until late on in each financial year which target the DoE intends to be decisive in controlling spending.

This directive financial role sits rather uneasily with the DoE's two other functions. First, the department is supposed to be the guardian of local government interests within Whitehall, with a brief to watch over the overall health and vitality of local democracy and to encourage improvements in local government efficiency. Second, the DoE is also a 'service department' in its own right, with extensive direct responsibilities for housing, planning and environmental service issues.

(ii) *The service departments* have responsibility for national policy-making on functions that are locally implemented, such as education, personal social services, transport and highways, police, fire and civil defence. In each of these cases a central department other than the DoE (respectively the DES, DHSS, DTp and the Home Office) is involved in setting out the kind of services that local authorities must provide under legislation, supervising this provision, and encouraging good practice more generally. In some cases, part of the services being supervised may be funded by specific grants which the service department negotiates with the Treasury and allocates itself to councils (for example, local transport planning projects are funded separately). But, for the most part, service departments are involved in protecting 'their' notional share of the annual block grant settlement against centrally decided cuts, and in making sure that local authorities actually spend something like this proportion on their service in practice. This concern makes the service departments, on the whole, the best friends local government has in Whitehall; it takes a very 'dry' Secretary of State for Education to favour cuts in local spending targets when some 36 per cent of all council current expenditure is on education or training falling within his or her area of responsibility.

(iii) *The Treasury* has no direct dealings with individual councils, although, since the mid-1970s, the department has become involved in regular consultation meetings on local government finance which involve the local authority associations as well as the DoE and service departments. The Treasury's key role, however, is in negotiating with the DoE (and service departments) inside Whitehall to set the level of central grant funding that it will permit (a level which once fixed is strictly adhered to in cash terms each year).

(iv) *Rival departments* comprise the domestic-spending ministries which have no services administered by local government. At the least, such departments have no interest either way in defending the funding of local services; indeed, in conditions of resource squeeze (such as those prevailing in the periods 1976–8 and since 1980) there is even some advantage for them in local authorities bearing the brunt of any cuts. There are also more specific rivalries where local authority policies conflict with the policy aims of a rival department. For example, many councils' efforts to promote economic development in their local areas were, by 1981, seriously eroding the effectiveness of *regional* development grants run by the Department of Industry. From the opposite direction, expanded youth training programmes were initiated in the late 1970s by the Manpower Services Commission (a Department of Employment QGA).

The original initiatives grew by 1982 into progressively more explicit attempts to wrest control of vocational training for older teenagers away from local authorities altogether (a move that would also transfer responsibilities within Whitehall from the Department of Education and Science to Employment).

For Scotland and Wales a slightly different pattern applies, since both the financing of local government and controls over most local services are in each case supervised by one department – the Scottish and Welsh Offices respectively. But many of the same tensions described here between Whitehall departments reappear within the Scottish Office and the Welsh Office between different divisions who look to their English counterparts for support.

THE INTERESTS OF LOCAL GOVERNMENT

Multiple conflicts of interest within local government are equally, if not more, important in muddying any simple patterns of relations between a homogeneous centre and united localities. Three lines of cleavage are particularly pronounced:

Top-tier and bottom-tier local authorities have different interests because their responsibilities and importance differ. Outside conurbations in England and Wales, the top-tier county councils spend 85 per cent of all local authority finance, and have responsibility for the big spending services such as education, personal social services and highways. District or borough councils in these 'shire' areas retain control only over local planning, environmental services and housing. Within the conurbations (or 'metropolitan areas') the picture is reversed, with 'metro' county councils being fairly weak strategic planning and transportation bodies in the main.

The districts or boroughs run education, social services and housing, which account for 80 per cent of all local expenditures within conurbations. In London the picture is more complicated, because the GLC has more powers than other 'metro' counties and a special Inner London Education Authority runs education instead of the inner London boroughs. In Scotland there is a different system again, with a dominant top tier composed of a few very large regional authorities, and, again, only local-planning, environmental-services and housing powers for the districts. Disputes between different tiers of authorities are frequent (Alexander, 1982). There are vocal demands by large free-standing cities in shire areas for the district to regain control of services such as education or social services. Some metropolitan districts in London and elsewhere have also backed Conservative government plans to abolish the metro-county councils and the GLC. Planning powers which were initially shared concurrently between the two tiers have mostly shifted to the districts after acrimonious conflicts throughout the 1970s. Rivalries remain intense in areas such as recreation and the arts, or housing improvements for the physically handicapped, where joint powers still exist.

Regional locations make a considerable difference to the ways in which councils react to central initiatives, even on quite technical matters. For example, proposals to use more up-to-date population figures as the basis for allocating central grants may seem fairly innocuous. But they would be staunchly opposed by councils in regions with declining populations and by inner-city authorities trying to preserve service standards in the face of continuing out-migration. For all these authorities, out-of-date population figures provide a cushion insulating them from the immediate effects of population decreases. Conversely, rapidly growing outer suburban councils around London (especially those with new towns) find their spending restricted by the under-funding that results from out-of-date figures.

Patterns of party control overlap with many of the divisions between tiers and regions. Labour support is high outside the south-east in large urban or industrial centres, and in inner-city areas generally. The Conservatives dominate a large majority of shire counties and rural, suburban and south-eastern districts. It is estimated that up to three-quarters of the people in England and Wales live in shire counties or metropolitan districts which are under the 'safe' control of one or other of the major parties (Dunleavy, 1980b, ch. 5). Of course this pattern is challenged by the growth of the Alliance (although they have so far failed to win control of councils), and by independents or nationalist councillors in Scotland and Wales. None the less, both Conservative and Labour governments at Westminster can still look to large and stable local government 'clienteles' for support when their policies attract criticisms from the opposition party, locally or nationally. Of course, national party labels conceal considerable variations in the character of different local parties. Governments may not get automatic support from councillors on the opposite wing of their party. In addition there are still sharp differences between local parties and councils in town and countryside areas. For example, Conservatives in metropolitan areas may be almost as far removed in policy terms from their 'shire' colleagues as they are from their Labour opponents. Often governments find that local elections between general elections bring sweeping gains for the opposition, as in 1981 when Labour captured control of all seven metro counties and an unprecedented number of shire counties as well. Such shifts invariably mean that resistance to implementing central-policy goals will grow, and the government's ability to control local government is usually weaker *ceteris paribus* in the second half of its term as a result.

THE ROLE OF LOCAL GOVERNMENT ORGANISATIONS AT NATIONAL LEVEL

Organisations representing local government at a national level are among the key arenas where divisions within local government are reflected. There are separate local authority associations for county councils, for districts, for metropolitan authorities, and for all Scottish councils. In each of these there is a Conservative/Labour split and a pattern of stable or contested party dominance. All the associations make efforts to cultivate some bi-partisan attitudes, for it is vitally important to them to go on attracting councils of different political complexions as members, and to be able to talk to governments of both the main parties. All the local authority associations are very active in consulting with Whitehall over issues that concern their responsibilities, in lobbying ministers and MPs over any new legislation, and in trying to influence the annual announcements of grant settlements and cash limits. Because Whitehall is several stages removed from operational knowledge of the services it is trying to control, the local authority associations have developed an important role in providing information about policy performance and authoritative reactions to new proposals. The associations' concerns range from the most general of issues (such as the defence of local government autonomy), through the particular interests of their type of authority, down to substantive policy questions which concern their membership. They draw leading councillors onto their committees, and key local government officers into their working groups and expert panels.

In Scotland, the existence of a single local authority association helps councils to present a united front to the Scottish Office, but this does not suppress the lines of division between different types of local authority as found in England. Where the associations come together most effectively is in a number of joint bodies which carry out particular functions for local government as a whole (such as manpower training and planning). From Whitehall's point of view, by far the most important of these joint bodies are those that negotiate national pay settlements with the local government unions, settlements of key importance for wage inflation in the public sector and the economy generally.

In addition to the associations and their joint bodies there is a wide range of promotional organisations which draw their membership from the local government world and which fall into much more subject-specific groupings, for example, on school education, or land-use planning, or social services provision. These groupings can be described as 'policy communities' formed by 'personal relationships between major political and administrative actors, sometimes in conflict, often in agreement, but always in touch [with each other] and operating within a shared framework. Community is the cohesive and orientating bond underlying any particular issue' (Heclo and Wildavsky, 1974, p. xv). There are as many different 'policy communities' as there are services, with the groupings changing or remoulding into new configurations on different issues. Policy communities usually involve the professions working in local government, parts of local authority associations, and often the trade unions, and the conferences or organisations of local councillors within the major parties. They can also absorb people working for central departments, including inspectors or regionally based civil servants in service departments.

A feature that local authority associations and policy communities both share is that they are not only a key means by which local government can convey a wide variety of different views to Whitehall, but they also provide a framework within which any individual local authority can situate their own problems, concerns and strategies. Local authority actors (both councillors and officers) do not decide policies for their areas in isolation. Instead they often look to their nationally organised associations and policy communities for guidance about what standard of service to provide, for ideas to imitate or to avoid, for ways of tackling common problems, and for justifications or philosophies of particular strategies. Some councils are innovators across a wide field of policy, but they are rather exceptional. Most councils most of the time follow national trends in the local government world, or national trends in their kind of authority facing their kind of general problems under their kind of political control. Each of them will innovate from time to time in one issue area or another, adding their own small contribution to the national picture. But most of the time local decisions are made within nationally defined parameters of what counts as good policy, rather than helping to redefine those parameters. This important role for local authority associations and their joint bodies on general issues, and for policy communities on individual functions, goes a long way to explain their influence with central government. It also suggests that it is plausible to talk of a 'national local government system' (Dunleavy, 1980b, ch. 4) or of a 'national community of local government' (Rhodes, 1981).

The Development of Central–Local Relations since 1970

So far we have discussed only the static framework of Whitehall's dealings with local government, describing the various actors involved on both sides and the fairly complex roles and attitudes that guide their overall behaviour. But how have central–local relations developed in practice since the start of the 1970s? There seem to have been four distinct phases during the period. The first phase was the tail-end of a long-standing bargaining/consultation pattern of relations which existed for most of the post-war period and which still survived under the Heath government. When Labour came to power in 1974 on a tiny Commons majority, the government adopted a strategy of trying to develop this pattern into a more corporatist system, especially after spending cuts in 1976–8 began to eat into locally provided services (see Chapter 10). This corporatist second phase was succeeded in 1979 by a radical attempt under the new Conservative government to reconstruct central–local relations on lines laid down unilaterally by Whitehall and imposed on an increasingly polarised and oppositional local government system. The Conservatives' 1983 election victory inaugurated a fourth phase of central government policy, this time aimed at radically reshaping local government organisation in the major conurbations, and effectively removing councils' discretionary power to raise local taxes, in order to achieve a 'final resolution' of central–local conflicts in favour of Whitehall.

BARGAINING

Consultation has been the 'normal' style of central–local relations throughout the post-war period until the mid-1970s. For most of this time local service spending was buoyant, and the numbers of local authority employees grew fairly regularly. Central governments of both parties kept an eye out for the electorally damaging implications of any slippage or non-performance by local government in areas of key importance. For example, slum-clearance and rehousing were major public concerns for most of the 1950s and 1960s, as was the reorganisation of secondary schooling from the mid-1960s until the mid-1970s. A whole series of expectations about reasonably consensual dealings between Whitehall and local councils were embodied in the concept of 'partnership'. Ministers often went out of their way to choose modes of implementing policy that maximised voluntary local authority co-operation. For example, in 1965 the Labour government inaugurated a major switch from a selective to a comprehensive system of secondary education via an advisory circular, rather than passing legislation to compel councils to change their ways. Nearly 90 per cent of education authorities went comprehensive by 1976, even though there were never any effective means by which the DES could unequivocally compel councils to reorganise their schools, as studies of Conservative 'rebel' authorities have now made clear (Pattison, 1982).

The bargaining phase lasted throughout the Heath government's period of office, despite some selective attempts by the Conservatives to develop more stringent controls over council policies. The government forced through changes in council housing finances against strong resistance (including the attempt by the Labour council at Clay Cross in 1972 to refuse implementation of the rent increases imposed). But elsewhere the government was cautious. Sales of council housing were successfully obstructed by all Labour councils. And although a full-scale reorganisation of local authorities was put through against much opposition from councils destined to lose many of their powers, the government adopted a two-tier system which was more popular with existing councillors and officers than previous Labour proposals for unitary authorities. Staffing and financing arrangements for the reorganisation were so much tailored to minimise opposition that the Heath government in fact presided over a bigger four-year growth in local service spending than any 1960s administration, a record that fitted oddly with the hard-faced 'Selsdon man' image with which it began its life.

THE CORPORATIST PATTERN, 1974–9

Central–local relations changed fairly gradually in the late 1970s towards a more corporatist framework. By 'corporatism' we mean a mode of integrating different sectors of society (for example, public and private sectors) or different tiers of government (for example, central and local) by means of formal-interest bargaining between central government and the outside organisations to be controlled. In a corporatist model we no longer have free-wheeling-interest group activity and open access for any potential group to influence policy. Instead, a few powerful outside interests are extensively co-opted into closed relations with central government, taking on a dual role representing their members to government and of controlling their members on behalf of government.

If the idea of corporatism is still controversial as a description of central–local relations on specific policy issues, there is clear evidence that the Labour government did make a sustained effort to introduce a kind of top-level, overall corporatism into its dealings with local government. Their essential innovation was to try to incorporate the powerful local authority associations (and their joint bodies) into a sort of 'social contract' about local government spending. For the first time, Whitehall set up a forum in which to discuss the long-run future of local spending with the local authority associations. This body, called the Consultative Council on Local Government Finance, was remarkable also in bringing the Treasury and local authority representatives into face-to-face contact for the first time, and in explicitly integrating the planning of local spending into the Whitehall system for projecting public expenditure five years ahead (known as the Public Expenditure Survey system). (There is a separate Consultative Council for Wales, but in Scotland there is direct negotiation between the Scottish Office and the Convention of Scottish Local Authorities.) The Council, plus the many influential joint working groups of civil servants and council staffs set up to serve it, have a brief which stresses:

> regular consultation and co-operation between central and local government on major financial and economic issues of common concern, with special emphasis on the deployment of resources both in the long term and the short term. In this way local government can be associated with the process of settling priorities for the whole of the [next] five year public expenditure period and local government would be consulted at an early stage when individual proposals for new policies directly involving local government are being shaped.

In practice, however, the government's hope was that by involving the local authority associations in policy-making affecting local government they would be able to persuade them of the 'realities' of the economic situation, and thus enlist them as allies in the battle to keep down the growth of local spending. In the Treasury's view:

> Through consultation and persuasion effectively done I hope we could get effective control. If we do not get effective

control we could not remain in the position where there
was not effective control, and therefore other measures
would have to be considered. (Layfield, 1976, p. 327)

How effective the Consultative Council on Local Government
Finance was in meeting this aim is difficult to say. Many of its
members argue that it was successful in getting the local
authority associations to persuade their members to behave
with restraint. But, of course, there were other forces working
in the same direction. The Council was set up at the same time
as a system of strict cash limits on central grants to local
authorities was introduced. And under a Labour government,
many of the naturally high-spending councils could be
persuaded to stay close to government guidelines out of a
feeling of party loyalty and concern not to rock the boat. In
addition, the swing against Labour in the mid-term local
elections meant that the government's policy of restraint
dovetailed neatly with the natural inclinations of the new
Conservative-controlled authorities. But the Council undoubtedly did succeed in increasing the volume of knowledge in
local government of Whitehall's problems, and in promoting
the local authority associations into greater prominence than
before. The associations' new role revolved centrally around
financial, 'manpower' and economic issues, and the main
bodies that found their influence decreased by this change were
the many different 'policy communities' promoting increased
spending in one issue area or another. Whatever else it
accomplished, the Council helped along a shift of influence
within local government away from service-orientated councillors and officers (for example, the school education lobby) and
towards local politicians and finance directors more concerned
with 'corporate planning', increased efficiency and financial
soundness. In effect, the Council was a Whitehall attempt to
build up the influence of the local authority associations and
local government finance managers, in order that they would
be better able to control the rest of the local government system
in return for consultation and a direct voice in future planning.

UNILATERAL ACTION AND CONFRONTATION

By contrast, the Thatcher government elected in May 1979

had little faith in consultation mechanisms, still less with corporatist devices. The new right (and 'dry') wing of the Conservative party argued instead that government must act with authority, without muddying its responsibility or intentions. And this authority has been primarily deployed in the service of a monetarist economic strategy which argues that government's overriding priority must be to control the money supply in order to reduce inflation. The main influence on the money supply is, in turn, the public-sector borrowing requirement, so that all forms of state activity that tend to push up the central government's need to borrow money must be firmly cut back. Any kind of central government spending may do this, but in local government only capital spending (on buildings or plant) has any implications for overall government borrowing. On day-to-day local spending the central government can simply cut its block grant to councils without worrying about what happens to total spending; if local authorities make up a loss of central grant by raising their own property taxes (the rates) this does not increase the money supply, nor is it necessarily inflationary (since total spending in the economy remains the same).

Given this background it was inevitable that the Conservative government would crack down hard on local capital expenditure. By 1979 the Conservatives were fiercely critical of council-housing programmes, and this service has accordingly borne the brunt of the capital cutbacks. In every other post-war year, three or four out of every ten new homes built were for local authorities; by 1982 this had fallen to well under one in ten as a direct result of central government refusing permission for any significant new building between 1979 and 1981. It was also very likely that Whitehall would cut back the extent to which it financed local service spending, as indeed it did: in 1979 the DoE paid for 61 per cent of council spending on staff and running costs for non-trading services, but by 1983 the proportion had fallen to just 53 per cent.

What came as more of a shock for local authorities of all political complexions was the determination of the new DoE minister, Michael Heseltine, to control *all* council revenue spending, whether Whitehall was picking up the tab for it or not. Heseltine's first Bill in 1980 gave the DoE unprecedented powers to assess how much they thought each local authority should spend in total, and to withdraw grant at a penalty rate if the council overshot this limit. No sooner did the DoE attempt to operate this system than they found several Labour authorities responding by deliberately overspending and meeting their penalty loss of grant by raising local property taxes. Business protests about these increases drove Heseltine to draw up drastic measures to force councils to hold local referenda before raising rates in mid-year. This idea was so radical that it was thrown out by the Cabinet before it could be put to Parliament. But Heseltine still sought other new powers to 'fine-tune' his withdrawals of grants, so that by 1982 the DoE had more paper controls over local authorities' spending than at any time in the past. Some Labour councils, such as the ILEA, still responded by overspending, so that they received no grant at all, and hence could not be influenced via these mechanisms. In Scotland, the growth of central control powers went one stage further. By 1982 the Secretary of State for Scotland could, in effect, order a local authority to cut its level of spending and lower its taxes (the rates) if he considered its budget 'excessive and unreasonable'.

The period after 1979 saw a general deterioration in central-local relations, largely but not entirely because of the changes in financial controls. Ministers initially promised that the government would remove many restrictive central government controls over councils, and some minor changes in DoE regulations have indeed been made. But many controls are operated by other service departments in Whitehall, and no discernible improvements in local 'freedoms' resulted overall. In other non-financial areas the DoE itself obtrusively interfered with councils' operations, pushing through measures designed to force council-house sales, to restrict the activities of councils' direct labour operations, and to encourage more use of private-sector accountants. At the national level, the DoE was stony-faced in its attitudes to consultations. Some junior ministers (such as John Stanley, who had responsibility for housing) virtually refused to talk to anyone, even the press. The local authority associations saw their special position slip away, and the Consultative Council on Local Government Finance was converted solely into a forum where ministers announce hard-and-fast decisions to unavailing protests by the local government representatives. Some of the Council's technical working groups remain important in spite of increasing restrictions on their work, especially when their 'shock' forecasts are leaked to the press to create a storm over possible cuts in services where the government is committed to 'maintaining standards' (such as education). But the Council itself ceased to have much of a role. Even within the Conservative party the lines of communication from Conservative councils to DoE ministers were strained by the government's reluctance to make any concessions to any but the most orthodox 'dry' Tory authorities.

In an atmosphere dominated by spending cutbacks, virtually all of the local government organisations at national level were permanently on the defensive, stigmatised by Whitehall as promoters of profligacy rather than as potential allies or partners. There were only two exceptions to this pattern. First, individual Conservative-dominated associations were able to wring some small concessions out of the DoE, by appealing to party interests. Second, and more important, the policy communities were able to mitigate some of the government pressure for cutbacks. Spending fell sharply in some services, such as council housing, but rose in others, such as police-authority funding. Cuts were selective, therefore, and central departments and policy communities in different areas were able to mount a rearguard action of some significance.

Above all, relations between Whitehall and local authorities were soured by a pervasive uncertainty about the sort of financial controls that were operating at any given moment. Very few local councils make any claim to understand the system that now operates, and public awareness of it is negligible. In some cases the DoE has acted unlawfully in failing to accept local authority representations before invoking penalties (*The Times*, 29 October 1981). The DoE's powers allow it to 'claw back' money it has previously told local authorities would be theirs, if it seems in mid-year that council spending is too high. Local authorities reacted by building up large contingency reserves to guard against sudden clawbacks or unexpected penalties.

What remains in doubt is how much the new style of central–local relations achieved, even in terms of the government's own policy objectives of reducing local government spending come what may. DoE ministers before 1983 were prevented by resistance inside the Conservative party from introducing the completely effective controls that they wanted. But the government's unilateral repudiation of previous modes of running central–local relations meant that the few remaining tactics by which local authorities could evade controls were fully exploited by an increasingiy adversary response by Labour councils. Their key response focused on massively subsidised public-transport provision, whose funding involves both the DoE and the Department of Transport in a tangle of different controls which the government only finally moved to clarify and tighten up in 1983. Although the Labour Greater London Council (GLC's) 'Fare's Fair' policy was unexpectedly struck down by the judges in the House of Lords, overspending of government limits in 1981–2 was almost £1,500 million, mainly because of the public-transport policies of Labour-controlled metro counties. Differences in spending patterns between Conservative and Labour councils widened dramatically under the first Thatcher administration, with nearly half the Labour authorities 'overspending' in 1981–2, while over half the Conservative councils were underspending more than 6 per cent below their DoE target levels (Cooper and Stewart, 1982). So, apart from its success in cutting council housing, the government may not have had as much effect in implementing cuts as is widely perceived. For example, the average expenditure cut in education in the last three years of the 1974–9 Labour government was 2.4 per cent, compared with 0.2 per cent in the first three years of the Conservative government, while the same figures for environmental services were –4.1 per cent for Labour and –2.5 per cent for the Conservatives (Duke and Edgell, 1981).

A second little-noticed dimension of the new central–local relations style was the creation of new problems for central government in other areas of policy. Whitehall apparently clamped down on local authorities' revenue spending, but at some cost in terms of other government objectives. Three unintended consequences were particularly noticeable. First, the tight revenue spending squeeze on councils caused a sharp fall in their capital spending (on buildings etc.) far below the levels that the government intended to produce. Councils claimed that they could not invest in buildings if their day-to-day spending was so squeezed that they could not afford to staff the facilities built or even cover the interest charges on the debts involved. Second, the squeeze on revenue spending more or less halted the process by which groups of long-stay patients being cared for very expensively and often inappropriately within the national health service were transferred over to local authority social-service departments (see Chapter 7). With their existing social-service spending badly squeezed, local authorities were in no mood to accept any new responsibilities, causing a growing problem for the NHS and Whitehall in funding much more expensive provision within the health service. The DoE's 'success' in curbing council revenue spending may thus have involved higher spending by the DHSS. Something similar happened in the field of housing rents. From 1980 the DoE compelled local councils to raise rents for council housing in line with rigid nation estimates of 'realistic' rent levels, which in some cases brought about increases of almost 80 per cent between 1980 and late 1981. By 1982, many councils were already making a profit on their council housing (so that council tenants were subsidising ratepayers). Since around half of all council-house rents are now paid by the DHSS (because tenants are unemployed or pensioners or on supplementary benefits), much of the rent increase simply put up the bill facing another central government department. Third, the clamp-down on capital expenditure for new council housing looks set to recreate a gross housing shortage in the UK (that is, a situation where there are fewer dwellings than there are households) by the mid-1980s, a situation which Conservative and Labour governments worked hard to abolish.

Centralisaton and Restructuring, 1983 Onwards

The fourth phase of development in central–local relations began with the Conservative's 1983 election campaign. Embarassed by her first government's failure to carry out a 1979 promise to abolish rates, Mrs Thatcher insisted that the new manifesto pledge radical action to allow her next administration at least to control rate increases. Two measures are involved here. First a 'rate-capping' bill provides that DoE ministers can: (a) intervene and take direct control of the rating decision on a selective basis in up to twenty of the highest 'over-spending' councils; and (b) fix limits on permissible rate increases for all local authorities. This general capability is said to be a 'reserve power' which will be used only *in extremis,* while ministers publicly anticipate that only Labour councils will be affected by the immediately implemented selective powers. Second, the Conservatives decided to abolish all seven (Labour-controlled) metropolitan counties in England, transferring their less important or shared powers to metropolitan districts in their areas, but shifting their big-spending functions (mainly police, fire and public transport) to newly created joint boards of the metro districts or to quasi-governmental agencies under Whitehall control.

Both these initiatives clearly imply major reductions in local government powers and responsibilities, and have aroused intense opposition, much of it tri-partisan. The general rate-capping power may well not be accepted by the House of Lords and will be fiercely contested even in the Commons. And the metro counties' reorganisation, especially the arrangements proposed for London, seems to most observers a hastily conceived initiative very unlikely to realise its claims to be 'streamlining the cities'. Accordingly, although the bulk of the two White Papers is likely to be implemented, major revisions may yet be made. Even when they are enacted, selective rate-capping and the metro reorganisations will certainly generate their own unanticipated consequences and new dimensions of central–local conflict. It is improbable that either measure will simply eliminate troublesome councils, as the government apparently hopes. The evidence that confrontation in central–local relations has proved a less effective strategy than co-opting councils into achieving central policy goals has apparently been ignored in favour of a further polarisation between Whitehall and the localities.

Conclusions

We have argued that the relations between central and local government are a vitally important influence on what gets done at national policy level. Quite apart from individual local authorities' discretion to make policy decisions for their areas (which we have not explored in any detail here), the cumulative impact of different councils' decisions and of local government lobbying at central level is seriously to limit both ministers' freedom of action and Whitehall's influence. Parallel conclusions could also be drawn from a study of the relations between Whitehall and quasi-governmental agencies, which we saw are involved in most other fields of domestic policy-making. This implies the way we phrase many of the traditional 'power' problems in British politics needs to be reassessed. We cannot go on arguing (in the way many textbooks still do) as if central government has unlimited 'power', and all we have to do is to parcel it out between the PM, the Cabinet, individual ministers, civil servants or Parliament. Instead we have to recognise that the UK's well-defined pattern of 'non-executant central government' involves Whitehall in power-dependency relations with QGAs and local authorities which are always complex, two-way flows of influence. Many of the key decisions confronting ministers and civil servants in British government are problems of inter-organisational relations, rather than matters under the direct control of a Whitehall department. Thus one of the crucial determinants of ministers' success, and a key field for the operation of civil service 'expertise', is the management of dealings with government organisations beyond Whitehall – organisations with their own autonomous powers, their own policy problems and priorities, and their own commitments and strategies. The lesson of recent developments in central–local relations for Whitehall seems to be that its potential to acquire new formal powers of control may not be a stable, long-run substitute for a system better able to secure voluntary co-operation from quasi-governmental agencies and local authorities of diverse kinds. Equally, the lessons for local government are that national economic priorities and the British tradition of strong executive government seem destined to radically restructure the practice of central–local relations. The key to any understanding of this area remains the unresolved tension between the interdependence of centre and locality on the one hand, and authoritive decision-making by central government on the other.

6

Economic Policy

ANDREW GAMBLE

Challenge to the Consensus

The importance of the economy as an issue in British politics
has been growing in the last thirty years. So has the number of
economists (especially economists with different opinions
about economic policy). Neither is accidental. As economic
performance has deteriorated so the economy has become
once again the crucial focus for debate between the parties
and within the parties. The post-war consensus on economic
arrangements and economic management has been challenged; parties have armed themselves with detailed economic
programmes designed to put right everything that has been
going wrong, and the economic record of governments has
become a crucial factor in determining electoral popularity.

Voters are naturally most influenced by those economic
developments that impinge directly on their lives. There is
little popular understanding of the technicalities and comple-
xities of economic policy, and the way in which economic
policy-making is conducted, and the manner in which
economic issues are reported do little to increase it. But
unemployment and inflation, taxes and welfare benefits are
real enough in their effects on everyday experience to provide
a popular awareness of the state of the economy and a basis

for evaluating the rival claims, promises and plans of the political parties.

What has made questions of economic policy so central to political debate has been, first, the relative decline suffered by the British economy since the war in comparision with similar economies, and second, the world recession. Despite a large absolute rise in the standard of living, the economy failed to achieve the still faster rate of growth that the electorate, encouraged by politicians and the media, had come to believe was possible. This produced growing political tensions over the conduct of economic policy during the Wilson and Heath governments. Inflation began to accelerate, and unemployment to rise. Industrial militancy revived and the public finances were plunged into a permanent 'fiscal crisis' (government spending showing a tendency to outpace government revenue), because government plans for expanding public spending assumed a rate of growth of the economy that was never achieved.

The impact of the recessions in the world economy since 1974–5 have brought gradual realisation that the Western capitalist economy faces an economic prospect as intractable and bleak as the depression of the 1930s, even though different in some important respects. If there was already talk before 1974 of Britain becoming 'ungovernable' and policy-making processes being overwhelmed by the irreconcilable demands of the electors and the major interest groups, such talk redoubled once the depth of the recession became clear. Not just relative but absolute impoverishment now threatened Britain. The relative weakness of the British economy in the previous twenty years made the consequences of recession more serious for Britain than for other states, because the contradictions and the inadequacies of previous economic policy were now exposed.

Varieties of Economic Policy

Since managing the British economy has proved so difficult a task in recent years and has brought so few dividends to politicians, it might seem surprising not perhaps that governments are so often held responsible for economic outcomes but why, at least until recently and the advent of the Thatcher government, politicians were so eager to make themselves responsible.

There are two main reasons. First, the interdependence of state and economy has developed in ways that oblige every government of a nation-state to formulate an economic policy in three main areas:

Foreign economic policy, to determine the relations of the national economy to the world economy, specifically the degree of freedom to be allowed for the movement of goods, of capital and of labour; the question of the relation of the national currency to other currencies; and the enforceability of contracts and security of property outside national frontiers.

Stabilisation policy, because the existence of a substantial sector of the economy which is publicly managed and publicly financed requires the use of monetary and fiscal instruments (e.g. interest rates and tax rates) both to raise the necessary finance for state activities and either to promote a stable monetary environment that encourages expansion and mini-mises uncertainty, or to achieve a balance between a number of different and partly conflicing goals, such as full employment, stable prices, economic growth, and a surplus on the balance of payments.

Industrial policy, because stabilisation policy, whether it concen-trates on managing demand or achieving sound money, may not achieve its objectives, and governments often supplement it with measures aimed at removing obstacles to the workings of free, competitive markets (restrictive practices of all kinds), or by measures to compensate for the failure of markets to provide the elements for successful production (of the right quality, in the right place, at the right time, and in the right quantity).

The second reason is that the actual historical path by which interdependence has grown has been shaped by the political process – the mobilisation, representation, and conflict of interests and opinion through political parties, the media, institutions, and pressure groups.

THE OLD POLITICAL LIMITS TO ECONOMIC POLICY

The recent changes and continuity in the three main branches of economic policy can only be understood if they are seen in relation to the post-war consensus on economic policy. What this consensus established were the priorities but also the limits under which economic policy was conducted. Whether this involved active consent between the parties, a true meeting of hearts and minds, or whether, more likely, it was the result of a common recognition of the impracticality of alternative policies, it certainly became in the 1950s and 1960s a significant feature of British politics. There was a high degree of continuity between the policies pursued by successive governments. Not until 1970 did a change of government bring a change in direction (and this was short-lived).

One crucial aspect of this consensus between the parties was the consensus on the priorities of Britain's post-war foreign economic policy. After 1945 all parties were committed to the Atlantic Alliance, and accepted the creation of a new unified international trading and financial system under American leadership. This entailed the eventual withdrawal of Britain from its Empire and the retention of other parts of Britain's traditional world role (such as the position of sterling as an international currency) only when they fitted in with American plans. Many options in economic policy were closed by this. It effectively destroyed protectionism as a serious position on the right of British politics. By renewing the old orientation of British foreign economic policy (freeing the movement of goods and capital from all avoidable restrictions), the policy dictated the framework in which stabilisation and industrial policy were implemented, and often their content. The decisions to maintain sterling as an international currency for example, and to permit the outflow of funds necessary to finance government military spending and private investment overseas, resulted in the succession of balance-of-payments deficits and sterling crises which dominated economic management in the 1950s and 1960s.

The other chief aspect of the consensus as far as economic policy was concerned were the concessions made to the Labour movement. What emerged in practice was agreement on an economy that was *mixed*, composed of a dominant free market sector controlled by private capital, and an enlarged public sector; second, an economy that was *managed*, in which full employment and economic expansion emerged as a priority of stabilisation policy, to be secured by the manipulation of the level of effective demand; third, agreement on a *public sector* enlarged through the nationalisation of key public utilities, through the increase in public spending on welfare, health, education, and defence, and through the development of new forms of public intervention to assist, subsidise, and regulate industry; and fourth, agreement on the need to recognise *trade unions* as a legitimate interest within the state whose views should be consulted and whose freedom to bargain collectively for their members should be protected.

THE CHALLENGES OF THE 1970S

All four of these priorities came under attack in the 1970s. A new framework for economic policy slowly evolved but it created fierce controversy. The 1970s saw a marked polarisation within and between the major parties – the rise of an assertive New Right in the Conservative party committed to the goal of creating a social market economy and rolling back the state and social democracy, and a revived Labour Left which developed an 'alternative economic strategy' in the 1970s, aimed at substantially reducing the autonomy of private capital and redistributing economic power and wealth. Both these challenges initially arose as challenges to the policies of Conservative and Labour governments in the 1960s and 1970s which continued to operate within the broad framework of the post-war consensus. Both parties, especially the Conservatives, moved a long way towards their radical wings in the later 1970s, and this created a space for the new Liberal/SDP Alliance to distinguish themselves from the other two parties by reasserting their commitment to the priorities the other parties were eager to discard. By the end of 1982 there was greater diversity in the economic programmes offered by the political parties than at any time since the war.

This was only partly due to the impact of economic decline. Whatever the outcome of the internal political reassessment of the causes of Britain's poor economic performance, the world recession would have forced changes in the direction and content of economic policy. It hastened and confirmed the polarisation of political opinion which the experience of economic management in the 1960s had begun. But the world recession itself was foreshadowed by a changing balance of forces in the world economy. The need to rethink traditional assumptions about foreign economic policy was already apparent after 1968, because of the noticeable weakening of American power. The breakdown of the international monetary system established at Bretton Woods in 1944, and the floating of all the major currencies in 1971–2, the entry of Britain into the EEC in 1973, and the quadrupling of oil prices in 1973–4, all were signs of this changing pattern.

The recession has powerfully shaped developments in economic policy in the last ten years. As in the 1930s the world economy has lacked one state with the power to impose its own solutions on other states. This has intensified uncertainties about finance and trade, protectionist pressures have grown, and there has been no agreement on co-ordinated policies of reflation to help end the slump. The issue of economic sovereignty has re-emerged and British political opinion has become divided on whether the priority of foreign economic policy should be to continue the close association with the United States, to promote common action by the EEC, or to pursue greater self-reliance and protection of British national economic interests and jobs. The right exchange rate for the £ to preserve UK competitiveness, the question of import controls to halt further de-industrialisation, the controls on movements of capital and on immigrants, have all become key questions.

The weakening of the major post-war check to domestic expansion of the money supply both reflected and contributed to the acceleration of inflation. The high rates of inflation distinguish this new slump from all previous slumps in the world economy. The containment of inflation had become the priority of all national stabilisation policies by the mid-1970s, and the International Monetary Fund (IMF) and the international financial markets assumed a greater role in attempting to push national governments towards sound money policies. Inflation has been contained, but at the expense of steadily increasing unemployment, over-capacity in many industries, fierce competition for markets, periodic currency instabilities, the piling up of debts by many countries and growing fears of a major banking collapse.

The domestic political argument has centred on whether priority should be given to containing inflation or unemployment. Monetarists have sought an explicit renunciation by governments of any attempt to maintain a particular level of unemployment. The traditional Treasury view of stabilisation policy has made a surprising comeback. Governments are not yet attempting simply to balance the budget, but they have moved a long way in that direction. Conservative governments in 1963 and 1972 responded to a rise in the number of unemployed towards one million by a rapid expansion of demand. In 1974 the Labour government initially attempted to maintain demand and its own spending to prevent a major deflation and the onset of recession. But after 1976 this attempt was abandoned. Unemployment had doubled to 1.5 million but no further significant attempt was made to reduce it. Acceptance of permanent high unemployment has become a major feature of British economic policy. Since 1975 the control of inflation has been given a greater priority than either employment or growth.

A second major issue has been the question of public expenditure. Here, too, the assumptions governing the great post-war expansion of public expenditure have been successfully challenged, and determined efforts have begun to control, and ultimately to contract, the share of resources taken by public expenditure. From a monetarist standpoint the inability of governments to fund public expenditure programmes through taxes or genuine borrowing has been a major contribution to inflation, and there have been major struggles over proposals to restructure social services away from universal to selective provision, whether by privatising the services or charging for them.

The sharp contraction of British industrial capacity during the recession, the squeeze on profits and the loss of markets, has sharpened the debate about industrial policy and reopened the question of the right balance between the public and private sectors. The initial policy response of the government in 1974–5, faced by the collapse of many industries, was to prop them up, often by taking them into public ownership. Subsequently the trend has been towards returning to the private sector all public enterprises on which the financial markets can be persuaded to put a price. The right size of the private and public sectors and the boundary between them has become an issue of major dispute once more, and it has become linked to the question of how far public agencies and public funds should be used to restructure and rationalise British industry and to retrain the work-force. Another major challenge to the post-war consensus has been the conflict over the legal position and political influence of the trade unions. Policy has oscillated between attempts to incorporate trade unions fully into economic decision-making through tripartite arrangements, and attempts to curb union power by market disciplines, especially mass unemployment, and legislation to reduce trade-union rights and privileges (see Chapter 10).

The Policy-making Process

We have already noted that governments need an economic policy and that their handling of economic policy has become central to their standing with the electorate. Governments, however, are far from having a free hand even in initiating, still less in carrying out, policies. The constraints of office are often more real than the powers, and the range of options open to ministers can be extremely narrow. This is not primarily because of the activities of civil servants or pressure groups, but because of the interdependence of state and economy. Policies have to be pursued that allow the private sector to remain profitable, otherwise the public sector cannot be financed. The public sector has to be maintained in order to create the conditions under which the private sector can be profitable. Access to world markets must be preserved so that essential imports on which the economy depends can be purchased. Pressure groups and influential civil servants may articulate and reinforce the case for a particular option. Their arguments are only part of the reason for the persuasiveness of the case.

THE ROLE OF GOVERNMENT

The initiation of policy is formally in the hands of ministers. In practice there are many other actors involved; the civil servants, MPs, (especially the Select Committees), the party organisations (through their manifestos and research departments), the major pressure groups, the economic experts (particularly the City editors and financial journalists), the international bodies (such as the IMF, GATT, and EEC Commission), and independent research institutes such as the Fabian Society, the Institute for Economic Affairs, the Centre for Policy Studies, and the Policy Studies Institute. The diversity of the policy-making community ensures a steady stream of advice, protests and information about economic policy.

Ministers and the Cabinet continue to play a crucial role, however. Many of the groups just mentioned such as the House of Commons' Treasury and Civil Service Committee normally attempt to monitor rather than directly initiate economic policy. Initiation of policy is still the carefully guarded privilege of the executive. What is immediately striking about the British economic policy-making machinery is the dominance of the Treasury. This has not changed in recent years. Indeed, since the failure of the attempt to create a separate Department of Economic Affairs concerned with the long-term expansion of the economy (created in 1964, it was finally wound up in 1969), the Treasury has once again successfully reasserted its grip on economic policy. One sign of this is that the Treasury now has two permanent members of the Cabinet – the Chancellor of the Exchequer and the Chief Secretary. Two previous Chief Secretaries, Jack Diamond and Joel Barnett, had eventually been promoted to the Cabinet, but since 1979 the Chief Secretary has been in the Cabinet automatically. The reason is because the Chief Secretary is in control of expenditure and that has become of central importance to economic policy since the mid-1970s.

The 'Treasury team' of ministers is completed by the Financial Secretary and two Ministers of State. While all Prime Ministers have tended to appoint to the Treasury those MPs who have specialised on economic and financial questions, the

Treasury team since 1979 has been unusual because the Prime Minister appointed to it only those holding one particular view of economic policy – a monetarist one. This, combined with the Prime Minister's own strong support for the economic policy of her Chancellor, Geoffrey Howe, gave great coherence and unity to the new Treasury doctrine and separated the Treasury team quite sharply from the great spending ministries, which were headed by ministers who often did not share monetarist views.

THE TREASURY

The Treasury's importance in economic policy stems from its crucial role in controlling expenditure and raising revenue, and therefore in stabilisation policy. In addition it has important responsibilities in foreign economic policy, because it monitors the balance of payments and, in co-operation with the Bank of England, it is in charge of the exchange rate. The traditional Treasury view of stabilisation policy was that it should be aimed at balancing the budget. This would minimise the burdens placed by the public sector on the rest of the economy and so create the best possible conditions for economic activity. This view was modified in the 1940s and stabilisation was conceived on Keynesian lines; policy became aimed at balancing the economy rather than balancing the budget. The Treasury began to manipulate the total level of demand by adjusting government spending and tax policies and by using monetary policy to regulate the flow of credit. The important point for the development of British economic policy is that this role was entrusted to the Treasury. Only in the 1960s, when ambitious programmes to modernise the economy and launch Britain into much more rapid economic growth emerged, was the position of the Treasury briefly threatened. The continuing balance-of-payments problem, however, allowed the Treasury to reassert control. The rise of monetarism in the 1970s and the repudiation of Keynesian demand-management, one of the major developments in economic policy in the last ten years, has further consolidated the Treasury's position.

The consequences of this institutional organisation of economic policy are that foreign economic policy and stabilisation policy have been accorded greater priority than industrial and commercial policy. The financial markets have had a greater impact on economic policy than the labour markets or the industrial and commercial markets. Economic policy has inclined more towards financial orthodoxy, and to the conception of the national economy as a set of open markets rather than a unified productive enterprise. The effects of this can be seen in the Treasury's attention to the responses of the financial markets, its dislike of detailed intervention in industry, and the much clearer dividing line that still exists in Britain, compared with many other countries, between government and industry.

None of the other main economic ministries has anything like the same importance as the Treasury in determining economic policy. The Cabinet Committee that considers long-term economic strategy always contains the Treasury ministers; the inclusion of others is less automatic. Many of these ministries are recent creations or amalgams, such as Industry, Employment, and Energy. Others, including the Board of Trade and Agriculture have a much more continuous history. The sphere of each one is fairly clear, although some overlap does occur. Their main tasks are regulatory or the provision of specific services. In addition there are the giant spending ministries, Education, Health and Social Security, Defence, and Environment. One of the major phases of the annual circus of economic policy-making has become the public-expenditure review in which the spending departments battle with the Treasury over their spending plans.

OTHER MINISTRIES

Although departments and ministers can initiate policies (occasionally ministers take such policies directly from the manifesto on which they have been elected), they do not always have the power to carry policies through to success. There are many decisions that need only the authority of the government for them to be carried out. A decision to raise taxes is normally entirely successful in generating the expected increase in revenue, because few citizens will refuse to pay it or manage to avoid it. But many policies, particularly those concerned with planning incomes or planning growth, require sustained co-operation from many separate interests and groups. The chance of a breakdown at some point in the chain and the ensuing frustration of the original aims of the policy is often great. In the past, governments have tried to strengthen the chain by creating new agencies to carry policies through into effect. There is a host of these ranging from the Departments under the Treasury (the Inland Revenue and the Board of Customs and Excise) to the Bank of England, the National Enterprise Board, Agricultural marketing boards, Industrial training boards, the Manpower Services Commission, the Monopolies Commission, the Forestry Commission, and many more. The Conservative government elected in 1979 declared war on all 'Quangos', but its achievements in reducing their number have not been impressive (see Chapter 4). But the economic strategy pursued by the Conservative government was also aimed at abandoning all policies that required a sustained effort by government and its agencies to secure agreement and co-operation among diverse groups and interests. Instead it aimed to concentrate policy on those decisions whose consequences were predictable and where the authority to take them lay wholly in the government sphere. Decisions on taxes, interest rates, money supply, public-sector borrowing, and cash limits are examples.

Foreign Economic Policy

THE EEC

The major developments in foreign economic policy in recent years have centred around, first, the uneasy role played by Britain in the EEC, and, more recently, renewed commitment to an open world-economy. The shift in Britain's pattern of trade towards the developed Western economies and particularly the EEC was one of the main reasons why EEC membership appeared attractive in the 1960s. In the 1970s, with membership of the EEC secured, Britain's dependence on trade with Europe grew still more marked. But popular enthusiasm for Europe waned, despite the energetic advocacy of the need to strengthen European links from the powerful European lobby.

Both Labour and Conservative governments fought bruising battles within the Community in defence of British 'interests', and declined to assist moves to speed the achievement of greater unity through common policies. The extent of import penetration of Britain's major industrial markets (much of which originated from the EEC), and the cost of the Common Agricultural Policy (CAP) made the EEC link seem increasingly disadvantageous. The EEC gave protection to British agriculture which did not need it, but not to British industry which plainly did. The government refused to join the European monetary system established in 1979 because that would have meant tying sterling to the German mark, and would have risked making British exports still more uncompetitive. The government fought strenuously to reduce the UK contribution to the EEC budget, which was thought disproportionately high in relation to the benefits Britain received. A temporary compromise was eventually agreed in 1980.

Although the 1975 referendum had registered a large majority in favour of Britain's membership, popular opinion soon swung once more against the Market; the Labour Party in Opposition after 1979 became committed to withdrawal, and a new anti-Market faction appeared on the Conservative side. The major initiatives of the Thatcher government inflamed rather than countered anti-Market feeling. In negotiations over the budget contribution the British demanded that contributions should be related to benefits, even though such a demand went against the concept of a community budget. The reason why the Thatcher government took such a strong stand was that the UK was due in 1980 to pay for the first time its full share of the EEC budget. Although the budget only amounted to 1 per cent of the total GDP of the EEC countries, it was financed mainly from the proceeds of the common external tariff. The interdependence of Britain and the EEC was increasing, but the dependence of the UK economy on non-EEC trade was significantly higher than it was for other EEC states. This made Britain's contribution to EEC revenue disproportionately high, while the efficiency of its agriculture made its net benefits from EEC expenditure disproportionately low. Some estimates of the

UK net budgetary contribution put it as high as £1.5 billion, a sizeable amount when the Public Sector Borrowing Requirement for 1979–80 was £9.9 billion.

The problem for British foreign economic policy in the 1980s was that the EEC was being visibly battered by the world recession. Its fragile unity had formerly depended on the spontaneous integration that had accompanied rapid economic growth, and the political commitment to the establishment of common policies – moving beyond a customs union to a genuine common market, with a single set of rules governing economic activity and a single currency. By 1980 forward movement of the Community had ceased and it appeared to be held together more by the external threat of world competition. The potential advantages of the EEC as a protectionist bloc in the event of a major collapse of the world trading and financial systems was given a further boost by the evident economic strains that began appearing between the United States, the EEC and Japan. The conflicts over steel imports (the EEC was accused by the Americans of dumping) and the Soviet gas pipeline in 1982 underlined the importance of a unified political and economic bloc in western Europe which could bargain on equal terms with the United States and Japan.

THE OPEN WORLD ECONOMY

The EEC remains a major priority of Britain's foreign economic policy, but the recession has also brought renewed emphasis on the long-standing commitment to an open economy and a liberal world economic order.

Import controls to deal with the problem of de-industrialisation and to permit a reflation of the economy have been strongly urged by some economists, by the Labour Left and by the TUC. But both Labour and Conservative governments since 1974 have so far refused to introduce any kind of general protection. British firms have been obliged to adjust to the harsh international conditions produced by the recession, either becoming as competitive and productive as the leading international companies or going out of business. The pressure on British firms was intensified by the decision in 1977 to allow sterling to appreciate. Following the collapse of sterling in 1976 the negotiation of a loan from the IMF brought a revival of confidence which was fuelled by the sudden perception of the UK as a self-sufficient oil producer in the 1980s. This made sterling to some degree a 'petro currency' and was partly responsible for pushing the exchange rate to a level far higher than was justified by the relative costs and relative productivity of British industry. The result was severely to squeeze profit margins of British exporters. This was a major factor in the severe UK recession in 1979–81. Although the pound subsequently fell, the drop in competitiveness had still not been overcome by 1983.

Faced with the dilemma of an overvalued exchange rate, the authorities chose not to hold down the exchange rate by exchange controls but began to lift all exchange controls in order to minimise the upward pressure on the exchange rate. The final step was taken by the Thatcher government in September 1979. Throughout the post-war period Britain had been characterised by a high net outflow of capital. This outflow grew to enormous proportions after the abolition of controls. In 1980 UK private investment rose to £7,100 million and in 1981 it reached £11,171 million (an increase of 40 per cent). By the end of 1981 the value of all overseas foreign assets owned by British companies and City institutions was £63,500 million (approximately two-thirds was direct investment by British companies and one-third portfolio investment). This policy increased further the openness of the British economy and significantly strengthened the international orientation of the dominant section of British business, the City institutions and British multinationals. An increasing number of British companies by 1980 had acquired overseas plants.

The opposite policy was followed with regard to labour. The free movement of migrant labour, which had been such a factor in the success of the Western European companies in the 1950s and 1960s, was subject to ever-greater controls in the 1970s. In the UK, because many of the immigrants came from parts of the Empire and enjoyed citizenship, the controls took the form of redefining British nationality so as to remove the right to entry from citizens of the Commonwealth and remaining colonies. The final step in this process was the British Nationality Act introduced in 1981 which defined British citizenship very narrowly and gave no right of entry even to citizens of the Dependent Territories such as the Falklands. This did not mean a complete end to immigration, but since the mid-1960s the number of new work-permits given to new immigrants had been cut to an annual rate of below five thousand. Much greater freedom of movement existed for EEC citizens.

Stabilisation Policy

After 1976, monetarism replaced Keynesianism as the major theoretical framework guiding the formulation of economic policy. This does not mean that monetarism was applied consistently or unambiguously. Policy is never solely the outcome of a particular theory. Interests, institutions and circumstances all play a major part in determining outcomes. The importance of monetarist doctrine is that it justified putting control of inflation ahead of the achievement of full employment or a faster rate of growth as objectives of policy. This meant giving monetary policy a new prominence and developing new ways of controlling public expenditure. The two key policies associated with this are the control of money supply and cash limits.

CONTROL OF THE MONEY SUPPLY

Since 1976 the government has been formally committed to controlling the growth of the money supply by publishing monetary targets. In order to meet those targets in a non-inflationary manner the government is expected to use monetary policy to control private credit and to keep its own spending and borrowing within specified limits. The Callaghan government chose to reinforce these efforts with a wages policy in the hope of keeping down costs in the public sector and unemployment in the private. The Thatcher government maintained a covert wages policy in the public sector (a requirement for all governments, otherwise projections for public expenditure would be completely arbitrary), but abandoned it in the private sector, arguing that such policies distorted the labour market and created inefficiency.

The main innovation of the Thatcher government was the announcement of a medium-term financial strategy in the 1980 budget. This had long been urged by monetarist commentators and economists. The government announced targets for the growth of money supply and public-sector borrowing several years ahead, committing itself to a gradual reduction of both. Such a strategy was intended to bind economic policy-makers to sound money policies in the way that the external discipline of the gold standard had once bound finance ministers. The aim was to restrict the room for discretion on the Chancellor's part so as to insulate him from the pressures of party and electoral opinion and special interests. Concentrating single-mindedly on the achievement of monetary targets to reduce inflation without regard to the effects on employment or output was considered the best means of laying the foundations for a secure recovery. What it implied in practice was that if monetary growth looked like being outside the target range, the Chancellor needed to tighten the squeeze on credit by raising interest rates to whatever level was necessary. In a monetarist world the authorities could control interest rates or money supply, but not both together.

CASH LIMITS

Cash limits were an integral part of this strategy, because excessive public spending and borrowing were regarded as major contributors to an excessive growth of money supply. Throughout the 1970s, public expenditure appeared to be out of control, rising much faster than had been planned and forcing governments to borrow or tax more in order to finance it. With a stagnant economy after 1974, with rising unemployment and pressure on take-home pay and living standards, the political limits to further general increases in taxation were quickly reached since the burden fell directly on the mass of wage earners. At the same time, the option of borrowing was extremely limited because it meant either borrowing from the banking system (which was equivalent to printing money and directly inflationary) or borrowing from the financial markets, driving up interest rates and crowding out other prospective borrowers. The only alternative was to find ways of permanently restraining public expenditure.

The control of public expenditure has become central to economic policy since the mid 1970s. The main flaws in the former system of control (The Public Expenditure Survey Committee – PESC – introduced in 1961) were that when the economy failed to expand, no automatic adjustment was made to the public-expenditure plans, and that because resources were allocated in volume not cash terms, there was always the possibility of an overshoot. In 1976 the much blunter control instrument of cash limits was introduced to impose financial ceilings on expenditure in particular areas. The idea behind cash limits is that any overspending will be clawed back in the next financial period, and that all spending, including items still to be determined such as wages and other costs, have to be met within the limits.

The severity of the fiscal crisis in the 1970s has thus brought the return of annual cash budgets. The wider goals sought by the PESC system of control, such as relating spending directly to economic resources and attempting to analyse the results of policies, were discarded in the interests of reasserting financial control. Cash limits have come to be applied to two-thirds of public expenditure which is voted by Parliament. But it has not been applied to programmes such as social security, where legal rights to benefit have been conferred on all who qualify. These are open-ended commitments and in meeting them governments have been forced to cut those programmes subject to cash limits even more. Capital spending has suffered most; all Departments have made their priority the preservation of current spending on staff and services.

The major change in policy introduced by the Thatcher government has been not in the methods used to control public spending but the distribution of the cuts. Among the big spending departments, Defence has been singled out for special treatment. The government pledged itself to increase defence spending in real terms by 3 per cent p.a.; it has also protected the budget for internal security, and has exempted the pay of the armed forces and the police from the pay curbs it has imposed elsewhere in the public sector. Given the extra money the government had to find to pay for the increased numbers of unemployed and to subsidise certain state industries, the squeeze on the other major areas of public spending – education, health, transport and housing – was intensified. One of the most protracted of these battles has been the attempt to impose curbs on local government spending (see Chapter 5). The impact of the cuts, however, has been most uneven and in certain areas, such as health, overall expenditure has risen not declined.

The new controls on public expenditure were aimed primarily at containing its tendency to expand faster than the economy, adjusting public spending plans to an economy of nil or very low growth. The Thatcher government also proposed to reduce the share of public expenditure in order to reduce taxation and increase incentives. This aim was not achieved in its first three years in office. Despite an initial tax-cutting flurry, the government was forced to increase, not reduce, the burden of taxation, despite the growing contribution being made to the Exchequer by North Sea oil revenues. The government has, however, encouraged a small shift from direct to indirect taxes (mainly by doubling VAT in its first budget). The government also substantially reduced the higher rates of income tax, just as the previous Conservative government had done. There was talk about more radical tax changes, such as the introduction of self-assessment and of a credit income tax scheme, but no firm plans have been announced.

Industrial Policy

The slow-down in the growth of the world-economy was accompanied by a severe squeeze on profits in British industry and a collapse of many financial institutions in 1974–5. The economy was plunged into renewed recession in 1979–81 partly by the appreciation of sterling and partly by the government's monetary policies which at one point raised interest rates to 17 per cent. In each of these two periods unemployment doubled, first to 1.5 million then to over 3 million. There were widespread bankruptcies, and many sectors of British industry came under intense pressure as overseas competition in a shrinking world market intensified. The policy response by governments has been to aid firms through tax reliefs and direct subsidies. Industrial strategy has been limited to a programme of identifying the problems and needs of each industry sector by sector. The more ambitious interventionist proposals represented by the Labour Party's plans for a National Enterprise Board (NEB) and planning agreements were discarded after the 1975 EEC Referendum. The budget for the NEB was drastically reduced and only one planning agreement was ever signed.

The Thatcher government was even more hostile in principle to industrial intervention, but in practice it has been closely involved in attempts at restructuring, and has been forced to increase state aid to industries like British Leyland and British Steel rather than let them go bankrupt. One estimate put the total job losses that would result from closing British Leyland at 750,000. This response has had important consequences for other aspects of policy, notably public spending. Aid to industry has always been regarded as a short-term expedient and the government has looked for ways to disengage itself from direct involvement in the running of business enterprises.

PRIVATISATION

This search has produced one of the major developments in policy in the last few years – privatisation. The most obvious form this has taken has been the sale of public assets. The Labour government sold some shares in BP but the Conservative government took the policy much further. Examples include the sale of a majority stake in British Aerospace, the sale of the NEB's shares in profitable companies, the sale of 49 per cent of the share capital of Cable and Wireless, the sale of 51 per cent of the oil-producing interests of BNOC, and the sale of the National Freight Corporation and some of the hotels owned by British Rail. Major plans already prepared by the end of 1982 included the sale of the oil interests and showrooms of British Gas (this has been delayed once by trade-union and management opposition); the nineteen ports run by the British Transport Docks Board; British Airways; and British Telecom. The government also hoped eventually to dispose of British

Leyland and British Shipbuilders. Other types of privatisation promoted by the Conservative government included ending the monopoly over services that some nationalised industries such as the Post Office and British Telecom enjoyed, and encouraging local councils and some central government departments to contract out public services such as refuse collection to private firms.

If the whole programme is carried through, a significant shift will have occurred in the balance of public and private sectors, and though it may ease some of the government's funding problems, in many cases the government will be denying itself direct contributions to the Exchequer from the surpluses produced by enterprises. How large such surpluses can be was shown by the government's decision to set very high financial targets for the gas industry, which resulted in annual payments to the Exchequer of more than £300 million. By selling public oil assets the government chose to rely exclusively on taxation of the oil companies to provide funds for the Exchequer from the development of the North Sea.

UNEMPLOYMENT

In the labour markets, the government attempted to mitigate the impact of unemployment and reduce the numbers officially registered by launching a host of new training schemes for various categories of the unemployed, particularly school-leavers, under the direction of the Manpower Services Commission (see Chapter 7). But policy-makers were clearly resigned to permanent structural unemployment of several millions for the forseeable future. The seriousness of the unemployment problem was shown by the fact that the number of registered unemployed was almost one million below the true figure according to the government's own figures. The Thatcher government was the first among post-war governments to disclaim responsibility for unemployment and to deny that stabilisation policy could do anything to reduce it. The level of unemployment was blamed on the world recession and the rigidities of labour markets, which were associated with the practices of trade unions and the level of social-security payments relative to wages.

The government in the 1981 Budget broke the indexing of social-security benefits but did not drastically reduce their real value as social market doctrine required. Two bills on trade unions were introduced which attempted to restrict picketing rights and the closed shop, and to reduce union legal immunities (see Chapter 10). The weakness of the opposition to these measures encouraged the government to treat them as first instalments in its plans for curbing union power and privileges. But by 1983 it had not yet become clear whether the change was only temporary, induced by the mood of resignation which mass unemployment had created among trade-union members, or whether it signalled a lasting shift in the balance of power and a decisive reversal of the trend towards corporatism.

The Agenda

The twin impact of decline and slump has begun to bring considerable changes to British economic policy. Between 1975 and 1983 monetarist and social market ideas were in the ascendant. Amid increasing pessimism about what governments could achieve, determined efforts were made to reduce the role of government in the economy, to encourage the electorate to scale down its expectations about what governments could deliver, and to relieve the 'overload' with which some perceived modern government to be afflicted. The policy response to the recession enhanced the role of the Treasury and the financial markets, and to a lesser extent the CBI, in the making of economic policy, while the role of the trade unions and some government Departments, like Industry and Employment, was reduced. The traditional foreign economic policy stayed intact, but major inroads were made on the traditional assumptions of stabilisation policy and industrial policy. A major programme of denationalisation was under way by 1983, trade unions' legal privileges had been reduced, while their membership and militancy had diminished. The citadel of public expenditure and taxation was under siege (though by no means stormed). The control of inflation had been declared the major contribution that government could make to the rebuilding of profitability, hence to eventual recovery. Mass unemployment might be the consequence, but it was blamed on the world economic blizzard and on interference in the workings of markets by trade unions and other groups. The government itself disclaimed responsibility.

The opposition parties and a section of the Conservative Cabinet between 1979 and 1982 argued for varying degrees of reflation, spearheaded by public-sector investment, to bring down unemployment and prevent the slump becoming ever deeper with catastrophic consequences for jobs, social order, and the public finances. They proposed to handle the risk of inflation politically, through some form of incomes policy or understanding with the trade unions. The Labour Party also supported a considerable expansion of public enterprise as the best means both to restructure and to protect the industrial base of the economy. Even more significant, the party was also opposed to the main priorities of the Conservatives' foreign economic policy; Labour favoured either a major devaluation or import controls, as well as strict controls on capital movements and withdrawal from the EEC.

In the 1983 election there were greater differences in the stated policies and economic doctrines of the political parties than at any time since the war. The scale of Labour's defeat in 1983 meant that the party's attempted revival of economic nationalism had failed. The initiative in policy had passed decisively to the Conservatives. But the prospects for a world economic recovery on which British hopes for recovery now depended absolutely were still clouded, and without a sustained recovery the difficulty of containing the problems created by mass unemployment would increase. The control of public expenditure would be harder and the chances of cutting taxes slim. At the 1983 election the Government accordingly proclaimed its belief that Britain was already moving out of the stagflation of the previous ten years. Yet some ministers were uneasily aware that any real recovery might revive trade-union militancy and popular expectations about rising living standards and improving public services. Whether a lasting political basis had been created for managing the different strains either of a further period of decline and recession or of a new phase of expansion looked like being the key question for the 1980s.

7

Social Policy

NICK BOSANQUET

How is Social Policy Made?

Social policy is made most visibly through decisions by government about the 'welfare state'. This has no formal boundaries but is usually taken to cover government expenditure for social security, health and personal social services, education and housing. Together these programmes add up to about one-quarter (25.4 per cent) of GDP and confer great potential power on a handful of people at the centre of politics. The social security programme accounts for nearly half (£25,840 m. in 1981–2) of welfare state spending, although as it consists of transfer payments it should strictly speaking be considered separately from the other spending which is mainly on goods and services.

Government also makes social policy through its decisions about tax reliefs. People who spend their money in certain ways, for example on mortgages for owner-occupied housing or on life insurance, are given special help. In addition there are less visible private contributions to social policy through occupational pension schemes and voluntary agencies. Titmuss wrote of the 'social division of welfare' with three different systems of social services: the welfare state, the fiscal system of tax reliefs and the occupational system of fringe benefits

(Titmuss, 1976, pp. 34–55). This chapter is mainly about the more visible decisions.

The welfare state deals with people who are peculiarly dependent on government, and with services of which the state often has a near monopoly. It is here that the impact of state decisions is most direct for the living standards and prospects of individual households. The job of Chancellor was recently described by one ex-contender for the post as two-thirds public relations. Certainly changes in economic or tax policy can be undone by unexpected changes in the non-government areas of the economy. But the welfare state is largely the government's own territory as paymaster and employer.

At Cabinet level, social policy in the narrow sense is a byproduct of choices about public spending. Certain programmes are labelled 'social' and others 'economic'. The score for the welfare state can be worked out by seeing how the social programmes fare relative to the economic. The key decision is on the general level of social spending relative to the other claims on resources from private consumption, other forms of public spending, industrial investment and exports. Spending departments do battle with the Treasury around the annual business of planning public spending with competing leaks to the media from the final stage of Cabinet argument in the autumn. Since 1976, social policy decisions have become more tightly constrained by the general decisions on public spending than in the past (Heclo and Wildavsky, 1981). In between public spending rounds much detailed social policy is made within the particular services. In this chapter we look first at the general decision at Cabinet level and then at the micro-climates of ideas, opinions and professional interests within the individual services.

The general level of social spending is the most important single decision in social policy; but it is made in the political stratosphere and is discussed, if at all, as part of the annual decision about public spending. Out of this decision come the budgets and cash limits for particular services. How these budgets are used – the results for particular groups of people – depends on the special world within these services.

The general history of social spending in 1976–82 tends to show rather limited impact both of a government's own intentions and of political ideology in the actual outcome. The outcome on the general level of social spending was not mainly determined by the government's own decisions. The inertia brought on by past programmes, political commitments and employment levels in the public sector meant that the scope for change was a small one at the edge of existing programmes. The overall outcome in levels of spending was influenced in the short term mainly by the state of the economy rather than by specific government policy. Government contributed to this outcome more through its general policy for running the economy rather than by specific decisions on public spending. The impact of its mandate or ideology was felt in few areas. Without its mandate, the Labour government would probably have made heavier cuts in social spending in 1976. The mandate certainly helps to explain the changes the 1979 Conservative government made in social security and housing. The immediate political pressures were different. For a Labour government, the influence of the Trades Union Congress was great: for a Conservative government, the ultimate test and source of power were the opinions of its own backbenchers. But both Left and Right were faced with common difficulties of control, in an economy of low growth, high tax levels on low incomes and increased producer-power in public services. There was no great difference between Denis Healey after 1976 and the early years of Sir Geoffrey Howe in some of the main essentials of their policy. Even at the technical level there was some continuity. The Conservative government's change to cash planning followed very easily from the Labour government's change to cash limits. The main differences between the governments were in their intentions and in their plans for the future rather than in outcomes achieved. A Labour government tended to see increases in social spending, usually in the future safely beyond the next general election; a Conservative one wanted to change track off the 'road to serfdom'. But in reality predestination seemed all too often to overcome political freewill.

Forces affecting Social Policy

Two different governments were in power over the period 1976–82, and we can compare the decisions made by the pragmatic administration of James Callaghan against the more ideological regime of Margaret Thatcher. Any government in power would have had to take account of some underlying changes in circumstances and opinion: changes that had their point of impact on policy during the annual public-spending cycle. How much difference did the change of government really make to the overall outcome in social spending?

The changed context. Decisions about the welfare state after 1976 were being made in a different context. The old welfare state established by the 1945 Labour government on the basis of the Beveridge Report and considerably expanded by Conservative governments in the 1950s had had certain financial and social foundations. These included:

(i)   *The possibility for major growth in spending without a rise in the burden of taxation on households.* This possibility was created by economic growth and by the decline of spending on defence from wartime levels in the 1950s.

(ii) *A shared social ethic.* The Beveridge/El Alamein ethic of solidarity carried over into a peacetime view that social services were 'good things'. As late as 1961–4 surveys of voters' opinions showed strong support for further expansion of spending on social services.

(iii) *An agreement about the role of the services.* When Nye Bevan set up the National Health Service everyone knew what health services were for. Stronger arguments about prevention and about community care have made the question much more complicated.

By 1976 each one of these foundations was being worn away. The level of taxation on households of average and below-average income had risen very sharply. Voter-opinion had begun to shift in favour of reductions in taxation and against expansion of services. Reduced economic growth made less room for social spending. The ethic of solidarity seemed a nostalgic memory and market solutions were much more prominent. There was disquiet both about the role of the services and about government's ability to run them effectively. Disquiet about bureaucracy in the health service and about the fiasco of high-rise building were only the most obvious examples of greater criticism (Dunleavy, 1981b). Deteriorating industrial relations in the public sector created a new and alarming range of issues especially as the old colonial system of industrial relations broke down in the NHS.

The Economy, mandates and rules. Within this new context the detailed decisions of the Callaghan and Thatcher governments were mainly influenced and conditioned by pressures from the economy, political mandates, and rules and practices in controlling public spending.

Chart	The main events
April 1976	Introduction of 'cash limits' for public spending
May 1976	Callaghan administration begins
September 1976	Sterling crisis
November–December 1976	Negotiations over IMF loan
November 1978–March 1979	'Winter of Discontent'
May 1979	Thatcher administration begins
1979–80	'Medium Term Financial Strategy' of restraining the money supply and reducing public spending developed
Mid-1980	Accelerating rise in unemployment to more than 3m. in 1982

Both governments had to face acute economic crises. For the Labour government this took the form of rising inflation and unemployment leading by the autumn of 1976 to a panic run on sterling. To restore foreign confidence the government had to apply for a loan from the International Monetary Fund. To get the loan it had to satisfy the IMF about its future policies on public spending. The crisis facing the Conservatives was that of the unprecedented rise in unemployment from mid-1980.

For both governments, the pressures from the economy threatened their mandates. Labour's traditional attachment to higher social spending remained powerful. The 1979 Conservative election manifesto had said, 'The State takes too much of the nation's income; its share must be steadily reduced.' On reaching office, its first White Paper on public expenditure began by stating that 'Public expenditure is at the heart of Britain's present economic difficulties.'

The Labour government initiated the change to cash limits, which was later taken further by the Conservative government in the change to cash planning. Cash limits set a cash budget for one year ahead; cash planning simply extended the principle of cash budgeting further ahead. From 1976 onwards, cash limits covered about 60 per cent of total spending, with the main excluded elements being demand-driven spending such as that on social security and unemployment pay. The system of cash limits was a major change in the so-called 'PESC' method. This method (named after the Public Expenditure Survey Committee which made the estimates) concentrated on planning spending at constant prices. If inflation rose more than expected the cash rations would simply be adjusted upwards to provide the planned volume of services. The aims of PESC were to get the planning of public spending on to a longer-term basis and to restrain its growth. First suggested by the Plowden committee in 1961 it fitted in with an age of planning and optimism about growth. This optimism became a major feature of the system through forecasts about future rates of growth. Public-spending plans were tied to these predictions and were not revised downwards when the growth failed to materialise.

Cash limits supplied an element of financial discipline which was not there before. Each major programme was to have a cash budget for the year and would have to stay within that budget. Concern about over-spending was not to be the prerogative of a few Treasury officials: it was now to be critical for all those senior civil servants who were in charge of the 125 or so cash-limited blocs of spending. The adoption of cash limits was an ominous change for all social programmes. It created a new test of the merit of any programme in the short term: did it go over its cash limit? Emotional arguments about the sacredness of social programmes would have less force.

Labour's Record

The only cut actually made by the Labour government was in the growth-rate of social spending in real terms. For example, revenue spending at constant prices on the NHS rose by 2 per cent a year from 1975–9 compared with 4 per cent a year from 1965–75. Yet this outcome seemed inherently unstable and seemed in fact on the verge of collapse when the Labour government left office. It kept its conscience intact – but only by a whisker. Its temporary success in squaring the circle between the state of the economy and its policital mandate owed much to a stroke of good fortune by which public spending unexpectedly fell in 1977. The government had not cut social programmes and yet circumstances and pay policies had led to the largest fall in the share of GDP for public spending that had ever happened in a single year. The government had set a priority of shifting resources into industrial investment: yet its last White Paper on public spending contained an ambitious programme for the growth of social spending. It had set cash limits for the financial year 1979–80 but had also agreed to honour the awards of the Clegg commission on public-sector pay which seemed likely to make those cash limits quite untenable. The 1978–9 'winter of discontent' left the Labour government in a deeply ambivalent position. It still had a strong emotional commitment to social spending – but the whole practice of cash limits and the conflict over public-sector pay suggested that there could not be the same open-ended guarantees to social programmes that had become traditional in post-war British governments.

From its first days in May 1976, the Callaghan administration had been dominated by the issue of public spending. To survive it had to find a credible policy for controlling public spending. It inherited the political consequences of a large unplanned rise in public expenditure which was mainly brought to public attention by Wynne Godley, a Cambridge economist and adviser to the Commons Select Committee on Public Expenditure. Real public expenditure was £5.8bn more in 1974–5 than had been planned in 1971, a figure fairly described by *The Economist* as 'staggering'. Part of the increase was due to subsidies on food and fuel prices but much was the result of higher social spending, especially on pensions. As the then Chief Secretary to the Treasury, Joel Barnett, later wrote, 'It was a period when public expenditure was allowed to increase at a pace we could not afford' (Barnett, 1982, p. 33).

Between 1974 and 1976, real public spending rose 20 per cent while real GDP rose 2 per cent. The situation was made much more critical by the new focus on a target for the PSBR (Public Sector Borrowing Requirement). Confidence depended on keeping to the target, although doing this presented many technical difficulties in practice.

A first round of spending cuts in July 1976 failed to restore confidence. A serious flight from the pound gathered pace and it became urgently necessary to secure a loan from the IMF. The autumn of 1976 was taken up with argument between some early Labour examples of wets and dries. In effect, there was a collision between the requirements for political survival and of the political mandate. The requirements both for survival and for economic growth pointed to some trimming of social spending. In the Chancellor's statement on the IMF loan, social services, which amounted to 50 per cent of total spending, were shown to contribute only 5 per cent of the cuts. The record was in fact very different from that of the cuts made after devaluation in 1967–8 which had fallen quite heavily on social programmes, including such measures as the postponement of the raising of the school-leaving age to 16. If the commitment to introduce child benefit is taken into account, the outlook for social spending was even more buoyant. The commitment to child benefit had been enforced by the TUC in mid-1976 after an inspired campaign by Frank Field on behalf of the poverty lobby.

The net effect of the actual decisions taken in 1976 was to raise the share of social spending in total public spending. This should have led to a rise in the share of GDP going to social spending. It did not, because of a large and unexpected short-fall in actual spending. Actual spending in 1977–8 was much below planned spending. Ironically, the underspending of about £4bn was four times as great as the cuts over which ministers had indulged in so much argument and dramatics in the autumn of 1976. The short-fall was in part an unexpected result of the change to cash limits, although pay policies also helped in a labour-intensive sector.

The main effect of the post IMF climate on particular social programmes was to stop initiatives. Even in the pre-election phase, plans for educational maintenance allowances for

16-year-olds staying on at school were blocked in Cabinet. The relative size of social programmes during this period was affected by:

(i) *The shift away from capital spending.* This hurt more capital-intensive programmes such as housing.

(ii) *Demographic changes* not usually linked directly to spending but which vitally influenced the context and argument.

(iii) *Past policy commitments.*

Total spending grew by 4 per cent in real terms from 1975–6 to 1978–9: but within this total there were significant shifts. Spending on social security grew rapidly while spending on housing fell. Public investment in hospitals, roads and housing is generally the softer option when spending has to be restrained. The fall in capital spending had especially serious effects on housing. Demographic pressure helped social security. Spending on pensions rose along with the numbers of elderly people and this increase also supplied a sympathetic background for arguments about more spending on the NHS.

The child population, on the other hand, was falling: this provided a context in which the demands of pressure groups and teachers for more educational spending could easily be contained. Policy commitment in favour of social security were other important reasons for the changed pattern of spending. The Labour government was committed both to a relatively generous treatment of pensioners and to replacing child tax allowances by child benefit. In real terms, the social security budget rose by 18 per cent from 1975–6 to 1978–9; but because of the falls in housing and education spending this growth could be accommodated with only an increase of 4 per cent in total social spending.

The commitments to social security had been entered into at the time of the Social Contract between the Labour government and the TUC in 1974 and represented the delayed effects of this agreement. They implied a very substantial rise in the living standards of pensioners in relation to the employed population. From October 1973 to November 1978 pensions rose by 152 per cent while average earnings rose by 108 per cent. The pattern of social spending represented a tribute to the power of the TUC and the trade-union movement over a Labour government, which gives even greater irony to the circumstances of the latter's downfall. The government left office with the industrial-relations problems of the public sector unresolved after the 'winter of discontent'. The focus had shifted from the 'outputs' of the public sector to the problems of the people working in it.

Conservative's Record

This shift in focus continued under the new Conservative government: there was less public attention on the actual results and more on the day-to-day problems of management. The critical issues about the general level of social spending were debated within a turbulent scene of industrial relations and management problems in the services. Once again a government was faced with an inconsistency between its mandate and economic circumstances. The mandate called on the government to hold the level of public spending in real terms: yet economic circumstances were causing social and other forms of spending to rise. The rise was so large that simply to reduce the rate of growth of spending the government had to challenge what had been an important taboo – that social security could not be cut. This taboo was broken, although the taboo against mass redundancies in the public sector remained. The Conservative government's record was a paradoxical one. It presided over a large rise in social spending in relation to GDP during its first years in office. Spending rose from 23.6 per cent of GDP in 1979 to 25.4 per cent in 1981. Yet there were very important reductions and changes in some programmes. Investment in housing was halved; pensions were indexed on a less generous basis and benefits to the unemployed were reduced in absolute terms. In practice these changes only held the total of social spending in real terms, in contrast to the previous government's plans for a general expansion. Once again the most critical outcome – the general level of social spending – was affected by forces outside the government's control. The decision was a *fait accompli* which the government struggled for three years to change.

The government came to office committed to cutting both taxation and public borrowing. It inherited both unplanned and planned increases in public spending. In the summer and autumn of 1979 it argued about how to contain the total level of spending. Among its own supporters it found assent for the general idea of reducing public spending but often violent opposition to particular proposals for doing this. In the summer of 1979 it was defeated in the Lords over the issue of charges for school transport. By December 1979 Thatcher was admitting defeat and telling the 1922 Committee of Tory backbenchers that she would 'have another go'. The 'go' was to last for three years until the autumn of 1982, when the government started to encourage more short-term capital spending in the public sector and recoiled from the long-term plans for reducing welfare state spending set out in an unpublished Think Tank report which suggested the extension of health insurance and the introduction of student loans.

The essential reasons for this failure were the recession and its effect on increasing unemployment. This led directly to an increase in unemployment benefits, from £1.4bn in 1979–80 to £5bn in 1982–3. It led indirectly to increased spending on employment schemes and to losses in tax revenue. The rising level of unemployment also tended to reduce the government's will to make other kinds of changes. It wanted a new monetarist dawn but it was also wary of being tagged as hard-hearted and extremist. The rise in unemployment sharply reduced the government's political, as well as fiscal, room for manoeuvre. It is probable that without the recession there would have been sharper changes in policies for the NHS and for education.

Sharp changes in policy were limited to housing and the more unpopular groups in the social security field such as the unemployed. Simply to stop the total social budget from rising the government had to make some important reductions, given its commitment to some increases for the NHS and the effect of rising unemployment on the social-security budget. As it was, the social security budget rose 16 per cent in real terms in 1978–9 to 1982–3. The government financed this increase and contained the total in two important ways. It increased the pace of reduction in spending on education and housing. These had already been moving downwards under the previous government but the fall was now even deeper for housing. The number of public-sector houses under construction was 149,000 in 1976: by 1979 it had fallen to 69,000. It fell further to 31,000 in 1981. Falling school-rolls were not directly linked to reductions in spending on education but provided a climate that acquiesced in them.

In social security the changes were of new kinds and it is fair to say that only a Conservative government would have been able and willing to make them. The changes affecting pensioners were less controversial than those affecting unemployed people. Any government might have changed the double indexation of social security benefits by which they were tied either to earnings or to prices, whichever rose fastest; this had the effect of bringing about continued automatic increases in the real incomes of all pensioners. But only the 1979 Conservative government would have legislated to 'de-index' unemployment benefits so that they could be increased by less than the rate of inflation; to abolish the earnings-related sickness, widows' and unemployment benefits; and to make unemployment benefits taxable. The net effect of these changes was to reduce the real incomes of the unemployed yet further: the costs of the recession were shifted even more from the employed population to the unemployed. At the same time, the government was greatly reducing the state contribution to income maintenance in sickness. Employers were to become responsible for the payment of short-term sickness benefit and, as compensation, to get a reduction in their national insurance payment. This change was originally planned to take effect in 1981 but after protest from employers it was postponed till 1982.

The Beveridge report (of 1942) and the legislation based on it had established a commitment to a minimum income for all in sickness, unemployment and old age. The government's changes taken together amounted to a further significant retreat from the Beveridge principle already eroded by the introduction of lower short-term rates of supplementary benefit for some groups in 1973. The government did not attempt further changes on other kinds of income support. Child benefit proved popular not just with the Child Poverty Action Group but with the Conservative Women's National Advisory Council, although the government was able to make some savings by stealth through its failure to index-link child benefit fully. It was committed both to the existing and to the new earnings-related pension scheme. It was impossible to unravel these commitments in the face of both the voting power of pensioners and the sentiments of the life insurance and pension funds who were strongly in favour of the Labour government's 1975 settlement on the right to contract out and the terms of the new scheme. However, government spending plans have not taken account of the increased health and social service costs arising from demographic changes, especially the growing proportion of elderly people in the population.

The Micro Climates of Social Policy

The most important single decision in social policy – on the amount of social spending in relation to other claims – is more a part of economic policy than of social policy as such. But out of this decision come budgets and cash limits that set the context for debate within each service. In detail, social policy is made in the day-to-day world of the professions and pressure groups.

SOCIAL SECURITY

The inside world of the social security programme is a small one. Within it pressure groups such as the Child Poverty Action Group are especially important. It also included until 1980 the Supplementary Benefits Commission which, under its then Chairman, Professor David Donnison, acted as a pressure group as well as administering payments. The wider public opinion is possibly a more powerful influence on shaping policy for social security than for the National Health Service. It was pressure from the TUC that, in turn, reflected the personal interest of Jack Jones, then General Secretary of the Transport and General Workers' Union, which led the Labour government to raise pensions so significantly in 1974. The poverty lobby influenced policy only when it was able to borrow power.

Thus the joint efforts of the TUC and the Child Poverty Action Group were successful in saving child benefit in 1976. On behalf of friendless groups such as the unemployed the lobby was able to do very little. There was therefore rather little opposition to very unfavourable changes affecting the unemployed after 1979. The main impact was the actual and the latent political power of pensioners and their ability to win more adequate levels of benefit than were available to less popular groups.

The National Health Service

The NHS is about rationing – about allocating scarce resources between people in need. From 1976 the general decision on social spending would in any case have forced some more rigorous rationing as the growth-rate of spending fell. But this change coincided with a much more intensive period in the NHS's own social policy. The NHS budget serves different client groups, among them the younger physically ill, old people, mentally ill people and mentally handicapped people. The social decision within the NHS before 1974 had always been in favour of increasing the share of spending on the 'acute' services for the physically ill. From 1976 the direction of change was the other way. The shares of so-called 'Cinderella' services started to rise. The first impulse for this change had come from ministers and goes back to the 1960s; but the change also reflected a change in the balance of opinion and power within the service. There was a more general recognition of the problems of chronic illness and mental illness. The power of the consultants in the 'glamour' specialties was less than it used to be. A new programme of joint-funding was also introduced in 1976 which made it possible for the NHS to subsidise local government in providing care in the community. One effect of the shift in priorities was to increase waiting-times in the acute specialties. Over the three years from 1974 to 1977 (the latest year for which figures are published) waiting-times for all hospital patients rose from 14.2 weeks to 16 weeks; even patients with cancer or suspected cancer found themselves having to wait for an appointment for 5.6 weeks on average rather than 4.7.

The NHS also embarked, after 1976, on a much more active reallocation of spending between regions. Again the impulse from this came from ministers and strongly from Barbara Castle, then Secretary of State for Social Services from 1974–6, and David Owen, Minister of Health over the same period. However, they had to create their own public opinion: there was little previous interest. This was a revolution from the top, although one that soon got strong political support from the regions which gained more money. At the beginning, in 1948, the NHS inherited a large degree of regional inequality and very little was done about it until 1974. In fact the concentration of the capital programme on Central London in the 1960s made some of these inequalities worse. Since 1976, 'gaining' regions such as Trent and East Anglia have seen their spending grow by 2.5 per cent a year in real terms, while spending in the London area has remained constant. The NHS's own social policy decision meant a considerable improvement in services for some parts of the country compared with South-East England.

These changes in priorities and in spending surprised and placated potential critics. The combination of low growth and redistribution has proved to be much more tolerable than either would have been on their own. In general, the NHS had surprisingly little difficulty from 1976 to 1982 in living within its cash limit. Technical influences contributed to this as well as the political ones. The growth-rate of spending had been faster on average in the past but had fluctuated more. The year-to-year change in the decade 1966–76 ranged from −1.1 per cent to +6.9 per cent. Growth was now slower but much steadier and this proved a tolerable combination. The scope for shifting spending away from support services such as catering and portering was also greater than suspected. The share of total spending in hospitals going to support services fell from 42 per cent in 1974–5 to 37 per cent in 1980–1 (Bosanquet, 1982, pp. 15–18). This meant that more was available for direct care of patients and offset some of the effects of the shift in spending towards the Cinderella services. The growing difficulty over the period was in pay-bargaining rather than in working within the cash limit: by 1982 the period of relative tranquility was at an end and the NHS was facing much greater budgetary difficulties.

PERSONAL SOCIAL SERVICES

These cover a wide range of support for children, old people, mentally ill, mentally handicapped people and the physically disabled. They are provided by local rather than by central government. Government policy on the NHS after 1979 was affected by the commitment in the Conservative manifesto to maintain the rate of growth of spending set by the previous Labour government; but its approach to the social services was not inhibited by any such commitment. The general level of spending here emerges from decisions made by different local councils. In 1979–80 they maintained spending in real terms on social services in spite of government pressure to reduce it: however, in the next two years total spending fell. Given increased need for the services implied by rising numbers of very old people and rising requirements for community care, this turn of events was potentially serious. However, actual crisis only materialised in a few places, such as the London Borough of Hammersmith, which had unusual combinations of rising demand with strong attempts to cut services.

The social services found a number of ways of adjusting to this new spending climate. Some councils tried to draw on resource of voluntary care which might offer a low-cost alternative to care by paid staff in residential homes. Many councils tried to find more foster-parents for children and a few also tried to extend community support for frail old people. There was a thinning-out of services to the old for whom councils had fewer statutory responsibilities than for children. This thinning particularly affected the home-help service. Councils had access to special funds from the NHS – joint-funding – which meant that they could continue to develop community services for mentally ill and mentally handicapped people. There also seemed to be a reduction in public pressure for expansion of social services. As a result of the public concern about the death of a battered child, Maria Colwell, social services had taken on large new responsibilities after 1973 for trying to protect children who were at risk of non-accidental injury. If anything, the pendulum of opinion had swung quite the other way towards concern about too much interference by social workers. Understandably, some social workers came to feel that they faced condemnation whatever they did – whether they left children with their parents or took them away.

EDUCATION

Not since the early 1960s has education had special priority in public spending. It enjoyed this mainly for its supposed role in promoting economic growth, but some also saw it as having a special power to promote social equality as well. By 1976, even the demographic arguments had turned against education, as the child population fell; but, more important, the old arguments for special priority were beginning to look very tired.

James Callaghan reserved his one personal initiative in social policy for education. In the autumn of 1976 he called for a 'great debate' about how to improve basic literacy and numeracy. The Labour government seemed to be moving towards the idea of a core curriculum. The Conservative government was to continue with these themes, though with less flair for publicity than Callaghan had shown. The connection between education and economic growth was hard to show after twenty years of low economic growth and rising spending on education; and the disciples of Tawney (1931) with his great faith in education had yet to come to terms with the findings of Jencks (1970) and others about how little schools changed the patterns of inequality arising from home background. By 1982 the educational world could show success only in its rearguard action against schemes for paying for education by vouchers (parents are given vouchers to present to their children's schools, rather than giving the schools a government grant). It had yet to register fully the most public and costly example of lost confidence – the growth of the Manpower Services Commission (MSC). This QGA had been founded under Ted Heath's government and had shown an astonishing capacity for growth under all successive regimes. By 1982 it was running a kind of shadow training and education system for the 16–19 age-group alongside the main system.

Higher and further education had had more priority before and fell into even deeper discredit. There was little public reaction against Sir Keith Joseph's reductions in university spending. The only strong local reactions came in a few areas of the country over standards in the schools. In the absence of agreed methods of measuring standards, the protests were rarely able to make much impact. The rain in the world of education fell on the just as well as on the unjust.

HOUSING

In housing there was a downturn in spending of a kind most unusual in a public-sector programme. It began under the Labour government but was much accelerated under the Conservative. The central government decision was much assisted by changes within the housing world: the most obvious was a loss of confidence in the large-scale redevelopment programmes that had been at the centre of post-war housing policy. But there was also a loss of confidence in the ability of local councils to manage their existing stock effectively. The image of council housing changed radically for the worse, among its own tenants and among local and national politicians. Those authorities who had done the most building in the past now faced the heaviest debts, the highest rents and the greatest problems of tenant-satisfaction. Other Conservative-controlled councils in the suburbs and shire counties which had done little building anyway were confirmed in their prejudices by the burdens passed on to them by their more profligate city cousins. Neither city nor rural councils were, therefore in a mood to invest in large numbers of new council houses.

Central government policy shifted first away from redevelopment towards rehabilitation, a change that began as early as 1969. It began to put the emphasis on indirect methods of dealing with dilapidation through improvement grants. By 1977, central government, in its housing policy review, was retreating from the idea of a general housing shortage or a national housing problem. Instead, it saw a series of different local problems for which councils were to apply different housing investment programmes. The Labour government also gave priority to forms of tenure other than renting through local authorities, especially by encouraging housing associations. By 1978, councils still started work on 68,000 new houses, while a further 18,000 were begun by housing associations. The growth of the housing associations was even more surprising given the very considerable suspicions shown about housing associations by previous Labour governments. By 1979, public-sector housing investment had only one friend left outside true believers: this was the construction industry. Although it lobbied the government hard this was not enough to stop further cuts in housing investment, so that by 1981 the number of public-sector starts had fallen further to 31,000 compared with 149,000 in 1976.

The growing stigma attached to council housing also prepared the way for the 'Right to Buy'. Surveys suggested this was a widely popular policy. In circumstances in which the most important form of rented housing had lost so much ground, there was almost bound to be a move of this kind. Council tenants were given rights to buy their own homes on very favourable terms. The argument that such a move would favour tenants in the better council properties, such as houses with gardens, as against those in flats on large estates, although strong was not widely influential. The low popularity of council tenants also made it possible for the Conservative government to bring about steep increases in council rents. The housing world is influenced by administrators in local authority housing departments and at the Department of the Environment. Local and national politicians also play a role, as do academics, to an unusual extent, and pressure-groups such as Shelter. Changes in government tended to follow changes in opinion within these worlds. Day-to-day discussion at many points in the housing sector came increasingly to be dominated by loss of faith in the old policies of redevelopment and council housing. In essence, there were no policies to carry on at the same level of spending when the credibility of the old policies decayed. Housing policy at the end of 1982 was only just beginning to evolve in a new and more pluralistic framework.

The Fiscal and Occupational Welfare States

The fiscal system of welfare became slightly more visible in 1979. The government then began to publish annual statements on direct tax allowances and reliefs in the expenditure White Paper. In total, these reliefs added up to more than £20bn (Field, 1981, p. 129): but the most directly relevant were those for payments to pension schemes and life assurance and on mortgage interest. These added up, in 1981–2, to £4bn. In 1974, a ceiling had been set on mortgage-interest relief so that the relief could only be claimed on the first £25,000 of the mortage. This was maintained so that the real value of the concession declined over the period. The reliefs on pension payments became even more deeply entrenched as a result of the government's concordat with the pensions industry, which cleared the way for the new scheme for higher pensions on an earnings-related basis in 1975. The fiscal system of welfare had shown considerable expansion since the late 1950s: but now it seemed to have reached a plateau. Towards the end of the period there was perhaps a stronger tendency to question the scale and permanence of the reliefs. The debate, however, was both intermittent and on the fringe of politics.

The occupational system of welfare had also shown rapid growth. The proportion of total labour costs accounted for by fringe benefits had risen sharply from around 10 per cent in 1960 to around 20 per cent in 1973 and 25 per cent in 1977 (Royal Commission on the Distribution of Income and Wealth, 1979, p. 130). The net gains from fringe benefits were much greater for non-manual than for manual workers. Both the fiscal and occupational systems reached a plateau in the period after a long period of growth. Their main effects remained those of increasing inequality and off-setting the income support provided by the official welfare state. The fiscal system could be particularly criticised as a form of income support to the better-off. Within the occupational system, the most important change was in the increased coverage of private health insurance schemes, mainly for group schemes organised by employers. The future role of private medicine looks set to remain a major issue in the 1980s.

The Welfare State and the Individual

While government was resolving its own problems, individuals and families were having to do what they could with theirs. To many the welfare services represented worry, complexity and possibly unwelcome attentions from professionals. The most obvious problem was the range of means-tested benefits. There were in 1982 over forty means-tested benefits, each having to be claimed separately and each involving a different calculation of family income. Some families were faced with the so-called 'poverty trap', by which as their gross income rose they got little net benefit. They lost most of the addition through higher tax payments and through the loss of means-tested benefits. The early 1980s saw a revival of proposals for reform ten years after the first discussions of the poverty trap and after the Heath Government's unsuccessful proposals for a tax credit scheme.

The complexity of the system certainly discouraged take-up of some benefits, although the effect seemed to be greatest for some of the smaller benefits, such as free school meals, than for the main ones such as supplementary benefit. The most troubling problem, however, was that of rising rates of direct taxation on low incomes. This meant that the state was increasingly trying to add to low incomes through the social security system while at the same time reducing them through the tax system. The rising tax-take from the working poor especially undermined the whole purpose of child benefit. The relationship between the tax and social security systems looks likely to be a major issue of social policy in the mid-1980s.

Reductions in the number of administrators had the perverse effect of turning bureaucracy into a do-it-yourself job. With fewer bureaucrats to fill in forms, customers were asked to do it themselves. By the end of 1982, people claiming supplementary benefit were being asked to fill in a form of 140 questions which would then be processed through the DHSS's computers.

The image of the social services changed for the worse in other ways. There was a decline in deference to and greater suspicion of administrators. Partly this was a question of the image being worse than the reality. The press was often unfair and one-sided in presenting issues. But there were also important changes in expectations and a greater awareness of rights. Another growing strand of criticism came from the Left: the researches of Le Grand cast doubt on whether the social services were at all redistributive (Le Grand, 1982). It seemed that the middle classes made much heavier use of the more attractive items on offer, such as free medical treatment and higher education. The old argument in favour of universal social services as a great integrating force in society was little heard. Little was heard too of another old argument, that voluntary organisations could replace large parts of the state service. Although active, they were themselves becoming more dependent on official funding. They retained however a particularly important role of innovation.

In the first years of the Thatcher government, the social services came through a rearguard action. Public opinion was seen to set a limit to 'privatisation', though not much to the increase of inequality. Public opinion wanted the welfare state in general to keep in being: but it was doubtful whether public opinion would provide the context for change, development and effective management in the welfare state.

After the June 1983 Election

Within weeks of a decisive election victory Mrs Thatcher's second administration was embroiled in conflict. The least publicised but perhaps the most important for the future course of the administration was about public spending. By November 1983 the Chancellor was announcing that 'we plan to hold public spending broadly constant in real terms over the next three years'. In the context of large planned increases in the defence budget and inescapable changes in spending on social security benefits, this suggested a much more intense struggle for shares of public spending. The conflict had in fact already begun: housing once again suffered worse with further cuts in the investment budget. Surprisingly strong pressure from Conservative backbenchers persuaded the Chancellor to up-rate unemployment and child benefit at the rate of inflation against his first proclaimed intention.

The most immediate conflict broke out over the National Health Service. The conflict seemed to have helped to turn voters to greater concern for the standard of public services and away from interest in tax cuts.

8

Foreign and Defence Policy

PETER NAILOR

Policy Machinery

Foreign and defence policy are traditional and fundamental tasks of government, and although the boundary between them and other governmental areas like economic and social policy has shifted over the years, their intrinsic importance is reflected in the seniority of the ministers usually appointed to the respective departments. Their political importance can be distinguished, however, using the difference that Clement Attlee noted. The Foreign and Commonwealth Office (FCO) is a 'policy' department, giving great political visibility: Defence (MOD) is an 'administrative' department where, although high policy is made, a minister must have good managerial skills as well. Politically, it is a less weighty appointment. Functionally, the two offices are closely linked nowadays because of Britain's dependence for security upon international alliances, notably NATO. The FCO and the MOD both see themselves as experienced instruments of policy-formulation and administration, supporting – indeed embodying – professional groups of activists in the diplomatic and military staffs. They have a high degree of *esprit de corps* and of internal cohesion. Indeed, it is this very professional cohesion that annoys some politicians, particularly politicians of a radical stripe (of either right or left).

The present shape and structure of the two departments only dates from the middle 1960s, when two groups of smaller departments were collated together (Nailor, 1973). This reorganisation, which was paralleled elsewhere in Whitehall, had a number of effects. So far as the political level of policy-making was concerned, it reduced the numbers of Cabinet-level ministers primarily concerned with overseas affairs, and it made the personal relationship between the fewer, more powerful, ministers and the Prime Minister rather more significant. And it put back into the departmental process some contentious issues that in earlier times might have come to Cabinet. Senior ministers at the head of these larger departments were expected to settle sectional arguments within their conglomerates themselves. This had particular importance for defence, where resource allocations between competing material projects and between the three Services are a periodic preoccupation (Hobkirk, 1976).

CABINET AND CABINET COMMITTEES

Foreign and defence problems frequently come to full Cabinet and there is usually a routine brief by the Foreign Secretary on current matters of concern. There is also a sub-committee of the Cabinet, chaired by the Prime Minister, on which is represented a range of departmental interests and which deals with much of the FCO and MOD business that needs ministerial approval. On occasion, this committee has been used to deal with specially sensitive items and, in effect, to by-pass the full Cabinet. We know that the decision in 1947 to manufacture A-bombs was taken in this way and there is no reason to think the practice has stopped. Below this is a set of specialist Cabinet Office committees, staffed largely by civil servants, which prepare the business, or in some cases regular briefs, for the more senior bodies. Of special importance is the Chiefs of Staff Committee which, chaired by the Chief of the Defence Staff, who now has quite extensive powers of his own, is the mechanism by which specialist military advice is given to the Cabinet. It normally meets with the FCO representation, and is illustrative of the extensive formal and informal links between the FCO and the MOD.

It is only to be expected that the Prime Minister will take a close interest in defence and foreign policy. In ordinary times, defence not only buys up very large resources (averaging between 4.7 and 5.1 per cent of GNP through the 1970s), but defence policy, especially as it relates to our alliances and to our other overseas commitments, can be a major instrument through which foreign policy objectives are pursued. Foreign policy, though much less costly in budgetary terms, is both the mode of expression and the instrument by which the country's interests, its standing, and, to some extent, its own values are transmitted to others and adapted to changing circumstances.

So, when there is a crisis that demands special attention, it is quite customary for the routine machinery to be overlain, and for a smaller group of ministers to take charge. The practice began in war, and it is most often used when, in practice, the executive responsibilities inherent in the Prime Minister's position as the head of the government require to be exercised. The practice was followed for the Falklands Campaign in 1982, and clearly has instrumental utility in shortening the chain-of-decision between, for example, the Prime Minister and the Chief of the Defence Staff. The membership of such groups is not fixed, but is determined appropriately. The Falklands combination included the Chancellor of the Duchy of Lancaster, Cecil Parkinson, who was given a responsibility for the ministerial co-ordination of 'the information war' halfway through the crisis. It seems to have been an expedient in the sense that his responsibility was not well defined, but it clearly had its origins in the confidence felt by the Prime Minister in Parkinson in so far as he was also at the time the Chairman of the Conservative Party. The choice may also have been intended to reassure the government's supporters in the face of the resignation of the Foreign Secretary and two of his colleagues at the outset of the crisis. The implication was created by this event that not only had there been a failure in foreign policy, in the sense that diplomacy had been unable to prevent the Argentinian aggression, but that by accepting the resignations the Prime Minister had acknowledged and disapproved of the failure. This is reinforced by the strengthening of the foreign policy and defence components on the Prime Minister's staff, announced in November 1982 (*The Economist*, 27 November 1982) (see Chapter 7).

THE PRIME MINISTER

The political dimension in all these arrangements and practices can be construed from the perspective that, in large part, foreign policy and defence are subjects where the government of the day has a prime responsibility to manage and direct. They are core functions of government, inherently technical in their complexity and procedures: they cannot be conducted as openly as other functions of government, because other governments and considerations of national security are involved. The government of the day is, in a sense, the trustee of the national welfare and is commonly given a relatively wide degree of discretion. Foreign affairs and defence do not habitually concern the mass of the population, like education or the health service do; although defence and its supporting industries are large employers. But when something goes wrong, or public concern is aroused, governments are taken to task freely. The *post hoc* nature of the criticism is almost inevitable, but because there may be fundamental issues at stake, criticism can be quite diverse, and often cuts across normal party boundaries. Sometimes, too, because prestige and attributed reputation, rather than some more easily quantified value, has been affected, the debate about the issues can become both subjective and emotional. For all of these reasons, the Prime Minister is bound to be closely interested, even when he or she has no extensive ministerial background. And, in recent times, the interdependence of the international community, and the alliance frameworks within that community, have highlighted the role of heads of governments. Wide media coverage is given to 'summit meetings'. In the same way that, in war, the Prime Minister really has no option but to become *de facto* Minister of Defence, so, in foreign policy, every Prime Minister now has to be ready to turn to, to perform part of, the representational function (and perhaps gain most of the acclaim) which formally is within the Foreign Secretary's ambit.

But there are corresponding difficulties when there are differences between either the Prime Minister and the Foreign Secretary, personally or between the opinions that – in either party or official terms – they represent. Soon after the Conservatives were returned to office in May 1979, it became difficult to hide the fact that the FCO's policy towards the settlement of the Zimbabwe question and the policy preferred by Thatcher and a segment of party opinion, to take a more direct initiative towards the refurbished Smith–Muzorewa regime in Rhodesia, were effectively irreconcilable. The FCO pattern was a 'continuous' policy, deriving from Commonwealth and Anglo–American discussions and proposals that went back several years, and it was only under pressure at the Lusaka Commonwealth Conference that Thatcher's desire to institute a novel policy was turned aside. It might be that her determination to end the chronic and unsatisfactory state of affairs in Rhodesia/Zimbabwe stimulated the quite remarkable progress that was achieved in the ensuing months; but the incident drew attention to differences of style, at least, and led to a more persistent criticism of the emollient performance and ethos of the diplomatic 'establishment' that resurfaced again over the Falklands campaign (*The Economist*, 27 November 1982).

The FCO is susceptible to criticism in this way since, in a sense, a large part of its function is to stay, as it were, in the middle of the road. This renders it vulnerable to the passers-by on the left and on the right. But the ability of any one state, except perhaps a super-power, to change the framework of international problems significantly or quickly is really quite limited, and it may well be necessary to manifest patience rather than initiative. To take the Zimbabwe issue as a case in point, although the final settlement was reached in a surprisingly quick way, during and after the Lancaster House Conference, and although that progress may have been stimulated in part by the new urgency of a new British government, we also have to take into account that the problem had existed, in its essentials, for nearly twenty years; that an increasingly fierce and destructive war was debilitating the 'front-line' states as well as Rhodesia itself; and that it was generally perceived – by more of the participants than ever before – that the combination of circumstances in 1979 provided what might be a final chance for a negotiated solution. Even so, the final shape of the outcome, with Robert Mugabe's sweeping electoral victory, was largely unforeseen in Britain (even by the FCO), and very disappointing to the Prime Minister's faction that had urged a quick deal with Smith and Muzorewa; disappointing enough to foster resentment about the 'soft' FCO, and their negotiating champion, Lord Carrington, and to lead, in the aftermath of the Falklands campaign, to a resurgence of the arguments about whether the Prime Minister should not have a separate department of advisers and staff ministers, large enough to superintend rather than collate the co-ordination of affairs.

Although it is a responsibility of Foreign Offices to seize upon the circumstances that will allow a *démarche*, the normal pattern of diplomacy is as much reactive as innovative; however well the national interest may be described in terms of general principle, it is unusual to find governments being able to move directly and consistently in pursuit of stated objectives. Their aims have to be set against the aims of other participants, who may have local advantages and more intense concerns, as British governments in the 1960s and 1970s found with Iceland, over a series of fishery disputes. The state may simply have to bide its time, as the British found out in pursuing the goal of membership of the European Community between 1961 and 1972. In the international arena, even more perhaps than in domestic affairs, the framework within which history and the pursuit of advantage have defined or united the state's freedom of manoeuvre makes little provision for electoral timetables. And in this sense, there is a distinct difference – at least in theory – between the interests of the state and the interests of any one particular administration. The difference is accentuated sometimes when different administrations, even though they may share a broadly comparable view of what the national interest requires, emphasise the differences of tactic and method they prefer rather than the similarities that exist. Bipartisanship may be responsible and important but it does not necessarily help to win elections. Personality, particularly the personality of the party leader, plays some part, although its significance is sometimes overdone. But, because foreign policy is importantly concerned with persuasion, confidence and style, as well as substance, personalities can be significant; the difference between a Callaghan or a Thatcher, a Carter or a Reagan, does say something about both policy and purpose, and sometimes style is as important as substance.

The Domestic Context

The Labour government that came to office in February 1974 found itself faced with a number of specific problems of overseas policy. In the long term, the most fundamental was the ending of the era of cheap power, which was ushered in by the OPEC oil price rises and the oil embargo imposed after the Yom Kippur war. In immediate terms, these problems required hastily contrived measures of alleviation and collaboration between the industrialised countries, that only slowly assumed institutional form and wider coverage. The general economic effect of the very large price rises undermined many of the plans and assumptions for international as well as domestic policy, and in particular significantly affected the prospects of the European Community Britain had so recently joined. The ways in which the world would develop became much less certain, much less optimistic, and the insecurity of oil supplies, before North Sea oil and gas became available in quantity to mitigate the immediate problem, became a major political concern. It had implications for defence, since the significance of oil supplies, and the vulnerability of the shipping in which they were carried, were thrust into prominence, in 1973–4 and again after 1978–9, with the overthrow of the Shah and the outbreak of the Iran–Iraq war.

DEFENCE AND PUBLIC EXPENDITURE

In 1974–5, the new Labour government reassessed its defence priorities, trying once again to reconcile the rising costs of military manpower and equipment, and the continuing need to provide for a wide range of defence commitments. By this time, the withdrawal from major extra-European commitments was accomplished, and largely accepted by both major political parties; but the relative prominence of the United Kingdom's contributions to a wide spread of NATO tasks, and the salience of Britain's military capabilities in Europe to her credentials as a 'good European' partner in European affairs, had frustrated government's attempts to reduce the burden of defence. It was not only the current costs that gave rise to concern, but the future costs of fulfilling the whole range of defence plans; the cost of high technology was increasingly alarming and new equipment would cost three, five or even seven times as much as the gear they were replacing. Moreover, Britain had assumed in 1948 a formal treaty obligation to maintain sizeable land and air forces in Central Europe; and from time to time the foreign currency burden that was involved was both a source of irritation in Anglo–German relations and a drain on the balance of payments, of a very substantial sort that became more and more disturbing as the nation's general economic performance continued to put pressure on our financial and economic standby.

The withdrawal from 'East of Suez' between 1967 and 1971 had relieved but did not solve the problem of how to maintain within a predictable cost-limit adequate and efficient forces to cover British defence interests that were still very extensive: to provide a nuclear deterrent, to contribute appropriately to NATO forces in the Central Front area, on the northern flank and in the Eastern Atlantic, to defend the home base and to look after the remaining commitments further afield (like Hong Kong, Belize, the Falklands). The Labour defence review of 1974–5 trimmed expenditure plans, and provided for a withdrawal from the Mediterranean; the equipment programme was cut, but an improvement plan for 'Polaris' was agreed. No more than a couple of years later, in 1977, the NATO allies were led to agree that the growth of Soviet military power, in quality no less than in size, required renewed efforts, that were, rather simplistically, settled as a need for a 3 per cent addition for some three to five years to national defence budgets. Even so, and in spite of an expressed determination by the new Conservative government in 1979 to give a higher priority to defence, another major review in 1981 again attempted to bring costs and plans into a politically more acceptable alignment. Five years of high inflation, a major economic recession and a more disturbed international environment presented even greater difficulties on this occasion.

The feature that marked the 1981 review was a more sharply defined attempt to redefine strategic priorities. Earlier reviews had been able more easily to trim each of the Services more or less proportionately: but the more efficient they became, in economic terms, the less 'fat' there was to trim next time. The redundancy of equipment and manpower which looks like waste in peacetime but provides reserve capacity in war had, by 1981, been substantially cut back. One of the major implications of nuclear war – which it was assumed any conflict in the NATO area would quickly become – was that such a war would be relatively short. The need for prolonged conventional fighting, and the time to mobilise reserves and production, would be much reduced. Although this enabled the Services to save on reserves, it also meant that the level of combat-ready forces had to be maintained at a high level. They would, in effect, be a very much higher proportion of the forces we could put into the field than ever before. This expectation was an important part of the policy, as well as of the doctrine, of deterrence, and a prime determinant of the high level of defence budgets.

In 1981, the new Secretary of State for Defence, John Nott, determined to restrict the role of the Royal Navy in the NATO area, and to give more emphasis to submarine and aircraft rather than surface-ship capabilities. This enabled two dockyards to be closed, and it was perhaps the most surprising political effect of this review, that electoral considerations in the Chatham and Portsmouth areas played a relatively minor part in the furore that followed. The Minister for the Navy, Keith Speed, was dismissed when he openly disputed the strategic implications of the decisions; and it was an irony of an unusually pointed sort that the flexibility and competence of the Royal Navy was so soon thereafter to be demonstrated in the South Atlantic. However, the basic substance of the government's view about the longer-term necessities was confirmed in the White Paper on the lessons of the Falklands campaign (Cmnd. 8758, December 1982) even though at the same time measures were announced to supplement provision for the conventional roles of the Navy, and in the short term to maintain a wider range of surface capabilities.

Nuclear Arms

Another defence issue of major political importance is the maintenance of Britain's nuclear strike force. The existing force of four Polaris submarines dates from 1969, and the Chevaline programme of the middle and later 1970s was intended to maintain the effectiveness of the force through to the 1990s. The scope and cost of it, some £1,000 million pounds overall, were not announced formally in the Commons until 1980, although there had been some speculation about it for some time, and some veiled references in earlier defence statements back as far as 1975. At about the same time, the government announced plans to replace Polaris in due course with another American submarine-based missile system, the Trident, under the same arrangements through which Polaris had been obtained. The plans have subsequently been altered to take account of the American decision to deploy a more advanced variant. It will be a lengthy and costly programme, even on the official estimates of some twelve years and some £7,500 million pounds. Arguments about whether the policy should be implemented have developed on two levels. The first criticism is that the cost may grow, but that even if current estimates are sensible, it will be so large and intensive a programme that it might divert resources from other, conventional equipment, plans. But the second criticism is of a broader and more essentially political sort: that the United Kingdom should not seek to remain a nuclear power and should certainly not go for a system that will militarily be more significant, and larger, than Polaris. Trident has, therefore, been caught up in the more general agitation about the high levels of nuclear armaments internationally, and is a prime symbol in the advocacy of specific British initiatives towards nuclear disarmament.

The movements that include this advocacy derived a new wave of popular support in 1979–80, in reaction to the NATO plans for a 'twin-track' policy that would, on the one hand, provide some counterweight to the growing Soviet superiority in nuclear weapons that has relevance only in Europe, by installing new medium-range missiles and cruise missiles in a number of European countries and, on the other hand, induce the Soviet Union to limit its own programme and also agree to some mutual limitations. It was a complicated plan that had important secondary implications about reassuring European governments about the United States' long-term intentions and, whatever its intrinsic merits, stimulated an unusually widespread range of concern, which led to large demonstrations in a number of countries. To a certain extent, governments were caught napping, in that few of them had made any recent attempts to lay before informed public opinion their own views about the intricacies, the risks and the benefits of what had by now become a traditional policy of deterrence, both nuclear and conventional. It was the first time for twenty years that nuclear weapons had become so wide and intense a source of concern.

In the United Kingdom, the disarmament movements recaptured Labour Party support and gained sympathisers in the Alliance (see Chapter 11), with more extensive consequences for official policy objectives than was the case in 1959–60 (Capitanchik, 1977), and there is a wider basis of encouragement for them in similar Western European and American movements, and support for some of their morally derived concerns from senior churchmen. Politically, 'nuclear disarmament' (to give a shorthand description to the variety of stances that are involved) is not a straightforward inter-party issue but, to the extent that many of the beliefs held by the protagonists on all sides of the debate are contentious, about what might or what should happen, and unprovable assertions about future possibilities and outcomes; it is a debate that sways backwards and forwards. It has both domestic and international implications (*The Times*, 29 November 1982) and featured in the 1983 election campaign. Although in form it is related to the relatively recent emergence of the Soviet Union as a military power of much increased potency, it also has some relationship to the apprehensions that arise from United States policies that are perceived to be 'hard' and, therefore, more risky. In that sense, in the same way that there is an historical link between the CND of the 1960s and its rather different modern counterparts, there is a connection between the days of John Foster Dulles and those of Caspar Weinburger.

The Foreign Context

Relations with the United States form one of the staple items on the British foreign-policy agenda. It is not so long ago that Churchill saw Britain at the centre of three overlapping connections: the Atlantic partnership, the Commonwealth and the European environment. By the 1970s, the United Kingdom had been forced to make some choices between these connections, in political and economic terms at least. Whether sentiment proceeded at the same pace as politics was less certain. The period after 1972 was taken up largely by discovering what membership of the European Community would mean in practice; but the connection with the United States remains fundamentally important in security matters. It is a relationship replete with historical and emotional overtones. It has also become increasingly important in recent years in financial and economic affairs, although in this field the United Kingdom is more on a par with the other OECD countries in its formal and informal patterns of relationship than in defence aspects.

The 'Special Relationship'

The United States connection seems so natural a partnership to most British people that it is easily misunderstood and mythologised, and Edward Heath's attempts to play down 'the special relationship' were both reasonable and disconcerting, in the light of our new European status. The condescension and mismanagement of Kissinger's 'Year of Europe', and the paralysis induced by Watergate and Nixon's resignation were disturbing; and the earnestness and confusion of the Carter period went even further to increase British bewilderment. At the official level, relations remained close; American support and assistance were instrumental in producing a new framework for resolving the Zimbabwe question and for engaging South African influence constructively, even when American policies towards Angola and Namibia were less coherent and less marked by consultation.

Britain had a higher expectation than some of the other allies of the capacity of American leadership (as well as a greater expectation of being listened to in Washington), and found it sometimes more difficult to participate in joint European initiatives that were distinct from American viewpoints, as over Afghanistan and, to a lesser extent, over the Middle East after 1979. The renewed prominence that Callaghan and then Thatcher gave to a continuing 'special relationship' accordingly emphasised two parallel strands of political significance: first, the extent, the importance and the familiarity of Anglo–US friendship which, it was inferred, had not been displaced by EEC membership. In so far as the 'special relationship' was based upon defence and foreign policy, it did not conflict with the limited spread of joint European activities. But, second, Britain was now in a better position to represent both British and, to a certain extent, common Anglo–European concerns to the United States; and that was both a good thing in itself and an enhancement of Britain's utility as a valued partner. The intricacy and some of the hazards of Anglo–American relationships were brought out in the 1982 Falklands campaign, when US concern, on grounds of principle as well as sentiment, to support a loyal ally, were intermingled with a national desire not to damage hemispheric relationships within Latin America. This tension illustrates, the complexity which a leading role in international systems can have, when all relationships can be seen, at some times and over specific issues, as special in some way or other.

THE EUROPEAN COMMUNITY

The United Kingdom joined the European Community in January 1973 and reaffirmed its membership in a constitutionally innovative way after a national referendum in 1975. With the advantages of hindsight, we can now see that the great economic problems of the decade, stretching into the 1980s, made any expectations of progress that the enlarged Community had, and which it itemised in a series of goals to be reached by 1980, were too optimistic. And the British experience of the

Community, and its own role and attitude within the Community, have led to strains and disappointments that, even in 1975, would have seemed overdrawn.

Since the early days of membership, the way in which the Community budget has been organised and used has been a matter of concern. In essence, the budget is a rather restricted type of equalisation fund, derived from contributions from each member state; and with the development of an extensive recession, the purposes to which budget funds could be applied, to industrial and regional support, have multiplied. But the chronic issue in budget politics is the dominance of the Common Agricultural Policy support, and the means by which it is deployed. The United Kingdom as a net importer of food and foodstuffs, but with a very efficient agricultural industry, sees itself as a victim of a system contrived in the early days of the Community of the Six. The perennial political problem of how to be fair – or, at least, just – to both the producers and the consumers of food, remains, for all the members, administratively intractable. In recent years, concern over the CAP has extended beyond purely financial adjustments to the way in which a very convoluted system could be developed to cope with the further enlargement of the Community, where Greece, Portugal and, eventually, Spain might be accommodated, without recreating the earlier problems of over-production and surplus management of particular regional products. Alongside this concern have run the problems of current over-production of dairy products, and the creation of a common fisheries policy: conserving fish stocks, resolving historic national concerns about reasonable fishing management and areas, and dealing with new littoral jurisdictions that are being created by the new international efforts to legislate for the resources and boundaries of the seas.

The issues are intrinsically complicated, and very large sums of money can be involved, by way of transfer and adjustment. The political problem is even more complicated: negotiations about agriculture and food prices touch domestic concerns of great sensitivity, and the nature of the negotiations brings, in national terms, a large number of departmental concerns into play. Politics in the European Community is not an exercise in traditional diplomacy; it is not 'foreign policy' in the conventional sense, and the FCO is the conductor of the orchestra rather than the composer of the symphony, as the departments of Agriculture and Trade and the Scottish Office, for example, play important solo parts. The inevitable tendency is therefore that persistent disagreements in the Community have to be referred to a more senior political level, even if the issues are detailed and technical in form. Policy may have finally to be agreed at foreign minister or head of government level. The succession of Community summit meetings that have been dominated by specific issues have tended to emphasise disagreements within the community, which have been over-dramatised by the media.

In 1979 the new Conservative government's willingness to make such demands explicit and dramatic owed its origin in part to a sense that the need both for reform and for short-term improvements was urgent – not least because support for the Community ideal was waning. By the end of the 1970s the benefits of membership, in day-to-day terms, were seen by a range of opinion within the country, especially by segments of the Labour Party, as being so marginal as to justify a renewed agitation to withdraw from the Community; and the generally worse economic environment, in which the Community's more general objectives were being slowed down, tended to highlight the significance of short-term gains and losses.

The attempts made by the Foreign Secretary, and more particularly the Prime Minister, to obtain what was seen as Britain's just due led to a series of intense negotiations, perhaps most notably in the Community summit meetings at Dublin and Luxembourg in 1979–80 and again in 1983. Britain's demands for budget adjustments, to ensure that her contributions were balanced out by receipts rather than requiring increasingly heavy payments, gave a tone of stridency to the relationship between Britain and the Community. This tone was quite different from the general feeling of British/Community relationship where the government was able to get along in a businesslike way with the Community's institutions but it undoubtedly dominated the public perception of the Community's vivacity and utility.

EUROPEAN FOREIGN POLICY

Recently there has been a stream of policy declarations on international matters that belies the apparent dissent on the CAP and budgetary negotiations. There was the Venice Declaration on the Middle East (proposing recognition of the Palestine Liberation Organisation), on the Soviet invasion of Afghanistan (both, incidentally, contrary to American policy and wishes) and the Argentinian invasion of the Falkland Islands. However, a consistent foreign policy is a long way off, as was shown in 1981–2 over the proposal to impose economic sanctions on the Soviet Union and Poland, in the wake of the declaration of martial law by General Jaruzelski. The domestic costs of forgoing participation in the energy pipelines being built by the Soviet Union to bring natural gas and oil to Western European countries, and the apparent unwillingness of the United States to make comparable sacrifices by maintaining a grain embargo, produced disarray in foreign-policy terms: a disarray that had a more immediate effect upon European–American relationships than upon Soviet policy, and the response by European countries to American pressure to react overtly to the Soviet action in shooting down a civilian airliner, in September 1983, illustrated how difficult it was to respond collectively to unexpected events.

In a time of recession it is difficult to pay attention to the broader aspirations of the Treaty of Rome about more fundamental unity; and Britain, like France, sees these aspirations as less useful than specific measures of co-opera-tion. But although the ideal of Europe as a unity has receded, it would be wrong to discount the progress that has been made in no more than twenty-five years, and which regular discussions and close personal contacts over a very wide range of levels support. Consultation is now a habit, and agreement is more common than headlines about disagreements imply. The direct elections to the European Parliament, which took place for the first time in 1979, also put down a marker for the future, which may eventually become significant in a more positive sense than we can, at the moment, assess.

PART TWO

New Worlds

9

The Police

MARTIN KETTLE

Challenges to the Consensus

A generation ago, the phrase 'law and order' had little political resonance. Although crime was then, as now and for centuries beforehand, a major source of newspaper headlines and a public preoccupation, crime policy was not an issue at elections, or generally between or even within parties. By the 1980s, however, it is clear that this is no longer so. While law and order is still far from being the dominant political issue of the era, it has certainly become part of the political vernacular in a new and significant way. One sign of this change is that political parties are now building up detailed policies on a range of law-and-order issues – public order, penal questions, criminal procedure, civil liberties and policing, for example – which have hitherto been uncontested within the political process. A tradition of consensus and non-engagement is undergoing a sustained, if unco-ordinated, challenge.

How far this process will now go is hard to assess. The challenge to the consensus is incomplete and the colonising of new territory for political controversy is uneven. However, it is hard not to conclude that law and order can never again recede into the political background. It has been well and truly captured by the public political process.

The very term, 'law and order', is problematic. As a political label it covers concrete policy areas such as crime and justice and a network of state-funded agencies such as the courts, prisons and the police. But it is unsatisfactory to suppose that this is what most people understand by the term. 'Law and order' also now presumes a much broader problem concerning the application of discipline in the home, the street and the workplace.

However, all perceptions of law and order inevitably focus on the police because of the police's central function as a socially coercive and disciplinary agency. The modern history of the British police epitomises the transition of law and order from a position of relative uncontroversiality to a new position near the centre of political debate. Writing in 1954, the first post-war Metropolitan Commissioner, Sir Harold Scott, described his relations with the successive Labour and Conservative Home Secretaries under whom he served: 'I was fortunate that during my eight years at Scotland Yard, there were never any serious differences of opinion between myself and Mr Chuter Ede or Sir David Maxwell-Fyfe. Their different political views were never allowed to influence their approach to police questions and we in this country can count ourselves very lucky that the police have always stood right outside the political scrimmage' (Scott, 1954, p. 21).

The belief that police questions were outside the politcal arena was tenacious. As recently as 1981, the former Labour Home Secretary, Merlyn Rees, was invited to address an Exeter University conference on the subject of policing and the lessons of the summer's riots. Unable to attend, Rees sent instead a copy of a speech by the current Conservative Home Secretary, William Whitelaw, explaining that it expressed his own view too. These examples of bi-partisan thinking on policing indicate just how little direct impact has been made on the government of the police by the development of modern democratic institutions. Parliament has traditionally exerted little interest in or control over policing. Until the riots of the 1980s, parliamentary debate on police was extremely rare, and detailed questions to ministers on the subject were frequently unanswered (on the grounds that it was not Home Office practice to answer for local forces), or indeed unanswerable (since the Home Office simply lacked the information). Even in regard to London, where the Home Secretary's role as the statutory police authority for the Metropolitan Police gives parliament a more direct constitutional role, policing has only rarely been raised except in private correspondence relating to individual cases.

Local authorities have rather more duties in respect of police. Even so, these duties are indirect, since they are exercised (in England and Wales but not in Scotland) at one remove, through a police authority which is not subordinate to the local council but which is independent of it and one-third of whose members are unelected magistrates. Thus, save in Scotland, policing is not dealt with as a direct local government function either. So the representative institutions that govern social policies and agencies in other areas such as housing and education, and whose members are answerable to the public for the way they have governed, have no real tradition or framework for dealing with policing.

Protecting the Police from Democracy

This distancing of policing from democracy is not a recent development. On the contrary. As democracy has become more representative so policing has been carefully placed beyond its reach.

It is always important to remember that Britain has an essentially devolved policing system, in spite of historically significant tendencies in recent times towards co-ordination and centralisation. With the important exception of the Metropolitan Police, much of nineteenth-century policing was locally controled by elected committees which broadly represented the enfranchised.

With the extension of the right to vote to all adults, this closeness came to an end. During the first half of the present century, the powers of local police committees were gradually whittled down. The local authorities were left with the job of paying for police, while decision-making was increasingly centralised in the hands of chief constables.

So, as the Willink Royal Commission on the police argued in a famous phrase in 1962, the problem of police accountability was in effect the problem of controlling chief constables. Though Willink supported the continuation of the devolved structure of police, he argued that 'general policies in regard to law enforcement' should be 'free from the conventional processes of democratic control and influence'. This brief background helps to explain why the political anaesthetisation of policing has come to be so well established. At the risk of caricature, by the mid-1970s, local police authorities had come to be little more than providers for and admirers of the police. Membership of such bodies was frequently seen as a politically marginal chore, redeemed only by the attendance allowance. At the parliamentary level, the attitude to the police was summed up in a forthright comment by Margaret Thatcher that 'what they need is support and not criticism'.

As a result, policing evolved in ways that were selected by the police themselves. The definition, prioritisation and implementation of policing tasks were made by the forces themselves. They decided what was a policing problem and what wasn't, and they did it without any effective or critical attention being applied from outside to their selection. This made for some important developments. Boring tasks, like enforcing parking restrictions, were hived off to traffic wardens. Dangerous tasks, like guarding bank shipments from physical attack were hived off to private security firms. On the other hand, industrial disputes and political demonstrations (but not domestic disputes or ceremonial processions) were redefined as policing problems. While there were not enough resources to deal with domestic burglaries, there were always enough to deal with young black men in shopping centres.

Reaction within the Parties

The evidence of a reaction against these developments accumulated fast in the late 1970s and early 1980s. At the national, party-political level the principal feature of this reaction has been the radicalisation of the Labour Party's stance. In this process the most notable element was the rapid ease with which a major transformation in policy was carried out in the years 1980 to 1982. Like so much else in the structure and policy of the post-war Labour Party, its existing police policy was completely incapable of offering any resistance to a determined radical challenge.

LABOUR

In 1978, the Labour Party conference, with more than one eye on the forthcoming general election, decisively passed a classically bi-partisan motion on law and order. 'Bold and resolute action is now urgently needed', began the motion, 'to combat the menace of vandalism, wanton destruction and needless violence.' Though suitably vague on points of detail, the motion called for greater support 'to law and order' and demanded a policy that 'will shatter the subculture that is developing as a result of ineffective action'. This motion, cobbled together by James Callaghan's advisers to provide the Labour Party with a tough policy on law and order, marked the end of an era. Over the next three years, policy was transformed as Labour conferences adopted a series of detailed resolutions of an altogether more radical kind, culminating in the passing by 6,035,000 to 849,000 at the 1981 conference of a motion calling for restrictions on police powers, democratisation of police authorities, a new police complaints procedure, extension of trade-union rights to police, the disbandment of the Special Patrol Group and an end to political surveillance.

Coinciding with these developments, the parliamentary Labour party and its leadership began to adopt a new approach to policing. The decisive moment in this process was the appointment of Roy Hattersley as Labour's shadow Home Secretary in December 1980, following the election of Michael Foot as party leader. Though firmly on the right of the party on economic and international policy, Hattersley identified himself with the civil libertarian initiatives being taken by the party's left wing. The change in Labour's approach was soon reflected in very critical responses to the publication of the report of the Royal Commission on Criminal Procedure in January 1981, in an unprecedentedly trenchant Labour attitude to policing during the 1981 urban riots, and in a generally more assertive frontbench approach to the Conservatives' Home Office programme. Legislation on nationality, criminal justice and police was opposed with a new vigour. These developments mirrored a much more extensive radicalisation of Labour attitudes on policing at local level. To some extent this was in turn merely a reflection of the regeneration of many Labour constituency parties through the influx of a more radical generation.

However, two important developments gave special force to this change. The first was the effect of public spending cuts. Between May 1979 and August 1982, basic police pay increased by 55.8 per cent. Recruitment soared and thus the wage bill to police authorities increased dramatically. But the new demands for expenditure coincided with pressure to trim even law-and-order budgets. From 1980 onwards, police authorities were faced with major budgetary headaches and a need to select between priorities. This meant that police-authority members were willy-nilly compelled to pay much greater attention than ever before to what they were spending on police – and why. The second vital development was the Labour Party's success in the local government elections of May 1981, coinciding almost exactly with the traumatic challenge to urban policing methods resulting from the 1981 riots. A number of police authorities came under Labour control and were filled with the new radical generation of constituency activists. Metropolitan areas such as Greater Manchester and Merseyside, which had experienced the worst riots, became well-publicised battlegrounds between the new Labour council members and the established police leaders.

Even where there was no overall change in the political control of the police authority, there were new challenges. In Thames Valley, where the force's computerisation of criminal intelligence records now became a local controversy, one veteran member of the authority complained: 'This authority isn't what it used to be. Then we were all pals together. Now it's a power struggle.' A particularly important conflict of this kind developed in London. The Metropolitan police is by far the largest, most expensive and most important force in Britain, employing a fifth of the country's officers. Londoners pay for the Metropolitan police through their rates but have no rights to representative control over their force, such as exist in all other forces.

The election of a Labour majority on the Greater London Council in May 1981, pledged to establishing a local police authority on the model set out in Jack Straw MP's private member's bill of 1979, therefore made little direct impact on Scotland Yard. The new GLC, however, took an important initiative towards local control of the capital's police when it proceeded to set up a police committee, with a support staff. Thus, paradoxically, the one British local authority with no powers over the police became the first British local authority to employ administrative staff working full-time on policing. The GLC initiative stimulated similar moves in a small number of London boroughs and the police committee also began a programme of funding local 'monitoring groups'.

LIBERAL AND SOCIAL DEMOCRATIC

If the decisive break from consensus came from Labour, important secondary challenges were also made from the Liberal Party and, to some extent, from the Social Democratic Party. With its civil libertarian tradition, the Liberal Party can be said to have resisted the policing consensus in several important respects at a time when Labour offered little challenge. The Liberals' special political significance in the 1980s debates on policing, however, was that they offered a political platform to opposition ideas on policing which had been largely developed within dissident police circles. (By contrast, Labour's policies were developed without any police input or co-operation.) A motion passed at the Liberals' 1982 assembly embodied this important dimension of the challenge to consensus. It called for the development of decentralised and various forms of 'community policing', involving a statutory police duty to consult with other local services in the hope that this would enable 'open, responsive and appropriate community policing' to take root. Significantly, the motion was supported by speeches from the two most celebrated senior police dissidents of the age, John Alderson and David Webb, both of whom had resigned from the force earlier in 1982 and were now pursuing political ambitions in the party.

CONSERVATIVE

These political changes in the Labour and Liberal parties were reflected in turn in the Conservative Party. The Conservatives' strong support for the police system led many within the party, and many outside it, to see it as the 'law-and-order party', a tendency that received a strong boost in the party's 1970 general election, and in subsequent campaigns. In reality, however, this rhetoric had significantly few policy implications when the party was in government, at either national or local level. For all that the 1979 general election manifesto contained a chapter headed 'The Rule of Law', and for all that the party leader Margaret Thatcher was well known to be a hawk on law-and-order policy, the manifesto contained no proposals on policing other than that the Tories supported 'strong, efficient police forces with high morale', and that they would pay in full a salary increase that Labour also supported.

In government since 1979, the Conservatives themselves demonstrated the fragility of the old consensus policies. Far from being able to hold their ground on the old 1964 Police Act basis, the Conservative government was, in practice, forced by the 1981 riots to set up an inquiry under Lord Scarman that led in turn to provisions in the Police and Criminal Evidence Bill 1983, which tried to create a new statutory settlement on accountability by making concessions towards more consultation (and, by implication, therefore more 'community policing') as well as changing yet again the police complaints procedure.

No single issue better illustrated the vulnerability of the policing system once the consensus broke down than the police complaints system. The system set up by the 1964 Act, and modified by the 1976 Police Act, held together as long as police nerve held. Once it broke, a point marked by the Police Federation's conversion to a fully independent complaints system in late 1981, any remaining political support drained into the sand. Newspapers that had never previously been known to criticise anything done by the police and that thrived on total uncriticism, suddenly discovered that the complaints system was as unfair as the radical critics had been saying all along.

Failures of Policing

These changes took place because of a series of failures within the British policing system. They were failures to which the narrow range of policy options available within the consensus had no answer, failures that those policies had manifestly failed to prevent and may even, said some, have helped to create.

These failures fell into three major categories – failures of organisation, of methods and of objectives. The failures of organisation consisted primarily of the tendencies towards centralisation and away from local (and individual) accountability. Prominent concerns included the greater regionalisation of specialist police tasks (training, technical support, criminal intelligence), the development of national co-ordination (computer services, public-order mutual aid, senior training), and the increasing influence of the national police representative bodies (Association of Chief Police Officers, Superintendents Association, Police Federation) over force policy and over pay and conditions.

'FIRE-BRIGADE POLICING'

The failures of methods were summed up in the term 'fire-brigade policing' – a system of co-ordinated incident response developed from the mid-1960s in which technologically superior intelligence, communications and vehicle systems absorbed the bulk of funds and training at the expense of police–community relations (and also, as it embarrassingly transpired during the 1970s, of police effectiveness in countering crime).

Two particular aspects of policing methods came in for special attention. The first was the mounting controversy over police violence in various forms. On the one hand there were charges of police maltreatment of suspects in the police station and of an increase in deaths in custody. On the other hand, three street deaths since 1974 were blamed on the police, and a major public debate took place concerning the appropriateness of various developments in police weaponry for dealing with crowds, and the sharp rise since 1970 in police firearms use. The second feature was the crisis over police surveillance and, in particular, over the computerisation of intelligence on the non-criminal population. Associated with this were a number of controversies about specific surveillance techniques, such as telephone-tapping and closed-circuit television, and about misuse of political-intelligence-gathering.

LOSS OF PROFESSIONAL CONTROL

However, perhaps the most important of all the crises that faced the police was the failure of police objectives. There can be few other institutions or services in Britain that take such pride in professional objectives, laid down before even the first Reform Act, as do the police in their devotion to a historical-fantasy memory of Sir Robert Peel. And there surely can be no other body that actually takes pride in the fact that its objectives and ideals have not changed in over 150 years.

Yet the police have consistently failed to reconsider their ideals. As a result, trapped in the latest brain-numbing ideology of 'prevention', they have developed (or have appeared to develop) an insensitivity to the changing popular aspirations, behaviour and culture, and any deviations from an often sentimentalised stereotype of white, male, lower-middle-class deferential honesty (i.e. the police's own self-image) are seen as increasingly serious and threatening.

'COMMUNITY POLICING'

The only alternative policing philosophy that can claim to have been at all thoroughly worked out has come from within the force, from a small but weak elite of senior dissidents – such as Alderson, above all – whose achievements are limited. The need for a clear set of policing ideals and objectives attuned to the late twentieth and early twenty-first century has not yet been grasped outside the police, where movements for reform have concentrated almost entirely in curbing the autonomy of police decision-making and action. In so far as they have considered the matter at all, political parties have tended to take their lead from Alderson, or from some vague sense of the progressive character of the phrase 'community policing'. Nevertheless, there can be no doubt that the gravest problem facing British policing is the need to forge a new framework of realistic, achievable, democratic, humane and acceptable goals for those who work in the force. There is no simple or single answer to this problem. But all the examples and causes of the current crises have a common characteristic. They all reveal the proven inadequacy of a system that allows police to enjoy spectacular autonomy in setting objectives, employing methods and organising themselves. By extension, they all suggest that other approaches might be more successful, more just and more acceptable.

Social Crises

The immediate causes of these crises of policing are the political and social events of our times – the unresolved issues of race relations, the struggle between owners and their workers, the future of Ireland, public corruption, and the rights of dissenters and minorities, not to mention the miscarriage of justice within the criminal process. Many police would leave it at that. They frequently argue as though the police are in the privileged position of being historically passive, and must simply respond to events; that they are there to clear up society's mess, and that there is no such thing as a policing problem; the only policing problems are society's problems. This belief is as unrealistic as the consensus that protected it and allowed it to flourish for so long. It has encouraged police and police-policy-makers to act as though all policing choices were inevitable – that greater powers, more spending, the investment in technology were all equally justifiable, and that none of these choices could possibly contribute to the problem rather than solving it.

There are signs in the post-riot discussion of policing that some lessons have begun to be learned. They are reflected in the more serious attention to law and order and policing policy and in moves away from determinism (both on the right and the left). But these developments are by no means unproblematic themselves and they are evidently politically vulnerable. If the old consensus has indeed broken down, it does not mean that the modest liberal reforming steps that initially followed the breakdown of 1975–81 are a true guide to the next stages of the policing controversy. If opinion surveys are to be believed, there would be wide public support for a more repressive and reactionary approach to policing. The breakup of the consensus and the challenge to police autonomy has so far been associated with social democratic and socialist political forces. The right has been slow to respond but it can be expected to do so, particularly because the overwhelming majority of police share its view of law and order.

The future of policing in British politics therefore appears extremely unstable. A radical assault has been begun against the traditional conservative consensus. But it is an assault that has taken place without very evident mass support. The next stages depend upon which approach wins the support of that mass. The relationship between democracy and policing is still at a very undeveloped stage.

10

Trade Unions and Governments

MARTIN HOLMES

To most of the general public, relations between governments and the unions are dominated by strikes, conflict and confrontation. The news media invariably concentrates on such newsworthy items as crisis negotiations, strike action and, in particular, controversies over picketing. To the participants themselves, ministers, management, and trade unions, the picture of government–union relations is often very different. While it is true that strikes have made the headlines – often justifiably – when relations have broken down, it is also true that for most of the past decade both government and unions have strenuously tried to co-operate to avoid industrial conflict. The Conservative government, 1970–4, under Edward Heath's premiership negotiated and talked to the unions on a variety of economic policy matters as no other Conservative government had done before. The 1974–9 Labour government, at first led by Harold Wilson and later led by James Callaghan, co-operated very closely with their trade-union allies, particularly with regard to legislation to extend trade-union rights. Essentially the approach of the 1970s whereby unions and government attempted to work together can be labelled 'corporatist' (see Chapter 5).

The End of 'Corporatism'

It is easy to pinpoint the fundamental change in union–government relations which transformed the, hitherto, cosy 'corporatist' approach to economic and industrial policy formation; from the moment Margaret Thatcher entered 10 Downing Street on 4 May 1979, a new non-interventionist, anti-corporatist, and anti-Tripartite policy was enacted. The changes initiated by the Thatcher administration were genuinely far-reaching, and constituted a real policy watershed.

Not only was the 'corporatist' approach of the 1970s rejected – Heath's Tripartite talks at the National Economic Development Council (NEDC) (Holmes, 1982) and Labour's 'Social Contract' (Barnett, 1982) – but also the philosophy of joint economic management between government, unions and the CBI, which originally the Conservatives under Harold Macmillan had fostered in the early 1960s. Indeed, the creation of the NEDC – itself the bastion of the 'corporatist' approach – had been part of the belief in the early 1960s in 'indicative planning', and industrial co-partnership. The move away from tripartism has left the CBI out in the cold as much as the unions, and, not surprisingly, criticisms of economic policy from the CBI since 1979 have been increasingly frosty.

What have been the major consequences of this change in style and policy? How successful has the Thatcher government been when judged by its own standards? How far can the unions' docility of the 1979–82 be put down to the severe economic recession? Answers to these questions are politically controversial; they are also, paradoxically, quite different from the expectations of government policy viewed from May 1979.

The Record since 1979

Up to the 'winter of discontent' (of 1978–9) which helped to destroy the Callaghan administration electorally, the Conservatives faced a major political problem: how to convince the electorate, wearied by strikes and industrial disruption, that they could work with the unions. The Conservatives were perceived as the party of industrial confrontation, while

Labour was portrayed – especially in its own self-image – as the party that avoided confrontation. In the October 1974 election campaign the Conservatives still had no argument to rival that put by Harold Wilson that a Conservative victory would return Britain to the three-day week and the industrial confrontation of the Heath period. The 'Social Contract' approach of close government/unions co-operation over legislation favourable to the unions was followed by an equally close association between the unions and the Labour government over the first three phases of its incomes policy. With the exception of the 1977 firemen's strike the period 1974–8 was a golden age of government/union collaboration on 'corporatist' lines. As late as October 1978 the Conservatives were widely regarded as likely to increase industrial confrontation if elected to office, especially given the monetarist and right-wing tone of Thatcher.

It is not the purpose of this account to relate the crucial events of the 1978–9 pay round and subsequent strikes, or the 1979 General Election campaign (Penniman, 1981). It is sufficient to say that it was the unions who, unwittingly, came to the Conservatives' aid. By their highly unpopular industrial action in the winter of 1978–9 they destroyed Labour's claim to be the party who could 'work with' (a phrase that itself betrays its corporatist origin) the unions and finally laid the ghosts of 1974 which the Conservatives had, themselves, failed to exorcise. Nevertheless many people still felt that, irrespective of Labour's failings, a Conservative administration would see a marked increase in industrial confrontation of the familiar set-piece variety of 1970–4.

In effect such prognostications have, hitherto, proved incorrect. Industrial disputes have decreased in number. Working days lost through strikes have declined to their lowest level, according to government figures, since 1940. Moreover, the severe effects of the recession have cut trade-union membership in stark contrast to the mid–1970s when union membership, fortified by the consequences of the Industrial Relations Act and the growth of white-collar miltancy, increased substantially. Falling trade-union membership has, in the 1980s, accompanied a decrease in the number of industrial disputes. Trade-union militancy – and trade-union power – have been, arguably, conspicuous by their absence. The docility of shop-floor reaction to Thatcher's monetarist experiment has been matched only by the failure on a political level of the TUC leadership to change government policy. The expected policy reversals of U-turns have not emerged. Government and unions have failed to begin, let alone maintain, a dialogue.

Two particular examples show the unions' sensitivity to the Thatcher government. The miners' rebuff in autumn 1982 to Arthur Scargill's campaign for a strike contrasted strongly with the miners' attitude in 1972 and 1974 (Holmes, 1982). The clear message was that even if a union leadership adopted a confrontationist stance the membership had other priorities – a factor that, given the lack of rallying cries from union leaders, has probably been evident in most other unions as well. A second contrast involved the 1982 Health Service selective strikes and campaign against low pay, and the 1979 strikes under the Callaghan administration. This example is, arguably, even more significant than that of the miners. In 1979 the Health Service strikes were conducted to lead to maximum inconvenience to public and patients in an effort to highlight the plight of low pay in the NHS. During the 1979 strike the sight of patients being turned away from hospitals was commonplace on the nation's TV screens; in 1982 the unions made sure to avoid such action. In 1979 the constituencies of Labour Cabinet ministers were targeted for special strike action and the Health Minister David Ennals, when unfortunately hospitalised, was the subject of industrial action; a NUPE shop-steward told the *Guardian* that Ennals 'is a legitimate target for industrial action ... He won't get the little extras our members provide patients ... He won't get his locker cleared or the area around his bed tidied up. He won't get tea or soup.' (*Guardian*, 7 March 1979). In 1982 the unions avoided any repetition of those tactics. In 1979 the stridency of Alan Fisher, the then NUPE leader, had become by 1982 the reasoned argument of his successor Rodney Bickerstaffe.

These two major examples could be reinforced by many which demonstrate an unwillingness to prolong strike action or intensify it: the ASLEF climb-down over flexible rostering in the face of TUC hostility and withdrawal of support in 1982:

the NUR's extremely brief strike action in the summer of 1982; the failure of the 1981 Civil Service strike; the absence of militancy at British Leyland which was in such sharp contrast to the record under the 1974–9 Labour governments. Many on the Left may regret the lack of union opposition to the Thatcher government, while in ministerial circles it is applauded; but the fact remains that since 1979, contrary to the expectations of strike when the government took office, the unions have demonstrated their lack of militancy and lack of power to change government policy. The contrast with 1974, or with 1978–9, is evident. There is no shortage of explanations for this state of affairs; the most important are considered below.

No Formal Incomes Policy

It is one of the ironies of recent British politics that an incomes policy, either statutory (1972–4) or compulsory non-statutory (1976–9) is often equated with moderation, consensus, the middle way and attempts to avoid confrontation. The hope on each occasion has been to restrain, and even control effectively, inflationary pressures in the economy presumed to originate with high wage demands. Indeed, the SDP/Liberal Alliance has modelled its incomes policy along these lines. Each successive incomes policy in the past, however, has led to severe industrial disruption and to polarisation and conflict between government and the unions (Brittan and Lilley, 1977).

Conversely the Thatcher government, while actually thought of as particularly right wing and inflexible, has been able to avoid much potential industrial trouble by allowing free collective bargaining to operate. Whatever its failures in other areas of policy, it is arguable that the Thatcher administration deserves credit for resisting what John Biffen has called the 'illiberalism' of formal incomes-policy constraints. The absence of such constraints had not led to the free collective bargaining 'free-for-all' chaos that was feared – one suspects particularly on the Conservative left (Edward Heath had publicly supported the 5 per cent policy in 1978–9) – before the 1979 election. Indeed wage levels have declined, along with inflation, during the Thatcher government's period of office, essentially by allowing free collective bargaining with the minimum of government manipulation and by deflating the economy. Even the public-sector pay targets set by the government have not become reliable guides to what is actually put on the table – or accepted. The 1982 4 per cent target has not become an official 'norm', as was the phase-IV 5 per cent norm 1978–9. Rather than being a directive as to the actual outcome of negotiations, the Thatcher 4 per cent target is simply a reference point. Different groups of workers in the public sector have therefore received quite widely differing wage increases: for example, the nurses received more than the hospital workers; the police have received more than the nurses, though not as much as the miners. Thus, although the Thatcher government – like any government – is responsible for public-sector pay, it has avoided its predecessors' policy of a blanket public-sector 'norm'. It is no coincidence that public-sector disputes have been, as a consequence, less prolific than in 1972–4 or 1978–9 when the earlier artificial restraints were ending.

Moreover, while previous incomes policies involved a period of initial acquiescence followed by an explosion of strikes it seems unlikely that such a pattern will trap the Thatcher administration. The Wilson incomes policy collapsed in 1969–70 with the 'dirty jobs' strike; the miners' strike against the Heath policy precipitated the first 1974 election (Holmes, 1982, ch. 7), and the 'winter of discontent' adversely affected the electoral fortune of the Callaghan government (Barnes and Reid, 1980, ch. 7). This is not to argue that government–union relations are the sole factor that determine a government's chances of re-election, particularly in an age of increased electoral volatilty. However, evidence from elections before 1983 suggested that deteriorating government–union relations have adversely affected the electoral attraction of the party in power. In each case the incomes-policy dimension has been crucial. The Thatcher government has avoided a fight with the unions over restoration of free collective bargaining by not having an explicit incomes policy in the first place.

One illustration relates to the motor industry. The Callaghan incomes policy began to collapse in 1978–9 with the question of government sanctions against the Ford Motor

Company. Both Ford's and the unions were prepared to settle for more than the government's 5 per cent; Ford's were in the private sector and were eager to avoid a strike which would seriously damage their production; the government threatened Ford's with the withdrawal of government business unless the company stayed firm; and a damaging strike occurred. Ultimately it was Parliament that came to the rescue by rejecting the sanctions policy, which in turn encouraged other claims of over 5 per cent. The contrast with the Thatcher approach is remarkable. Ford's can settle, and the unions can bargain freely, without government norms and guidelines. Indeed the Ford settlements since 1979 have hardly made headlines. By allowing free collective bargaining to operate, the government has depoliticised and decentralised such potential confrontations and thus avoided much unnecessary industrial action. Those who argued, long before it was politically fashionable, that the 'corporatist' incomes-policy approach actually engendered industrial conflict have regarded the recent decrease in strikes as a vindication. It is not the only factor that explains the low level of union militancy under the Thatcher government, but the lack of a formal incomes policy has greatly contributed to the situation.

Limited Scope of Legislation

With the exception of the 1969 battle over the Labour government's proposals contained in the *In Place of Strife* White Paper, when the Wilson government abandoned its proposals for legislative reform of trade-union law, it has usually been the case since 1964 that the Conservatives rather than Labour offend the unions by legislative reform, either threatened or actual. The Heath government's Industrial Relations Act produced a gigantic and concerted opposition from the unions but the legislation of the Thatcher government, although ritually denounced in Parliament, is far less comprehensive, and to the unions, less objectionable. This is not because the Thatcher government in general, and Employment Minister Norman Tebbit in particular, are less anti-union than in 1970–4. Indeed Tebbit's anti-union stance is quite

genuine and is not mere Tory-conference rhetoric. It is rather
that the nature of trade-union legislation since 1979 has been so
limited.

The reason why there has been no repeat of the Industrial
Relations Act legislation is that the Conservative leadership
learned the lesson that such comprehensive, all-embracing
legislation failed, to the point of being counter-productive.
Indeed, even the October 1974 Conservative manifesto – let
alone May 1979 – pledged not to reintroduce the then
just-repealed Act. The party leadership has therefore avoided
the main pitfall of the Industrial Relations Act, the National
Industrial Relations Court (NIRC), which tended to prolong
disputes and to politicise them, as in the infamous case of the
jailed 'Pentonville five' dockers in 1972 (Moran, 1977). Thus
both the Prior legislation and the Tebbit legislation have
concentrated on the periphery of trade-union power – secret-
ballot provisions and closed-shop-victims' compensation –
rather than the central issues as perceived by *In Place of Strife*
and the Industrial Relations Act.

Furthermore such then-central issues as the numbers of
unofficial strikes (accounting for 90 per cent of all strikes in the
late 1960s) and the question of secondary action have been
inconspicuous since the 'winter of discontent'. The reaction of
the union leadership – and the rank and file – has been far less
strident to the Thatcher legislation than it had been to the
Industrial Relations Act and the NIRC. Although, as already
explained, this is partly because the Thatcher legislation is
much more limited, another factor lies with the union
leadership itself.

Change in Union Leadership Styles

It is arguable that the TUC leadership has been less
consistently anti-Conservative and pro-Labour since the
retirement of Jack Jones and Hugh Scanlon in 1978. Jones and
Scanlon typified the politically committed union leaders who
saw the preservation of a Labour government as an end in itself
and who, for that end, were prepared to support strict
incomes-policy controls over their members (Castle, 1980).

The £6 flat-rate policy, which was the first of four stages, was Jones's creation in the summer of 1975. With subsequent phases, except phase IV, supported or acquiesced in by the union leadership, the period 1975–8 saw the apogee of corporatist co-operation between the unions and a Labour government. Jack Jones was as frequent a visitor to 10 Downing Street as many ministers, and as committed as those ministers to keeping Labour in office.

However, with the retirement of Jones and Scanlon a new generation of union leaders, typified by Moss Evans and Terry Duffy and, to a lesser extent, David Basnett, Ray Buckton, and Alan Fisher, took over the TUC leadership. Len Murray, who had been somewhat dwarfed by Jones and Scanlon and who had only become General Secretary in 1973, failed to emerge after 1978 as a TUC leader with the stature of Vic Feather. Significantly it was not Murray who made the running in the various oppositions to the 5 per cent pay policy in the 'winter of discontent'; similarly, Murray, who orga-nised the 1980 Day of Action against the Conservative government, may have expected greater support from a number of his colleagues on the General Council. His failure to rally union opinion significantly against the Thatcher government contrasted with Vic Feather's successful opposi-tion to the Heath government.

Murray's lack of authority, the right-wing shift in union opinion (particularly evident at the 1982 Labour Party Conference), and the absence of a 'Jack Jones' figure to act as a successful political influence have all contributed to the unions' docility since 1979. A generation of union leaders who contributed so clearly to Labour's unpopularity in the 1979 election seems set on weathering the Thatcher storm as best they can, preserving not the political credibility on which a new Labour government would rely but the interests of their members above all else. Thus, as Beloff and Peele have argued, 'perhaps the final paradox was that the events of the 1970s had pushed the theme of the defence of the unions back to the centre of the public's image of Labour just as the Labour Party itself was establishing its credibility as a national rather than a sectional party' (Beloff and Peele, 1980, p. 160).

Clearly in 1978–9 both the Labour Party and the unions got it wrong. In the 1977 Richard Dimbleby Lecture Jack Jones put it that, 'as trade unions try to force a result from employers or the government, pressure has often been applied to the public. All too often the ordinary people have been made the victims. They have felt the brunt of industrial action. We cannot afford to be indifferent to the effects of our actions on the public – indeed such indifference would be contrary to good trade union principle.' (Jones, 1977, p. 7). The post-Jones leadership, in failing to take such advice, helped to bring about the Thatcher government. While that same leadership has now, arguably, taken the Jones line to heart, it has not yet consistently adopted the political stance that proved essential *inter alia* to Labour's victory in 1964 or in both 1974 elections. Until this happens the main beneficiary may be the Conservative Party.

Unemployment

One of the most common explanations for the lack of union militancy and ability to challenge more directly the Thatcher government's policies is the high level of unemployment. The actual number of people unemployed more than doubled between 1979–82, to 3.3 million, or 14 per cent of the working population. The shop-floor workers, so the argument runs, are fearful that high wage settlements may jeopardise jobs, particularly if companies hard hit by the recession in the manufacturing sector, are unable to pass on wage increases in price increases to maintain profit margins. To the government, such attitudes are examples of a new realism among the work-force, particularly with regard to the chronic overmanning that Thatcher's government has sought to eliminate with considerable vigour in industries such as steel and motor manufacturing; to the Left, the government is deliberately creating unemployment as a weapon to break the unions and induce fear among working people. Whichever explanation is preferred the fact remains that high unemployment has affected shop-floor expectations and consequently weakened the hand of those who advocate more direct action.

This factor has been starkly demonstrated in the private sector, where many groups of workers have accepted zero wage increases for the 1981–2 round; however, in the public sector, where job security is more – though not absolutely – guaranteed, there have been no zero increases but merely small percentage rises. The issue of rising unemployment, which clearly broke the nerve of the Heath government in early 1972 when the dreaded 1-million threshold was crossed, has served to strengthen the nerve of the Thatcher administration and undermine trade-union power. Furthermore, following the Falklands conflict, it was proved that the unemployment issue alone was not sufficient to maintain the government's unpopularity.

Government's Handling of Disputes

The saying that oppositions don't win elections but governments lose them has much basis in truth; it is equally the case that the unions have not so much won battles with governments but that governments, by blundering, have lost them. This is particularly true of many of the failures of incomes policy, especially with regard to 1978–9. The Heath government blundered several times over the handling of the 1973–4 miners' crisis, from the 1973 secret meeting in July between Heath, Joe Gormley and William Armstrong, to the leaked Pay Board relativities figures just before polling in February 1974 (Holmes, 1982, chs 7,8). To many in the Labour Party, the Callaghan government blundered by using troops to break the 1977 firemen's strike, and in so doing set a precedent for the Conservatives.

The Thatcher government has not blundered in its handling of pay rounds, negotiations and actual disputes. In 1981 Thatcher overruled the Energy Secretary, David Howell, and ordered a climb-down to the miners over pit closures. Arguably this was the politically astute course of action. Equally politically astute – though perhaps less economically defensible – was the decision to respect the generous awards of the Callaghan government's Clegg Commission which finally settled the disputes of the 'winter of discontent'. On the other hand, the government successfully overcame the ASLEF flexible-rostering dispute by leaving the matter essentially in the hands of the British Rail management. Even long-running disputes, such as the 1980 steel strike and the 1982 Health Service dispute, were competently handled from a government point of view. The government's success also stems from the fact that while cash limits on public corporations (Hood and Wright, 1981) can be stretched without breaking publicly visible political principles, no such flexibility pertained to previous formal incomes-policy arrangements. Thus when the Thatcher government suffers a defeat in a dispute with the unions it can extricate itself with greater ease and dignity than its predecessors. The 1972 defeat of Heath by the miners still brings back memories, but who now remembers Thatcher's 1981 climb-down?

Difficulties for Labour

The Thatcher government has decisively rejected the 'corporatist' approach to governing through some form of consultation with the unions, and indeed the unions are, for the first time since the early 1960s, actually excluded from any influence on policy formation. This major change, however, has not led to a union reaction in the form of increased militancy and political action against policies the unions publicly oppose. Instead the number of industrial disputes is decreasing and union power is at a low level. The main explanation for such a reaction by the unions, and for the success the government claims, lies in the absence of formal incomes policy. But other factors are also important: the limited nature of the Conservatives' reforms of trade-union law; the leadership changes in the TUC; the effects of recession and high unemployment; and finally the politically astute way in which the government handled those disputes that led to strike action.

In an era of high electoral volatility those factors alone may not be enough to guarantee electoral success for the Conservatives. But the fact that three and a half years into its term of office, and despite over three million people unemployed, the

Thatcher government was contemplating electoral victory, demonstrates how difficult Labour's and the unions' task had become.

Moreover the scale of the Conservatives' electoral victory, when it came in June 1983, demonstrated how the vote of trade unionists, once Labour's bedrock of support, had become as volatile as that of other electoral groups. Unlike the elections of February and October 1974, and 1979, the 1983 election was not dominated by the question of trade-union power and government inability to deal with it. In 1983 one Conservative televised election broadcast proudly stressed the lowest level of strikes since the Second World War – a complete contrast to the Heath experience of only a decade before.

Following the 1983 election victory the prospect of the reversal of the anti-corporatist trends of the Thatcher first administration now seem remote. The TUC, at its 1983 conference, voted to re-examine its links with the Labour party – a euphemism for jettisoning left-wing unpopular policies – and during the *Stockport Messenger* dispute the TUC General Council failed to support the NGA's willingness to defy the law. The contrast between the 1983 approach, and the successful defiance of the 1971 Industrial Relations Act by unanimous TUC backing for unions defying that legislation, again emphasised the weakening of trade-union power in the Thatcherite post-corporatist era.

Thus mass picketing, which defeated the government in 1972 at the Saltley coal depot during the then miners' strike, was unsuccessful in the *Stockport Messenger* dispute and trade-union opposition which successfully forced the Heath government to 'put on ice' the 1971 Industrial Relations Act was unable to invalidate the 1980 and 1982 Employment Acts. Such contrasts reflected the wider changes in attitudes brought about by the Thatcher government regarding the role of trade unions in the post-corporatist economy. Given the evidence from 1979–84 it is not unrealistic to speak of such changes as revolutionary. Who, during the 1978–9 Winter of Discontent, would have predicted the extent of trade-union impotence that was self-evident by 1984?

11

Two New Protest Groups: The Peace and Women's Movements

PAUL BYRNE and JONI LOVENDUSKI

The standard approach to the study of political groups has concentrated on political parties and interest or pressure groups. This has led to an underestimation of less conventional kinds of political activity. Thus political scientists for a long time failed to notice that Britons were becoming less enchanted with most of the political parties, and that many people had either lapsed into resigned indifference to politics or were channelling their energies into new kinds of organisation. People look to interest groups, not just parties, to realise their demands, and interest groups have altered in ways that render the conventional classification schemes inadequate.

This does not mean that the old categories have ceased to be useful. Indeed, so long as groups such as the trade unions and the Friends of the Earth continue to exist and to make demands on government, we must continue to use the traditional distinction between protectional (or sectional) and promotional (or cause) groups, and keep in mind the clear differences in the compositions, aims and tactics of the two types. But the 1970s and the 1980s have seen the emergence and consolidation of new political movements which seek to pressurise government, but which do not fit into either of the traditional categories of interest groups.

Possibly the simplest and certainly the most popular new term that might be used is 'protest group'. Protest groups may be defined as groups that aim to bring about fundamental changes in public policy, political institutions and sometimes society itself. They differ from parties in that, like other pressure groups, they do not seek to exercise the formal powers of government. They differ from protectional pressure groups in that their membership is not drawn from one particular section of the community, and they have a relatively loose organisation. Contrasts between protest and promotional groups are less categorical, but a key factor is that protest groups have more radical aims which cut across and into established policy and issue areas. While both protest and promotional groups aim to influence public attitudes, the former are more prone to mass-action tactics (such as demonstrations). The controversial nature of their aims means that although protest groups have strong collective agreement on basic values and attitudes, disagreements on tactics occur frequently.

We believe that this differentiation between 'old' and 'new' styles of group activity can be taken a stage further. Within the general area of protest groups, at least one distinction may be drawn. Some protest groups restrict their efforts to achieving changes in governmental policy (albeit radical changes, with implications for policies outside the immediate area of concern of the group), while others not only want to change governmental policy but also social attitudes generally. A good example of the former type of protest group in Britain today is the peace movement, which aims to change official policy in just one area, but with obvious repercussions for the whole of foreign policy. By contrast, the latter often look to their supporters to adopt and propagate new attitudes even in their personal lives. The women's movement, for example, has a clear interest in changing public policy in such areas as employment and taxation, but also is intent upon promoting change in attitudes throughout society; hence it would be more accurate to state that those supporting the feminist cause comprise both a protest group and a social movement.

These 'new' protest groups do not fit readily into conventional views of British politics. Indeed, it has long been commonplace for those describing Britain's political culture to stress the prevalance of pragmatic, deferential and corporatist attitudes among Britons. Comment is often made on the apparent reluctance of most citizens to engage in any political participation outside of the established channels of political influence – parties, sectional groups and Parliament. Such views suggest that British society is not fertile ground for the mobilisation of significant numbers in radical social movements and protest groups, but this is no longer wholly true. Despite the fact that their supporters' ethos challenges conventional politicians, both the peace and feminist movements have attracted sufficient support to force their causes onto the issue-agenda of all the major political parties and recent British governments.

Although neither peace nor women's rights have ever been completely missing from the issue-agenda in twentieth-century British politics, both movements have experienced lengthy spells of political dormancy. Disagreements over tactics have contributed to this uneven history, but both have survived, and in their present form demonstrate many similarities. Both are organised into interconnecting networks, have loose definitions of membership, and draw their supporters from diverse sections of society. Both attempt to change political attitudes not only directly, but also by work within other pressure groups and the political parties, and each has had mixed success. Although there are differences between them, their forms are only really distinguished by the existence of an identifiable organisational centre in one of them – the Campaign for Nuclear Disarmament (CND) in the peace movement. The two movements have more in common with each other than either have with any political party, even with the Ecology Party or the parties of the extra-parliamentary left, despite some overlap in aims and memberships between all these groupings. To appreciate this, and to arrive at an assessment of

these particular protest groups, we must examine their aims
and origins, their membership and support, their organisation,
their strategies, their achievements, chances of success and
future roles in Britain.

Origins and Aims

Prior to its revival in the last decade, British feminism had
gained strength during the suffrage struggles of the early
twentieth century, and maintained some vitality until the
Second World War. During the post-war period, falling levels
of employment for married women and a cultural preoccupation with home-based motherhood undermined the movement's sense of purpose. A the end of the 1960s, however, the
frustration felt by increasingly educated and qualified women
who failed to obtain suitable employment, the formation of
liberation groups by women dissatisfied with their surrogate
status in the anti-Vietnam-war movement and similar protests,
and the increased control over personal lives made possible by
new contraception technology, all combined to create a
responsive audience for women's-rights campaigners. This led
to the first Women's Liberation Movement (WLM) conference
at Oxford in 1970, which adopted four basic demands: equal
pay, twenty-four hour nurseries, free contraception and abortion on demand. Subsequent annual conferences added the
demands of legal financial independence for women, and the
right to self-defined sexuality. A bitter dispute at the 1978
conference occurred over a proposal that all six demands be
scrapped and replaced by a single resolution against violence to
women. No national conferences have been held since that
time, and the movement has remained without a central
organising body, but it can be assumed that the seven demands
taken together do constitute the movement's basic programme.

  While CND is not the only organisation of note within the
peace movement, it is easily the most significant. It has been a
feature on the British political scene since the late 1950s when,
together with other groups, it headed a movement capable of
mass mobilisation. The other main group was the Emergency
Committee For Direct Action Against Nuclear War (DAC),

formed in 1957 and effectively replaced in 1960 by the Committee of 100. While the original CND was based around a number of nationally known figures who believed in the efficacy of reasonable argument with political decision-makers, the Committee of 100 stressed instead the importance of direct action and visible protest. Such differences over strategy provoked considerable disagreements between the two organisations, but they were able to co-operate to the extent of mobilising up to 100,000 participants for their early-1960s joint Aldermaston–London protest marches (Taylor and Pritchard, 1980, *passim*). As detente progressed during the 1960s, so support for the peace movement declined; it revived, however, with the return to a cold-war atmosphere in the late 1970s and early 1980s. Of all the groups involved in the early phases of the peace movement, only CND has benefited substantially from this revival. Its national membership has risen from around 3,000 in the early 1970s to over 40,000 (and still rising) in 1982. The current general secretary, Bruce Kent, estimates that there are also over 200,000 people in local peace groups affiliated to CND. This 'bottom-heavy' membership profile is stressed by the contemporary CND as being very different from the original CND, with its nationally based and somewhat elitist approach to organisation and decision-making.

Like the women's movement the revival of the peace movement is attributable to a number of factors. Particularly important have been technological developments such as the neutron bomb and the Cruise missile, and political developments such as the Thatcher government's decision to replace Britain's Polaris with the new Trident system and to allow United States deployment of Cruise missiles in the UK (see Chapter 8). Other factors include increased tension between East and West following the Soviet invasion of Afghanistan in 1979, and the establishment of a military government in Poland in 1981, as well as the adverse publicity given to the British government's civil-defence preparations (see Thompson and Smith, 1980). The aims of CND have remained largely unchanged since the late 1950s. Their essential argument then as now is that nuclear weapons are morally indefensible and are bound to be used sooner or later. Much stress is placed on Britain's vulnerability as a target in the event of any nuclear conflict and on the difficulty (indeed, in their view, the impossibility) of effective civil defence. Although there are, and always have been, convinced pacifists amongst CND's members, the group does not campaign against conventional weapons. While CND's ultimate aim is general and complete nuclear disarmament, the thrust of its short- and medium-term demands is that the possession of nuclear weapons hinders rather than aids an effective defence policy, principally because it dramatically increases Britain's attractiveness as a target area. It is also opposed to British membership of NATO, favouring the dissolution of both NATO and the Warsaw Pact. Finally, CND supports peace education in schools and redeployment schemes for those employed in military industries.

Organisation and Membership: The Network

A strong element of the feminist ethos has been resistance to organisational hierarchy accompanied by a prevailing distaste for designating leaders or spokespersons. Both of these attitudes are reflected in the WLM's practical and ideological commitment to the small-group structure developed in the early consciousness-raising groups. This apparent structurelessness makes it difficult to estimate the membership of the women's movement, a problem that is compounded by the fact that many women (and men) support some or all of the basic demands of the WLM but are reluctant to call themselves feminists. The absence of a single, encompassing national organisation prohibits a detailed outline of the movement's formal structure. In general, the WLM has taken the form of various local and sectional groups loosely interconnected into networks of support. Women have organised as women over issues such as health and child care, wages for housework, freedom of sexual preference and sexism in language. Women's caucuses are to be found within established groups as diverse as churches, trade unions, professional associations, some of the political parties and even within the civil service. In addition, various national single-issue groups have emerged – for example, the National Abortion Campaign set up in 1975 to defend the provisions of the 1967 Abortion Act. By the beginning of the 1980s, many permanent associations in Britain contained a women's group which pressed women's demands for greater status within the association. Finally, several important organisations (notably the Labour Party, many trade unions and the TUC) saw women's sections dating back to the 'first wave' feminism of the suffragists become revitalised during the 1970s. Thus women's organisations are diverse and various in form and location. And although not all of the groups possess formal links with each other, communications are good and the network has proved a sufficiently robust organisational form to assure the British WLM an appreciable political presence.

The peace movement also favours network forms of organisation, its major structural difference from the WLM being the pre-eminence of CND as its largest group. But even CND is loosely organised. CND membership is large, but there is unfortunately little reliable data on its composition. Preliminary investigations made by the national office suggest that it is safe to assume that their members are mainly middle class, under 40, mostly (but not exclusively) Labour Party supporters and that about one-fifth of them hold strong religious views (local branches may have a broader composition). Although CND has a national dues-paying membership, an annual conference that decides broad policy, a national council, an executive committee charged with implementing policy, and all the other hallmarks of a centralised organisation, it is in practice highly de-centralised. There are few full-time employees at its London offices and the impetus for many CND activities comes overwhelmingly from affiliated local groups and sections within the professions, the parties, trade unions and religious organisations. The national office offers support to such groups, endeavouring to keep them in touch with one another via a newsletter, but it makes little effort positively to direct their activities. It is only in the organisation of the annual conference and national protest marches that the centre plays a systematic organisational role. Links with other groups are either the formal ones allowed for by the constitutional provision for affiliation, or the more informal kinds of overlapping memberships and regular personal contact. Local groups may be founded wherever ten members can be attracted, and only the officers of these groups need be national members for full affiliation to be possible.

With a membership at all levels of over 250,000 and even greater numbers willing to turn out for national and local activities, the head-count of supporters of the peace movement is impressive. Only one political party – the Conservative – is larger. The overall organisational and membership pattern bears a striking resemblance to that of the women's movement. In both cases it is difficult to determine the limits of membership, a boundary problem that arises from the network form of organisation.

Strategies

Clearly their organisational forms and the composition of their memberships have a considerable bearing upon the activities of the two groups, with differences between them arising largely from differences in aims. The women's movement seeks fundamental change in a range of attitudes that cuts right across traditional social cleavages and political issues. Gaining equal status for a previously oppressed fifty-plus per cent of a society is a considerable task and accordingly activity proceeds on a number of fronts. The most visible of these are the increases in political participation and the establishment of several defensive single-issue groups. The revitalisation of previously dormant women's sections, the emergence of women's caucuses in seemingly monolithically male institutions, and the establishment of numerous single-issue groups (for example, Rights of Women, the National Women's Aid Federation, Rape Crisis Centre) are all characteristic women's-movement activities. Like the peace movement the WLM has been prone to internal conflict, and in particular deeply divided along radical-libertarian *vs* socialist lines. The reason is the fear of organisational hierarchy and elitism felt by a substantial number of British feminists. At its most extreme, this fear leads to the position that hierarchy is essentially a male construct used mainly to oppress women. Feminists want none of this despite the advantages that a national umbrella organisation (however loosely constructed) would bring to the movement. However, debates since the 1978 conference suggest that at present there is an insufficient basis of unity for a formal national association encompassing all of the movement.

The peace movement does in fact illustrate some of the difficulties a broadly based women's organisation might encounter. The low-key strategy of the CND centre reflects the leadership's break with the elitist and centralised structure first adopted by CND. The 1980s CND concentrates on being as broad a movement as possible; not only, it should be said, in order to keep the movement intact, but also because the contemporary leadership is firmly convinced that CND will only gain credibility with those in 'the middle ground' of the electorate if it is seen to keep a distance from what their general secretary has termed 'a crowd of cranks and partisan extremists on the left'. Consequently the strategy is one of building support among local authorities, the professions and the churches, as well as maintaining and increasing support in the political parties and trade unions.

These policies have not been pursued without opposition, however, and CND today also shows evidence of becoming conflict prone. There are two main points of opposition within the movement. The first is comprised of those who argue that, of the major political parties only Labour presents a realistic possibility of implementing disarmament. Therefore CND should concentrate on developing its strength within Labour to the virtual exclusion of the other parties. By contrast, those on the left within CND regularly attempt to establish a connection between the possession of nuclear weapons and the capitalist system in Britain, and from this basis argue that CND should concentrate its efforts on building on support in the trade-union movement. Both arguments are resisted by both the leadership and the mass membership of CND who may be wary of Labour's record in office, but the presence of such tendencies is a reminder of previous dissension in the movement.

Certainly in the early years there was a clear split between those who saw nuclear weapons as a direct consequence of a particular form of social structure (the DAC and much of the Committee of 100), and those who saw disarmament as a single policy issue to be pursued within the existing political system (the original CND). The potential for disagreements is high, and CND's very existence as a national organisation should be seen as the major accomplishment of the peace movement. But a split may yet occur. Apart from strategic differences, there is also an important division over the tactical issues of civil disobedience and direct action. Although national conference has given its support to 'considered non-violent direct action', the organisational implications of the decision have been fudged by leaving implementation to the discretion of local groups. Furthermore, the CND leadership stresses that such direct action as the establishment of 'peace camps' outside British nuclear bases is independent of CND itself (although obviously it has been sympathetic to the Greenham Common protest). Such equivocation is unlikely to be possible indefinitely. Following the deployment of Cruise missiles in the UK in 1983, CND will sooner or later have to develop an explicit position on what it considers to be legitimate direct action.

There is no ready parallel in the women's movement to the dilemma the debate over direct action poses for CND. The single organisational form, however loosely constructed, does imply a membership unity over tactics, a problem the WLM has yet to face. On the one hand CND does not wish to alienate the sympathies and energies of its activists, while on the other it is convinced of the necessity of maintaining a broad appeal and largely respectable image if it is to counteract the nationalism and militarism of British political culture. Facing even more deeply rooted cultural obstacles the women's movement may well be wise to eschew organisational distinctiveness, and to adopt national structures only over single issues.

Achievements and Prospects

Internal dissension apart, there is no doubt that both the peace and women's movements, comprised as they are of thriving sets of organisations capable of mobilising large numbers of people, are effective political forces. Neither, however, is anywhere near achieving across-the-board success, although both have made progress. To measure that progress we need to consider the effect each has had in influencing public opinion and mobilising mass support, in gaining the support of powerful interests, and in achieving significant changes in public policy.

The available evidence suggests that the WLM has experienced mixed success in each of these three areas. Survey evidence indicates substantial increases in the number of both men and women supporting the demands for equal pay and more representation of women in political elites (Eurobarometer, 1979). Periods of economic recession have had some impact, however: in 1980, 38 per cent of working men and 28 per cent of working women agreed that, where jobs were scarce, married women should be discouraged from working (MORI Poll, 1980). In more general terms, more than 40 per cent of British voters in 1979 preferred that men should occupy various positions of authority and responsibility in political and social life (MORI Poll, 1979). Such data suggest that while there may be majority support for the principle of sex equality (and one must not forget the problem of biased and induced responses when dealing with survey data), there is at least a substantial minority that would resist its actual implementation.

The pattern of support by powerful organisations for WLM aims is also mixed. The TUC has long supported the principle of equal pay, as have most of the component unions; most major trade unions have also adopted some kind of pro-abortion stand (Coultas, 1981, p. 77). But women continue to be underrepresented on trade-union decision-making bodies, and women's issues continue to receive relatively low priority (Coote and Kellner, 1980, pp. 8–11). The Labour, Liberal and Social Democratic Parties all have sex-equality platforms, but Labour and the Social Democrats have failed to adopt the positive discrimination proposals that might serve to bring this about. Indeed, the 1982 Labour Party Conference rejected a motion designed to guarantee a limited right for the Labour Party Women's Conference to table motions at National Conference. Success at capturing the support of parties and trade unions has been limited when it comes to securing practical support; it has also been limited to the centre-left of the political spectrum with the Conservatives proving highly resistant to any feminist influences (Coote, 1978, pp. 462–3).

Some feminist demands have become public policy, but here too the pattern is mixed. Free contraception, the only one of the four original demands to be met, is now available, rape victims are guaranteed anonymity and sexual privacy and the law offers some protection to battered wives. The women's movement must rely heavily on various kinds of self-help. Neither the Equal Pay Act of 1970 nor the Sex Discrimination Act of 1975 have been far-reaching. Average women's industrial earnings in 1982 were only 71 per cent of those of men's, and this was largely due to the persistence of the occupational sectoralisation the Sex Discrimination Act was designed to alleviate. The Equal Opportunities Commission set up to oversee these acts has been unsuccessful at getting loop-hole-closing amendments passed, and sex discrimination remains difficult to prove and difficult to correct (see Byrne and Lovenduski, 1978). In addition, discriminatory taxation policy is outside the scope of these acts. The Employment Protection Consolidation Act (EPCA) of 1978 confirmed certain maternity rights, but nursery provision remains scarce and abortion provision is inadequate and has been under consistent attack.

Signs of 'backlash' have threatened even these gains. Protection supplied by the EPCA was reduced by the 1980 Employment Act, the 1983 election returned only 23 women to the House of Commons, and all the major parties tend to leave women's issues to women MPs. Policy successes so far cannot be taken for granted, and the political climate at the end of 1983 was not auspicious for further feminist gains. It is only because of pressure from our EEC partners that the government has seen fit to close some of the loopholes in the law.

CND has also had mixed progress in each area. During 1982 the government became increasingly concerned with the impact that the peace campaign, and CND in particular, had on public opinion. National polls showed a steady rise in opposition to nuclear weapons, with up to 63 per cent of respondents opposed to the deployment of Cruise missiles and 53 per cent opposed to the purchase of Trident, although there was considerably less support for withdrawal from NATO. Such opinion-trends represent impressive accomplishments given the generally unfavourable media coverage the movement has had. Among the national press in Britain, only the *Guardian* and, to a lesser extent, the *Daily Mirror* has been prepared to comment sympathetically. The issue of disarmament has received considerable exposure on television, but both BBC and ITV, constrained by the necessity to give a 'balanced view', have been hampered by the reluctance of the Ministry of Defence to engage in open debate. The BBC in particular has found coverage of the topic to be problematic. Too much air-time devoted to the possibility of disarmament would, it is felt, lay the corporation open to charges of bias – hence the by-now infamous decision to withdraw the invitation to E. P. Thompson to deliver the 1981 Dimbleby Lecture. Media attitudes are significant for a movement intent upon attracting wide public support in a policy area in which there is a long tradition of minimal public participation, and in which deferential attitudes on the part of the electorate are at their strongest. Changing public opinion is crucial for the peace movement, as it lacks the traditional strengths of successful conventional pressure groups – it neither possesses information which the government needs, nor is it in a position to exercise effective and direct sanctions against central government.

Progress among powerful interests has been made. Since 1981, the Labour Party and some unions have, (in their annual conference decisions), committed themselves to the cause of unilateral nuclear disarmament, as have the Communist Party of Great Britain, Socialist Workers' Party and the Ecology Party. The membership – but not the leadership – of the Liberal Party have demonstrated sympathy with the unilateralist cause. However, the Social Democrats, like the leadership of the Liberals, remained committed to multilateral rather than unilateral disarmament. Even the Conservative Party has been sufficiently impressed by the growth of the peace movement to seek to contain it by launching its own Campaign for Defence and Multi-lateral Disarmament at its 1982 conference, but has otherwise remained steadfastly committed to the independent deterrent. There are also growing levels of support from the major churches.

At policy level, perhaps the greatest success has been the more than 140 local authorities who followed the lead of Manchester City Council in declaring themselves Nuclear Free

Zones, and refusing to implement central government civil-defence planning. This was the main reason that central government had to postpone its major civil-defence exercise (Operation 'Hard Rock') in 1982 until it could devise a legal method of forcing local authorities to comply with civil defence plans.

Despite the rapid growth of the peace movement, it would be foolish to assume that the battle was almost won. Although there is some evidence of headway among the membership of parties, there are rather fewer signs that the leaderships are similarly convinced. Equally worrying for the peace movement must be the possibility that if limited success were achieved (for example, a reversal of the decision to purchase Trident or deploy Cruise missiles), the campaign might lose much of its dynamism, as membership drifts away in much the same way as it did after the signing of the Partial Test Ban Treaty in 1963.

Conclusion

Both CND and the women's movement have succeeded in pushing their cause into the realm of public discussion and onto the policy agenda of parties and governments. Both groups are well known, and there are continual reminders of their existence in all branches of the media. In short, they are popular movements, which have grown as ideas have struck a chord, and as new attitudes have spread. They were helped in this by the radicalisation that overtook much of Britain's youth (and especially middle-class youth) in the late 1960s – although objective data is not available, subjective impressions suggest that these 'children of the sixties' have proved a good source of recruitment as they have grown older. Both movements will suffer (in particular, the WLM) as economic recession concentrates minds on economic security and little else. But it would be foolhardy to predict their demise at any time in the near future, unless their demands have first been met.

At the level of government policy the women's movement has achieved more success so far than CND. When in power both parties have been prepared to advance women's rights. However, although goals of sex-equality were given some statutory expression in the Equal Pay and Sex Discrimination Acts, neither Labour nor Conservative governments in recent years have felt it necessary to do any more, or to show much interest in the defects that have become apparent in these laws. CND, on the other hand, has in the past been effectively 'frozen out' by both parties who, when in government, have viewed disarmament and the independent deterrent as the exclusive preserve of government and experts.

Such off-handedness on the part of government is encouraged by the ambivalence or opposition of other influential sections of society toward the two protest groups. The trade unions, for example, are less willing to advance the cause of sex-equality when the jobs of male workers are at risk. Senior officers in the armed forces and their counterparts in Whitehall are well placed to offer 'informed opinion' to their Ministers that may well outweigh unilateralist opinion among party activists and supporters. In addition, on issues like these the weight of inertia is a significant factor against radical policies.

Although a less-than-favourable political environment is undoubtedly a factor, on balance, it is probably the very magnitude of the tasks to be accomplished that has led sections within CND and the women's movement to advocate caution, adherence to legitimate channels of protest and a gradualist perspective. Leading figures in both are evidently mindful of the tendency of the political elite and media in Britain to ridicule those who might be labelled as 'extremists' – and of how effective this can be. Thus they find themselves having to distance their organisations from their more enthusiastic supporters. Internal tensions are never absent from the two groups and may serve to distract supporters' attention and energies from major goals. Leaders from both the women's movement and CND are aware that they must walk a tightrope between effective and noisy championing of their causes and the risk of provoking a backlash from those who are, at best, grudging supporters, a problem that is endemic to protest groups. It would, of course, be surprising if such problems were absent from organisations formed to challenge deep-rooted and traditional social norms and values. It was, after all, largely the fundamental nature of their challenge that originally excluded peace and women's-rights activists from the established channels of promotional group activity and turned them to the protest group as a basis for political action.

12

Northern Ireland

PAUL ARTHUR

Northern Ireland is a tiny region on the periphery of the United Kingdom. This fact has had two significant consequences. First, geography and the constitutional settlement of 1920 quarantined the Northern Ireland problem from British politics until recently. Devolution was administratively convenient for Westminster but politically unfortunate for the province. Second, political life in Northern Ireland deviated from British practice. It had the appearance of being British but, in fact, it was more reminiscent of the divided societies of Europe, such as inter-war Austria.

On the mainland, political debate during the 1970s was dominated by the collapse of the post-war social-democratic consensus, and centred on the merits of free-market monetarism *vs* the centralised collectivist control of the economy. Commentators of Left and Right welcomed the removal of the straitjacket of centrist politics. In Northern Ireland, on the other hand, London was attempting to sell consensual politics to an electorate who could barely tell the difference between a Keith Joseph and a Tony Benn; 'setting the people free' was not about the advantages of freedom over planning but about the liquidation of republican terrorism and/or the British link.

Political schizophrenia has been the result. Rational Man operating in an irrational environment has hidden behind the convention of 'government as arbiter' – Britain is above the conflict but is prepared to use her good offices and vast experience to fashion a solution. The purpose of this chapter is to explain how Britain has approached the problem since she imposed direct rule in 1972, and to examine the impact of the Ulster problem on British politics.

Direct Rule

Ultimately, it was the introduction of internment without trial in August 1971 (to quash nascent armed republicanism) and Bloody Sunday in January 1972 (when paratroopers killed fourteen unarmed civilians in Londonderry) that forced the hand of the sovereign power. On 24 March 1972, Stormont, the seat of government in Northern Ireland, was prorogued and direct rule imposed. Since 1972 Westminster has resisted the temptation to integrate Northern Ireland fully into the British political system. Instead it has created another territorial ministry, the Northern Ireland Office (NIO), and has concentrated on constitutional initiatives. No less than six successive sets of political institutions have been authorised for the province in the past decade – direct rule with an appointed advisory council, devolved coalition government, temporary direct rule, a Constitutional Convention, temporary direct rule again, and, James Prior's 'rolling devolution' initiative. Such constitutional innovation gives the NIO an extra dimension missing from the Scottish and Welsh Offices.

With the imposition of direct rule Northern Ireland was ruled directly from London for the first time since 1921. The former powers of Stormont were vested in a Secretary of State, William Whitelaw, and a small team of ministers responsible directly to Westminster. Direct rule entered its most creative phase after October 1972 when the government produced a discussion paper, 'The Future of Northern Ireland'. It introduced the concepts of power sharing and an Irish dimension. The former recognised that in a divided society political power must be shared proportionally among those communities committed to a constitutional settlement. The latter acknowledged the (Catholic) minority's sense of Irish identity, and the practical realities imposed by two sovereign states sharing the same (disputed) land border. Thus it combined symbolism (Irish unity but only by consent) and hardheaded functional and security co-operation. The feasibility of these innovations was tested in a general election to a seventy-eight-seat Assembly on 28 June 1973, and in subsequent negotiations between the province's elected leaders and representatives of both sovereign governments. The outcome was the appointment of Northern Ireland's first coalition containing an antipartitionist party, the Social Democratic and Labour Party (SDLP).

The experiment lasted less than five months, brought down not so much by divisive conflict within the coalition of three parties, as by the insistence of some 'loyalist' parties outside government on operating the adversarial Westminster model. The means of election (proportional representation), the type of government, and the implications of the Irish dimension made the whole sorry business 'unBritish' in their eyes. With the intimidating assistance of the paramilitary Ulster Defence Association (UDA), and the control of key sectors of the power industry, they called the Ulster Workers' Council (UWC) strike which brought the Executive to its knees.

Caution has been the keyword ever since. Whitelaw had returned to the mainland before the Executive met. His successor, Francis Pym, was Secretary of State for too short a period to make any obvious impact. With the change in government in February 1974 he was replaced by Labour's Merlyn Rees. Rees presided over the collapse of power-sharing and succeeded in alienating virtually every section of the community – the powersharers through his acquiescence in the UWC blackmail, and the Loyalists by his dismissive attitude towards their political pretensions. Nevertheless, he did make one serious effort at political movement. In July 1974 he announced that the defunct Assembly would be replaced by a seventy-eight-member Constitutional Convention which would be given the opportunity to produce a viable constitution. The election on 1 May 1975 gave a comfortable majority to those firmly committed to having 'British parliamentary standards'. Consequently, Convention debate and the majority Convention Report was predictable. Westminster rejected this plea for a modified version of Westminster practice but accepted that it could not impose a settlement on the recalcitrant majority.

Subsequently Britain has adopted what one NIO officical calls a 'cotton wool policy', that is the avoidance of disaster and an acceptance of the less ambitious task of making direct rule more amenable to local convenience.

'Ulsterisation'

In September 1976 Rees was replaced by Roy Mason who was to remain in the post until Labour lost the May 1979 election.

While he made some efforts at establishing a form of 'interim devolution' after a series of desultory discussions with local political leaders, Mason is remembered chiefly for his impact on the security situation. As Defence Secretary he had permitted the introduction of units of the SAS into South Armagh in 1976. In his Ulster post during 1977 he increased the covert tactics of the Army and allowed the SAS to operate throughout the province. Additionally, he embarked on a policy of 'Ulsterisation' whereby an enlarged police force and Ulster Defence Regiment (UDR) took the frontline places of the Army. This was an important decision. It paid obeisance to the growing professionalism of the local security forces; it recognised that the Army was too blunt a weapon for civilian control; it bestowed a confidence on those who believed that there was a security solution; and it appeared to augur the death of the Irish dimension. Certainly during Mason's time, loyalist violence and, for long stretches, republican terrorism were kept under wraps.

Since Margaret Thatcher became Prime Minister, Northern Ireland has had two Secretaries of State. Her first appointment, chosen to replace her close friend, Airey Neave (who was assassinated by the Irish National Liberation Army (INLA)) was Humphrey Atkins. He was without Cabinet or Ulster experience, and during his two years in the job he managed to convey an air of concerned bewilderment. Like Mason he tried unsuccessfully to engage local politicians in reaching enough agreement to form a government of Northern Ireland. But his chief concern was on the security front, in particular trying to solve the hunger strike.

Hunger Strikes

The antecedents to this protest go back to William Whitelaw. In July 1972, following a hunger strike he granted 'special category status' to convicted paramilitaries. These privileges turned the prisons into schools of terrorism and distanced the paramilitaries from 'ordinary' criminals, thus giving them a degree of respectability in the outside world. Whitelaw recognised his mistake, but it was not until March 1976 that a successor, Merlyn Rees, ordered the phasing-out of this category. Republican prisoners objected strongly to this 'criminalisation' policy, and protested by going 'on the blanket', refusing to wear prison clothing. Two years later they intensified their campaign through a 'dirty protest'. They smashed up cell furniture and refused to wash or use any toilet facilities. When that bore little fruit in terms of concessions they engaged in a series of selected hunger strikes. They reached a culmination on 18 December 1980 with one prisoner very close to death. At last the authorities had made some moves in their direction. But the whole issue was botched with charge and counter-charge of bad faith. So republicans began a second series of hunger strikes in March 1981 when Bobby Sands, the Provisional commander in the Maze prison, began a 'fast to the death'. He was to be followed at carefully chosen intervals by other prisoners. Atkins was under strong pressure from Thatcher not to bow to blackmail. Equally he was aware that the strike was alienating most of the minority population and driving out what remaining goodwill there was in the province.

The Provisionals had struck a brilliant propaganda blow against established authority. There has always been an ambivalence in Northern Ireland about the use of political violence, and hunger-striking had claimed twelve republicans earlier in the century. The organisers made great play of the symbol of Christ crucified, and appealed to a wider world attuned to humanitarian cries. They organised mass demonstrations which had a huge emotional effect on Catholic

Ireland. The folk memory of '800 Years of British Repression' was tapped yet again, and as the strike progressed the terrorist coffers were filled with funds from the United States, and constitutional antipartitionists were marginalised. Republicanism was resurrected, and those who had turned away from it because of its atrocities raised it once more from being a sect into a mass movement. All of this was confirmed when Bobby Sands fought a by-election for the Westminster constituency of Fermanagh/South Tyrone from his death-bed. His victory represented the nadir in community relations in Northern Ireland. It did not prevent his death nor that of nine other strikers. And it was only when the remaining strikers' relatives demanded medical intervention that the hunger strike came to an end.

By this stage (September 1981) Atkins had been replaced by James Prior. From a position of strength he used his considerable negotiating talents to fashion a compromise that stopped short of granting political status to the prisoners. In any case it was meaningless to speak of 'victory' and 'defeat'. By the following year Sinn Fein, the political wing of the IRA, were demonstrating their new-found political prowess in Assembly elections called by Prior. To explain the genesis of the Prior initiative we need to make a few comments about the manner of his appointment and about the current political background.

If we discount Francis Pym's very short tenure, Prior is only the second real political heavyweight to serve in Northern Ireland. The other, William Whitelaw, started with many more advantages. He had the absolute support of his Prime Minister and of a Cabinet intent on finding a lasting solution to the problem – hence the sharp burst of intense and creative activity that culminated in the 1974 partnership government. Prior's appointment on the other hand was seen as the removal of an unruly baron from the centre of power in London. In effect, he was exiled from Westminster because he represented a 'Wet' threat to the Prime Minister. Moreover, the inventiveness of 1972 had been replaced by a pervading sense of distaste and despair in Whitehall in 1981: the foul Irish actually enjoyed conflict, so let them find their own solution.

That is not entirely true. One of the most hopeful developments since 1979 appeared to be burgeoning Anglo–Irish
relations. At first sight this might appear odd; after all,
Margaret Thatcher was 'rock hard on the Union', and the
Taoiseach, Charles Haughey, had the reputation of being a
hard-line republican. However, both saw the IRA as a real
threat to their respective politics, and, after security co-operation began to flourish, they realised the necessity of a summit
meeting. During 1980 they met in May and December. Their
second meeting referred to 'the totality of relationships within
these islands' and established joint studies by senior officials
covering possible new institutional structures, citizenship
rights, security matters, economic co-operation and measures
to encourage mutual understanding. At last there was a
realisation that moving from the eye of the storm to working at
its edges might be more fruitful. At the very least, functional
and security co-operation would benefit both countries.
Confirmation of growing rapprochement was established at a
third summit between Thatcher and a new Taoiseach, Garret
FitzGerald, in November 1981 when they institutionalised the
relationship. They created an Anglo–Irish Council, the first leg
of which was an Anglo–Irish Inter-Governmental Council, to
be followed, it was hoped, by an Inter-Parliamentary Council.
The latter has not been established, and the former met only on
20 occasions to the end of 1983.

Anglo–Irish Relations

In fact, Anglo–Irish relations were being slowly eroded by
distinctive domestic considerations. Unprecedented economic
and financial difficulties and constantly rising unemployment
produced no less than three separate governments in under
eighteen months in Dublin. In 1982 alone there had been two
general elections, three budgets, a change of leadership in the
Labour Party, and two direct challenges to Haughey's
leadership of the Fianna Fail party. To divert attention from
the economy Haughey tried to make more of his meetings with
Thatcher than was warranted. Playing the nationalist card
made little impact on the Republic's electorate, which was

deeply concerned with immediate bread-and-butter issues, but it had a depressing and inevitable effect on Ulster loyalists. Thatcher had to draw back and reassure her Unionist allies.

Second, the Anglo–Irish process was badly shaken by the hunger-strike saga. It was obvious that, good relations notwithstanding, Dublin could not shift Thatcher's resolve on no concessions to blackmail. That may have made sound political sense in Finchley, but Irish nationalist politicians knew that the hunger strike was aimed just as much against their constitutional approach as it was at 'British imperialism'. Third, Ireland's attempt to remove EEC trade sanctions on Argentina during the Falklands war had a catastrophic effect. She could cite the sinking of the Belgrano and her own tradition of neutrality as justification for her action, but given the very long history of mutual suspicion it is not altogether surprising that Thatcher saw such action as a stab in the back.

The 1982 Assembly

Finally, the 1982 initiative at finding yet another internal settlement to the Northern Ireland problem set back Dublin/London relations. Haughey reacted to the Prior plan by declaring that it was 'unworkable'. He was correct in the sense that since 1972 every Secretary of State had failed to persuade enough Unionists of the advantages of sharing power. Admittedly, Prior acknowledged the futility of trying to impose agreement; instead, like his two predecessors, he sought no more than the highest level of acceptance that would bring both communities together in their own Assembly. And his scheme was more subtle than previous efforts. He offered elections to another Assembly which would permit representatives the facility to make direct rule more accountable. Initially they would have scrutinising powers, and if they could demonstrate a real measure of 'cross-community agreement' Westminster would devolve functional powers either partially or *in toto* – hence 'rolling devolution'. The Secretary of State claimed to be motivated by the very sad plight of the Ulster economy. If local politicians could unite in trying to make the province more prosperous their unity might encourage overseas investors that

Ulster was a viable proposition. Thus the Assembly was to be a school of reconciliation.

Charles Haughey's initial reaction may prove to be the correct one in the long term. Assembly elections were held on 20 October 1982 with a predictable outcome. The Official and Democratic Unionist Parties won 47 (out of 78) seats, the SDLP 14, the biconfessional Alliance Party 10, and Provisional Sinn Fein 5, with the remaining two seats going to independent Unionists. Prior had gambled on the upsurge of the middle ground and failed. Only the Alliance Party actually believed in his version of rolling devolution; the SDLP and Sinn Fein refused to take their seats; the two big Unionist parties have used the forum to continue their longstanding hostility against each other. Prior had made the crucial error of assuming that a fundamental constitutional issue could be subsumed by more mundane matters. It may be that his 'exile' impelled him to produce something spectacular in Ulster. If so, there is little movement in local political life – where the only common ground is that of mutual distrust.

The Lessons of Ulster

Two stark facts stand out: the Ulster polity has lived in a pathological condition since 1968; and the problem involves a value conflict of national allegiance which does not appear to be amenable to compromise.

... FOR THE ARMY

By June 1982 more than 2,200 people were killed in political violence. The conflict has claimed the lives of such notables as a British Ambassador to Ireland, Airey Neave MP, Lord Louis Mountbatten, and Rev. Robert Bradford (Unionist MP for Belfast South). Republicans have shown the ability to hit targets in Britain, and while the level of violence may have diminished from the bad years of 1972–4 the authorities have not been able to bring it under total control. They accept the cynical view of the late Reginald Maudling that there is 'an acceptable level of violence'. Clearly, there have been major security successes and terrorism is not quite the potent force of a decade ago. The security forces have become much more professional, have received much more information from the ghettoes as people weary of yet another atrocity, and have adapted a much more sophisticated intelligence-gathering machine.

But a price has had to be paid. Northern Ireland may be good training-ground for analysing the challenges from internal wars in the late twentieth century. It may even provide instances of the politicians being overruled by the military, as occurred during the UWC strike (see Fisk, 1975, p. 153), and that had led some to assume that the lessons of Ulster will be used against the Left in some future 'doomsday scenario' on the mainland (see Ackroyd *et al.*, 1977, *passim*). On the other hand, the Army has learnt some little respect for the tenacity and ingenuity of the terrorist; and the UWC strike did teach it that it is not equipped to run a high technological society at the point of breakdown. Like the politicians the Army has learnt as well that it is the terrorist who controls the agenda. There have been several occasions when terrorism seemed to be defeated but it has bounced back. The IRA in particular will not be unduly concerned about temporary setbacks. They have a moral certitude about their cause and they believe themselves to be engaged in a war that is 800 years old. It is very, very difficult to defeat an idea.

... FOR LIBERAL DEMOCRACY

More important, terrorism challenges the pretensions of liberal democracy. In several respects the campaign had a debilitating effect on British democracy. Originally London's response to the 'Troubles' was to disarm and 'anglicise' the Royal Ulster Constabulary (RUC), and to place its (permanent) emergency legislation under close scrutiny. It did not take too long to ascertain that Belfast was not like Surbiton. The temptation to repress violence by whatever means were considered necessary, regardless of the legal constraints – the security response – became paramount. The Diplock Report (1972), for example, recommended that non-jury trials should be introduced for a wide range of terrorist offences, and that there should be easier admissibility of confessions. The recommendations still stand. Following the Birmingham bombings of 1974, Parliament passed a Prevention of Terrorism Act which the Home Secretary, Roy Jenkins, recognised as giving the authorities 'draconian' powers. Incidentally it created two classes of United Kingdom citizens – those who could be deported to Ireland as suspected terrorists, and those who were welcome on the British mainland. In general, London is open to the charge of imposing repressive legislation on Northern Ireland, much of it consolidated in the Emergency Provisions Act 1978 (Flackes, 1980, pp. 207–9). Finally, the European Court of Human Rights in January 1978 found that post-internment interrogation techniques used by British soldiers constituted 'inhuman and degrading treatment'. It may be objected that there is no other way to defeat terrorism, but the experience of devolution in Northern Ireland illustrates that the security response can become a way of life.

One could add to this checklist of woe. For instance, the problem has taken up an inordinate amount of parliamentary time when MPs would prefer to get on with 'the real business of politics'. One could discuss the financial cost of Northern Ireland in some detail. Suffice to say that the UK subvention to or on behalf of Northern Ireland was calculated at £52 million in 1966–7, whereas a special report in the *Guardian* (19 February 1980) set the figure at £1 billion twelve years later.

The price might be worth paying if there was any evidence of political movement within Northern Ireland. The sad fact is that the only real movement occurs within communities. The introduction of proportional representation did not herald the rise of centre politics. It seemed to smash the Unionist monolith, but that was shortlived and now there are two major Unionist groups vying with each other for the title of super-loyalist. In the Catholic community the SDLP emerged as the most outstanding antipartitionist party in the history of Northern Ireland. But as time wears on and they cannot deliver a share of the political limelight the 'children of the Trouble' turn to more simplistic solutions – hence the success of Sinn Fein in the 1982 Assembly elections. Indeed even the IRA faces a challenge from the more reckless and vicious INLA. Formed in 1975 from the old Official Republican movement (which had renounced violence in favour of the political road) it sees itself as the Irish equivalent of the Red Brigade, part of an international Marxist campaign against bourgeois society. Although it has less than 200 activists it has carried out some spectacular atrocities, such as the Ballykelly bombing of 7 December 1982, and the murder of three innocent Protestants at their place of worship in the village of Darkley on 20 November 1983. Perhaps the only hope lies outside NI in a body entitled the New Ireland Forum. It was established by the three major democratic parties in the Republic and the SDLP for 'consultations on the manner in which lasting peace and stability can be achieved in a new Ireland through the democratic process'. In other words, it was examining the flexibility and the positive properties of Irish nationalism. Following its first meeting in public on 30 May 1983 it invited submissions from a wide spectrum of public opinion, and over the following six months it heard evidence, much of it unpalatable, which challenged the myths of traditional nationalism. Its real test would come by March 1984 when it is expected to produce a blueprint which will woo northern Protestants towards a new Ireland. In the meantime the Anglo–Irish process continues to stress security and functional co-operation – the best example of the latter was the arrangement signed on 10 October 1983 whereby the Republic supplied the Northern Ireland gas industry over a 22-year period.

This chapter has not discussed the economic debate within the poorest region of the United Kingdom. It is not that Ulster people are economic illiterates. It is simply that politics in the province is a matter of life and death. The population cannot control its own destiny. The people are a subordinate part of the United Kingdom, and another state makes irridentist claims on their territory. They resent being treated like a sideshow and the political troglodytes of the western world. Unless, and until, the other actors play their role to the full then peace will not descend.

One might argue that the current position is as it was in the seventeenth century ... only more extreme.

PART THREE

The Political Science of British Politics

13

Analysing British Politics

PATRICK DUNLEAVY

This chapter outlines some recent developments in the way academic political scientists have described and analysed British politics. Political science is an inherently multi-theoretical discipline. Almost invariably, on major questions there are a number of rival interpretations, framed from different perspectives and often appealing to different kinds of evidence. Some of these models are arguments specific to one area of the political process, while others are building blocks in much broader theories of society or the state.

To understand the current state of the discipline it is important to discuss both kinds of views. The main part of the chapter considers some major empirical topics in British politics, in each case looking at two or three alternative approaches that are important in current discussions. The topics covered are: four political input processes – electoral behaviour, party competition, the interest group process, and the mass media; five institutional areas – Parliament, Cabinet government, the civil service, quasi-governmental agencies, and local government; and one overarching problem – the post-war growth of government intervention. For each topic alternative views are presented in summary, followed by a brief historical account of how analysis of the subject has evolved in recent years.

The chapter's conclusions look at some recent patterns of political science explanation, each of them built up from a selection of the topic approaches. Four contemporary perspectives are explored: a revival of classical pluralism; the new right approach; Marxist theories; and the neo-pluralist view.

Topics

Topic 1: Electoral Behaviour

Key question: Why do people vote the way they do?

Party identification model. Voters find that deciding between party policies on their merits is too complex. They tend to short-circuit a closely rationalised decision by voting in line with people they know or meet in everyday life – parents, occupational class ('people like me'), workmates, neighbours, etc. Most voters develop long-run, emotive or habitual 'identifications' with one party by the time they are middle-aged. People tend to be pretty consistent in their voting over time, and only a minority 'float' between elections. But since 1974 previously strong social influences (particularly occupational class alignments) have decayed, and electoral volatility has increased.

Issue voting model. Individual voters act 'rationally' by choosing the party that offers them personally the greatest net benefits – that has policy positions closest to their individual views on those issues they see as salient. People are basically self-interested and economic issues are usually most important. Voters treat manifesto promises with considerable scepticism, so that the existing government's performance is an important influence on their decision. Citizens have shortish memories and a prosperous election year can make up for harder times in the past. Some voters who are consistently better off under one party than its rivals may develop a 'brand loyalty'; but this can always be reconsidered if it no longer works in the voter's interests.

Structural model. Individual voting decisions cannot be scientifically explained, only aggregate shifts of alignment in a mass electorate. Political alignments predominantly reflect people's social locations – their positions in a complex structure of inequalities and conflicts of interests. The UK social structure is dominated by social class cleavages, but has been changing quickly since 1945 because of the impacts of increased state intervention. The number of state employees has grown (to 30 per cent of the workforce), the state-dependent population has greatly increased, and government provides many consumption services (e.g. council housing, public transport, the NHS). Previous class-based political cleavages have increasingly been cross-cut by private-sector *vs* public-sector conflicts. Labour has gained some votes in the public-sector 'middle class', but lost more support among privately employed and home-owner manual workers.

* * * * * *

The party identification model was first defined in the early 1950s by researchers at the University of Michigan. It became accepted as the orthodoxy in Britain fairly quickly, largely on the basis of evidence from commercial opinion-polls. But the first in-depth political-science surveys of British electoral behaviour were only begun ten years later by David Butler and Donald Stokes. Their book *Political Change in Britain* (1969) provides the most comprehensive account of the party-identification view, and numerous extensions of the original model. They found that voters know relatively little about political issues, and to some extent may adjust their views on specific questions to fit in with their long-run choice of party. People may also go on voting for a party while disagreeing with many of its policies. Four-fifths have some kind of long-run party identification, mostly for the two major parties. Only 15–20 per cent are 'floating voters' at any one election. People can be influenced by the political climate when they first start voting. For example, the generation of voters who entered the electorate during the 1940s are overall somewhat more left-leaning than those who started voting during the Conservative-dominated 1950s.

The issue voting model was set out theoretically by the US economist Antony Downs in his path-breaking 1957 book, *An Economic Theory of Democracy*. But his 'rational man' model was not applied in empirical work in Britain until the early 1970s, when the growth of third-party support and increased electoral volatility raised questions about the party-identification orthodoxy. The 'partisan de-alignment' thesis developed by researchers at Essex University argues that party identifications are being 'hollowed out' by voters' loss of confidence in the traditional policy commitments of the major parties, especially Labour's links with the unions and advocacy of nationalisation (see Chapter 2). Essex researchers have not completely abandoned the party identification model, but argue that it now captures only a part of people's voting behaviour. Voters are increasingly reconsidering party loyalties in the light of specific issues most salient for them. Dissatisfaction with the polarised options offered by the two main parties has produced a sharp growth in third-party support and encouraged up to 40 per cent of people to switch their votes between elections. The only 'pure' statement of the issue voting model is provided by Hilda Himmelweit *et al.* in a 1981 study, *How Voters Decide*, which looked at how the same small group of (mainly 'middle class') voters behaved over the five elections from 1962 to 1975.

The structural model is the most recent and least well-known view, and is formulated largely from radical work on theories of the state and urban politics developed in West Germany and France. It criticises both party identification and issue voting accounts for treating British society as if it were static, and for ignoring the growth of state intervention as a possible cause of political change. It strongly suggests that the influence of union membership and housing tenure on voting cannot be seen as part of occupational class impacts on alignment. Instead, these are part of more general conflicts between the public and private sectors, and hence are sectoral in character. At present the structural model is fully set out only in rather difficult articles by Dunleavy (1979, 1980) but its broad implications are discussed in Chapter 2.

* * * * * *

Topic 2: Party Competition

Key question: Does competition between political parties provide a clear mechanism by which citizens' votes can control government policies?

Responsible party model. Party competition can guarantee effective citizen control over government only when voters are offered distinct options on most issues, when they can unambiguously ascribe responsibility for unpopular policy decisions to one party, and when the possibility of elite collusion is ruled out. These conditions are best achieved by two-party competition in an electoral system that normally delivers a secure majority to the election winner. It helps if both parties also have open membership policies, mass memberships and essentially democratic internal structures.

Parties win elections by persuading voters to see the issues their way, rather than simply accommodating themselves to voters' current preferences. Voters are motivated primarily by party identifications (see above), and activists and leaders primarily by ideological convictions.

Economic model. Party leaders are basically concerned with winning the next general election. Since voters choose parties from their issue positions (see above), the winning party will be that which more successfully changes its position to match the preferences of a majority of voters. Party competition tends to produce a convergence by both parties on the position of the most centrist (median) voter along the ideological spectrum. In a three-party race, the middle party is always squeezed by its more polarised neighbours moderating their positions. Citizen control over government policy is most complete when whichever party wins the elections will implement the same (median-voter) policies, and the parties are minimally differentiated from each other.

Adversary politics model. Although citizens vote on issues and party leaders are basically vote-maximisers as the economic model suggests, two-party convergence on the median voter does not occur in Britain because:

(i) Party activists (the mass membership, or its most active elements) control the parties' policy stances. They are motivated by a desire to see their party expressing their own ideological standpoint, and they care much less than leaders about winning elections. They use intra-party democracy to prevent leaders lapsing from an ideologically 'pure' line. Leaders need the support of a majority of their activists, and hence may be locked into artificially 'extremist' policy positions which they know to be unpopular with voters but cannot change for fear of putting their leadership of the party at risk.

(ii) The UK's plurality rule elections normally protect the two major parties from third party competition or new party entrants. Voters are continuously presented with a 'Hobsons's choice' between two equally polarised and unattractive manifestos. Dissatisfaction with this situation can be measured in lower turnout, increased electoral volatility and increasing cynicism about party politics.

*   *   *   *   *   *

The American economist Joseph Schumpeter founded the modern study of party competition in 1944, when he argued that liberal democracy is basically a system where two or more elite groups continuously compete against each other for the endorsement of a mass electorate. But controversy continues to surround the precise mechanism by which political parties are kept responsive to public opinion. The responsible party model was the orthodoxy of the 1950s, closely linked to party-identification accounts of voting behaviour. Party leaders were seen as strong actors, capable of remoulding voter opinion to some extent and well placed within their parties to command assured support. Robert McKenzie's *British Political Parties* (1954) argued that despite their apparent differences the internal organisation of the Conservative and Labour parties worked in very similar ways. The memberships acted as influential sounding-boards for the leadership to use in trying out new policy directions, but they did not directly control party strategy. Open membership policies and internal democracy served more to facilitate long-run shifts of party position in response to changes of public opinion, than to reduce the day-to-day control of policy by party leaderships. The responsible party model provided the standard defence of the two-party system as securing strong government and clear choice for voters, and it endured into the early 1970s with little effective challenge.

The economic model was formulated by Downs's *An Economic Theory of Democracy* (1957) along with the issue voting model of voting behaviour. Downs's prediction of two-party convergence was given some empirical support by changes in party competition during the late 1950s and early 1960s, when there was a consensus on growth-orientated economic policies, the development of the welfare state, decolonisation and the maintenance of a unilateral nuclear deterrent. The 1970 election was the high-water mark of party convergence. Since then the model in its original form has seemed decreasingly applicable to British experience.

The adversary politics model is a British variant of the economic model that was formulated by a number of authors in the mid-1970s, particularly responding to the Labour party's leftward shift in opposition up to 1974, to the confrontational quality of the February 1974 election, to the sharp decline in two-party voting at both elections in 1974, and to the Conservative Party's shift to the right from 1975 under Thatcher's leadership. A leading exponent in the late 1970s was S. E. Finer, whose book *The Changing British Party System, 1945–79* (1980) summarises trends in the fortunes of the major parties and the explanations that political practitioners have used to account for them. But the adversary politics model has gone out of fashion with conservatives such as Finer since 1979, perhaps because a Conservative government pursuing an uncompromisingly ideological line has appeared to attract considerable popular support. The adversary politics model is now rather closely associated with an SDP/Liberal position, particularly in its stress on the adverse policy implications of having parties with polarised policy positions alternating in power, reversing previous governments' legislation, and destabilising the management of the economy with rival economic doctrines.

A sceptical note about these alleged policy impacts is struck by Richard Rose in *Do Parties Make a Difference?* (1981). Looking at Britain's experience in the 1959–77 period he finds little evidence that shifts of party control at Westminster coincided with significant changes in economic or social policy indices. Continuity of trends and performance from one government to another seems to be the norm in those policy areas where quantitative measures are available.

* * * * * *

TOPIC 3: THE INTEREST GROUP PROCESS

Key question: Does the interest group process provide equal access to policy-making for groups in proportion to their numbers?

Pluralist group politics model. Interest groups are organised by many different sorts of people to promote almost any kind of collective aim – common interests, moral commitments, or minority social identities. Voluntary organisations such as interest groups depend on their members for money, unpaid help, and support. They are active on issues of which citizens have direct experience, so that members can more easily control group leaderships. Open membership policies and internally democratic organisation are the norm. Resources to form groups are widely available, and politicians, the media and the public see them as a legitimate form of political action. Group influence depends on the size of their membership, on the proportion of potential members who join, and on the strength of members' feelings. There is a continuum of progressively more costly actions that groups can take to demonstrate the intensity of their preferences – ranging from consulting with government agencies at the 'low-cost' end of the spectrum, to civil disobedience at the 'high-cost' end. Governments use information about group-members' depth of feeling on issues to 'weight' preferences, often moderating proposals with majority support but arousing fierce minority opposition. Because group memberships overlap, the interest-group process also allows an aggrieved minority to campaign to persuade members of the majority to change their minds. The most successful groups will be those that are involved at the earliest stages of policy initiation and have good consultation contacts with the civil service. Because it is easy to form interest groups and have some influence on policy the group universe is usually in flux, with changing alliances and patterns of influence over time. But a more stable configuration will exist in areas where two well-organised groups oppose each other on the same issue, creating a system of 'countervailing powers' (for example, the TUC and CBI). To some extent, therefore, very powerful groups tend to offset each others' influence.

Logic of collective action model. People only join an interest group if a rational calculation of costs and benefits shows that their personal welfare would be improved by becoming a member. Interest groups exist to promote 'public goods' – i.e. benefits that require collective action if they are to be produced, but that once provided accrue to everyone in a particular situation whether they joined the group and helped produce them or not. For example, securing a wage increase requires that a majority of workers in a factory join a union and perhaps take industrial action – but everyone there subsequently gets the wage increase, not just union members. Hence the key problem for all groups is to prevent 'free riding' – to stop people gaining the benefits of group action without incurring the costs of membership. Successful groups will be those that can develop 'selective incentives' (benefits available only to members). These may be positive incentives to make joining individually worthwhile (e.g. free legal representation for workers disciplined by management), or negative incentives to increase the costs of not joining (e.g., a 'closed shop' rule or informal social sanctions against strike-breakers). Where groups cannot offer such private goods to attract members they will commonly remain latent or badly organised. Groups seeking to organise large numbers of people have greater problems with free-riding than those with a small potential membership (where one person staying out of the group will be more noticeable). Groups will also be easier to organise on issues where one person's non-participation will adversely affect the likelihood of the group achieving its objectives. Variations in the level of group organisation reflect a whole range of extraneous factors, not just people's differing preference intensities. The group universe is marked by major long-run inequalities of influence and access. It tends to be stable, and 'countervailing powers' will be the exception rather than the norm.

Corporatist model. Major social groups tap strong solidaristic loyalties and have developed into large organisational blocs (e.g., the labour movement, trade associations) often with distinctive political leanings and linkages. These macro-groups are hierarchically organised with powerful peak associations, to co-ordinate numerous interest groups of the same kind (e.g. the TUC unifies the trade unions). Business and union peak associations (plus some professions in particular areas) have extensive control over resources that governments need. Hence they can bargain from a special position, achieving privileged or exclusive access, closed and permanent relations with state agencies, and creating a 'corporate bias' in policy-making which excludes lesser interest groups from influence. Major groups have become integrated into government (e.g. via quasi-governmental agencies) and group–government interdependencies are extensive. Corporatist interest bargaining is now crucial for economic policy, with the pluralist interest-group process influencing what gets done only on less important issues.

*   *   *   *   *   *

British political scientists discovered interest groups with a sudden flush of enthusiasm in the late 1950s. A whole crop of books listed examples of successful voluntary associations or recorded the details of particular campaigns. A stress on the importance of group politics in policy-making became a brand characteristic of pluralist behavioural studies reacting against the sterile institutional approaches of earlier periods. But after 1965 the interest group literature itself became frozen in aspic; case-studies multiplied but the framework for handling more information remained sketchy. A contemporary restatement of the pluralist approach is provided by J. Richardson and A. Jordan, *Governing under Pressure* (1979). Their thesis that the 'group process' is crucial in policy-making is weakened by a tendency to apply the 'group' label to everything that moves on the political scene (e.g. the Ford Motor Company is described as a 'group', and so are government agencies). But if everything is a group, the group process in turn becomes everything and nothing.

One opportunity for sharpening up and testing pluralist claims was provided by the American economist, Mancur Olson, whose 1965 book, *The Logic of Collective Action*, followed Downs in developing a 'rational man' picture of political life, but applied the technique to explaining why people join interest groups. He concluded that rational actors will rarely join groups unless they can provide specific membership benefits as well as public goods, and insisted that group-joining be interpreted as self-interested behaviour. This model provides a whole series of suggestive empirical questions that could be investigated. In practice, however, the Olson model has not yet been applied by any major study, and the more general picture of research into interest-group activity remains one of piecemeal, descriptive studies. For example, the only comprehensive data on how many groups exist in British political life (and how politically active they are) derive from a local study of Birmingham by Ken Newton (1976, chs 3 and 4).

Corporatism became a major topic for British political science under the 1974–9 Labour government, whose 'social contract' with the trade unions broke new ground in integrating group behaviour with government objectives. For example, the implementation of tax reductions was made conditional upon the unions delivering their members' agreement to abide by 'voluntary' norms limiting the scale of wage increases. Of course, corporatist practices had emerged much earlier in some areas, such as economic planning in the early 1960s. Indeed, Keith Middlemas's *Politics in Industrial Society* (1979) claims that this mode of operating the political system has been developing continuously since the inter-war period. Middlemas takes a conservative view of corporatism, seeing it as no more than a fairly weak form of tri-partite co-ordination between government, business and unions to try to secure greater growth. A summary of the more ambitious versions of 'corporate theory' and a discussion of liberal and radical modes of thinking about corporatism in a British context is given by Otto Newman's *The Challenge of Corporatism* (1981). All exponents of the model agree that the pluralist picture of a free-wheeling, open and egalitarian interest-group process is an anachronism. But they diverge sharply on whether the shift to a corporatist pattern is a benign or pernicious phenomenon, on whether corporatist relations are a stable and permanent solution for problems of economic management, and on the social group interests that are characteristically advanced or disadvantaged by the growth of corporatism.

*   *   *   *   *   *

TOPIC 4: THE MASS MEDIA

Key question: Do the mass media provide sufficient unbiased political information for citizens to make autonomous judgements on party alignments and policy questions?

Public opinion control model. Any system of mass media provision carries risks of biased news and political coverage. British practice combines two differing systems, which to a great extent act as a check upon each other's distortions and problems:

(i) Newspaper production is organised in line with the liberal theory of a free press. Papers are privately owned and run on partisan lines, with direct proprietorial control of editors and staff. But to make a profit owners must attract a paying readership, and hence deliver something that readers positively value. Free-market forces will produce newspapers espousing a diversity of views and appealing to different readerships. In normal times under a two-party system we should expect a rough partisan balance of newspaper readerships. Public opinion control via market forces remains important, despite the very striking concentration of newspaper ownership in Britain and despite the impact of advertising in blurring the relationship between papers' sales figures and their profitability. In addition, most people are well aware of newspapers' partisan biases and discount for them. People relatively rarely read papers primarily for their political coverage; many readers vote against their paper's political line; and increasingly a large majority of people rely on bi-partisan TV news for their knowledge of politics, largely because TV news is seen as more 'trustworthy' than newspaper coverage.

(ii) TV and radio news and current affairs are (in contrast to the press) organised in line with a public-service ethic. Here close regulation by quasi-autonomous state agencies (the BBC and the IBA) is used to enforce bi-partisanship in coverage, 'balanced' reporting and discussions, and equal access for 'mainstream' political views. British broadcasting practice has developed high standards of objectivity and journalistic integrity while remaining remarkably sensitive to the public's reactions and concerns.

Overall, the UK mass media convey a great deal of political information at low cost to citizens, with progressively greater expertise and professionalism, providing multiple outlets for publicising issues under conditions of extensive control of news production by public opinion.

Dominant values model. The production of 'news' is a social process in which a great deal of discretion rests with journalists and media managers. News output systematically reflects a set of 'dominant values' influenced by the major established institutions: business, media corporations, the major parties, high-status social groups, the Royal family. Private ownership of the press promotes capitalist values out of all proportion to the numbers of owners of capital, and allows the rich to buy some political power. Advertising values have undermined any direct connection between mass appeal and papers' viability. The buying-power of a paper's readership is crucial, and their numbers not very relevant – hence the phenomenon of multiple 'quality-press' titles for high-status groups and decreasing choice for working-class readers. Private ownership of the press also structures journalistic values to the right. And the pooling of common values across the press and broadcasting pulls supposedly 'neutral' TV news into the same configuration. For example, press and TV both display the same obsession with industrial disputes and continuously present their coverage with a strong anti-union slant. Since broadcast agencies are ultimately dependent on government for funding (BBC) or for franchises (ITV), and since they are immediately controlled by elite boards of governors, there is a great deal of censorship practised on topics where there is an elite consensus – e.g. on the dangers of nuclear war in the 1960s, or on the reality of the Ulster situation now. There are no effective channels by which mass media coverage can be democratically controlled or influenced by an autonomous public opinion in contemporary Britain. By controlling news production the mass media help to manufacture a 'public opinion' that legitimates their own practices.

*   *   *   *   *   *

Political scientists in Britain have tended to leave the job of researching the mass media to sociologists until quite recently, partly because their techniques were not particularly appropriate to studying the broadcast media, and partly because the topic was seen as not especially salient or controversial by mainstream approaches. The public opinion control model was well developed by the 1950s in relation to the press, while radio broadcasting was treated as *sui generis*, something to be explained in terms of the particular history of the BBC as a broadcasting institution. The advent of television sparked a keen interest in the medium's alleged or expected impacts on political life in the period from 1959–64, particularly in relation to election campaigns. The apparent promise of this research largely petered out, however, as study after study found little evidence of distinctive impacts from television on political perceptions or behaviour. By the early 1970s, as the prospect of establishing any dramatic behavioural implications from TV's political coverage receded, the public opinion control model was simply extended to include the broadcast media, and a strong argument was added about the partisan press and bi-partisan TV news as a system of 'countervailing powers'.

A major shift of focus took place in media-studies during the early 1970s, however. Research started to focus less on the impacts of media coverage, and more on its production. A key stimulus was the pioneer work of the Glasgow University Media Group in undertaking the first comprehensive documentation and analysis of TV news output, published in a series of *Bad News* titles since 1976. Their claim, backed by systematic research, that TV news output shows a characteristic anti-union, pro-establishment and anti-left-wing bias has considerably revived the dominant values model of the mass media. Previously espoused by radical critics in a largely unresearched and assertive way, the dominant values model had always been plausible if applied to the press alone, but not clearly applicable to a complete mass media system where broadcasting played an increasingly central role. By attacking the linchpin of the pluralist defence of the media, the *Bad News* studies contributed to rehabilitating radical critiques across the board. J. Curran and J. Seaton's *Power Without Responsibility* (1981) sums up the dominant values model in its current form.

* * * * * *

TOPIC 5: PARLIAMENT

Key question: How important or residual is Parliament as an influence on policy-making?

Legal ('Golden Age') model. The legal supremacy of statute law – the ability of parliamentary legislation to rewrite previous statutes and to override common law, crown prerogative or constitutional conventions – is matched by the practical importance of the Commons in making policy decisions and scrutinising the administration. Parliament retains the *potential* to act indicated by the 'golden age' of Commons power between 1832 and 1868 – when it could remove governments between elections, enforce sanctions on individual unpopular ministers, consider government legislation as separate measures decided on their specific merits, and initiate some significant legislation itself. The fact that these powers have very rarely been activated in this century reflects continuous majority support for the government within the Commons, but does not demonstrate that any major parliamentary powers have lapsed.

Westminster model. Parliament's major functions are to provide a forum for debate between the government and the opposition, publicise the executive's proposals, subject them to rigorous criticism and scrutiny, and allow the party battle to be kept before the public and the media. Parliament is run on party lines, with strong discipline on individual MPs via the whipping system. The Commons' standing orders allow a government with a majority to control debate and enforce a strict legislative timetable, while excluding private members' bills with financial implications. Consequently the government is the prime initiator of legislation and its success rate is virtually complete (except in the case of minority governments). Only the internal debates within the majority parliamentary party will have any effective influence on legislation, but the Opposition can use delaying procedural devices to indicate very intense hostility to some bills. Floor debates and questions to ministers are key Commons activities, but the committee stage of legislation normally makes little impact. Party dominance of the Commons means that opportunities for detailed scrutiny of administration or finances have tended to be converted into forums for mainstream party controversy, further enhancing the executive's predominance and the Commons' removal from involvement in effective policy-making.

Transformative model. Three key changes since the 1960s have indicated a resurgence of Parliament's corporate ability to act as a check on the executive and an independent force in policy-making.

(i) The 'Parliamentary rule' whereby a government defeat on major legislation should precipitate an election has greatly relaxed in the 1970s and 1980s. MPs on the majority side are less willing to accept blanket party discipline, increasing the incidence of overt dissent on particular bills and even causing a few government defeats in floor debates and standing committees.

(ii) The political parties have increasingly withdrawn from a range of 'social morality' issues. Private members' legislation on issues such as capital punishment, divorce reform, abortion, homosexual-law reform and the censorship or liberalisation of pornography have become increasingly important. Over quite a wide range of 'conscience' issues, therefore, the collective policy views of individual MPs have become decisive.

(iii) Demands for increased facilities and specialisation among MPs have increased in line with the development of select committee scrutiny over executive policy-making which does not require legislation. In 1979 a major reform introduced the first comprehensive apparatus for such Commons' scrutiny, with committees organised to match the structure of government departments.

* * * * * *

The legal or 'golden age' model of parliament is not put forward by any major group of political scientists. Although some institutional or public administration writers spend a great deal of time advocating 'reforms' designed to make the Commons' role approximate to the model, no one seriously claims that parliament actually operates on these lines today. But the model is still important empirically because it defines the constitutional or legal fictions on which the courts operate. For example, objectors to new motorways who tried to obtain the right to question the need for such roads at motorway inquiries, have been prevented from doing so because the courts consider that such 'policy questions' have to be decided in Parliament – even though the Commons has never debated or approved the Department of Transport's motorway strategy since it began operating. The legal model is still the basic account given by constitutional-law textbooks and British public law has not yet evolved any effective way of recognising the reality of a party-dominated legislature.

The 'Westminster' model is a hybrid rationalisation of British practice as it has become established since the late nineteenth century – when Commons procedures were transformed by the growth of mass parties establishing strong party discipline over MPs, and by changes in standing-orders to combat the obstructionist tactics of Irish Nationalist MPs trying to bring Commons' business to a halt. This model has been the orthodoxy among institutional and pluralist writers for many decades and has changed very little over the post-war period. It characteristically portrays a party-structured Commons as the central element in a political system combining an unwritten constitution and strong two-party competition. Parliament is seen as a crucial forum for defining the informal checks and balances and self-restraint among political leaders that are needed to make the British system work in a stable fashion. Gilmour (1978, p. 226) is by no means alone in describing the Westminster model as 'the highest form of political development' (a conviction that underlay the numerous unsuccessful attempts to export the model to UK colonies achieving independence in the post-war period).

The 'transformative' model of Parliament's operations is much more recent, and represents a belated (if still small-scale) recognition that the changes detected in voting behaviour and party competition outside Parliament are likely to be accompanied sooner or later by changes in its internal operations. Phillip Norton's work (1975, 1980) on intra-party dissent at Westminster, together with work on earlier periods by Finer *et al.* (1961) has been crucial in providing for the first time systematic evidence of the influence of MPs on policy-making. The central implications of Norton's findings are presented in a very accessible manner in a short article by Schwartz (1979), and in a lengthier and rather more difficult way by Norton's book, *The Commons in Perspective* (1981). Parliament's role on conscience issues and the operations of the select-committee system remain unsatisfactorily described outside the research literature, partly because the committees are rather new, while private members' bills have been underplayed in mainstream accounts. Most private members' bills, of course, fail to get passed, normally because they are obstructed enough by other MPs to fall foul of time constraints. Writers who employ the Westminster model commonly contrast the great volume of government legislation with the pitiful trickle of successful private members' bills. But quite apart from the enormous impact of some private members' bills on social life (such as the 1967 Abortion Act), the transformative model insists that it is simply inappropriate to use the amount of legislation passed as an index of Parliamentary 'power' in this aspect of its work. In a genuinely 'transformative' legislature Parliamentary power would be indicated both by the passage and by the failure of bills in response to the balance of opinions within the legislative body: there is no presumption (as in the Westminster model) that the locus of power rests with those who get things done.

*   *   *   *   *   *

Topic 6: Cabinet Government

Key question: Which actors or institutions in the British central executive fix the overall direction and co-ordination of government policies?

Cabinet government view. The Cabinet remains the key policy co-ordinating institution in British central government. In particular it acts as a constraint on Prime Ministerial power because of the need to accord some representation to different party factions and potential rivals for the party leadership. The PM cannot 'rig' the whole Cabinet committee structure nor fully offset the weight of departmental resources controlled by other ministers. Similarly the 'collective responsibility' of Cabinet members extends beyond simple ministerial solidarity to include the right for a significant minority of Cabinet to debate any key issue before it is finalised as government policy. Cabinet government is desirable because it introduces a measure of collegial decision-making into government, encouraging a more balanced and restrained judgement than unitary decision-making by one chief executive. It also multiplies the number of political perspectives and departmental interests that are taken into account in the making of important decisions.

Prime Ministerial government thesis. British Premiers occupy a dominating role at the core of the executive machinery. Their control over Cabinet personnel and the allocation of posts, their ability to tailor the Cabinet committee system to their purposes, their control over agendas, and their involvement in key issues – all place them in a position of great scope for personal influence. The growth of the Cabinet Secretariat, the Central Policy Review Staff (CPRS) in the 1970s, and the PM's staff since, have combated the previous lack of departmental back-up. Modern Cabinet conventions and practices have hollowed out the independent capabilities of the Cabinet, so that except in periods of extraordinary personal or political weakness a PM can be assured of a secure majority for her or his policies. Trends towards a strong role for party leaders have brought changes elsewhere in the political system that further enhance the Premier's position.

Segmented decision-making model. The PM *vs* Cabinet government debate is misleading, because instances of direct conflict between the two are rather rare. The Premier is primarily concerned with policy in three key issues; economic policy, foreign affairs, and major defence decisions. Over most areas of domestic policy, however, Prime Ministerial involvement is very sporadic, and the final resolution of controversies and co-ordination of policies remains with the Cabinet as a whole. PM and Cabinet co-ordination primarily operate in separate spheres of decision-making.

Bureaucratic co-ordination model. Co-ordination of government policy rests chiefly with the centralising institutions of the civil service – official committees paralleling Cabinet committees, the Treasury and Cabinet Secretariat, weekly meetings of permanent secretaries, developed Whitehall information networks, etc. The PM plays a central arbitrating role in this machinery, resolving inter-departmental disputes, and providing a central point of policy definition to which civil servants can appeal in bypassing troublesome Cabinet ministers. The PM's 'presidential' role is fostered by Whitehall in order to undermine the individual responsibility of ministers – producing a standardised policy line across all departments that is far more susceptible to civil-service pressure than a variety of individual ministerial policy positions.

*   *   *   *   *   *

The dispute about the relative power of Cabinet and Prime Minister in Britain is one of the great 'chestnuts of the constitution' (Heclo and Wildavsky, 1974, p. 341). Endlessly debated in the daily papers and first-year-undergraduate essays, the controversy has been locked in a time-warp for at least twenty-five years so far as academic political science is concerned. Since even the most basic information about contemporary Cabinet operations – such as the number of Cabinet committees – is unavailable, the scope for professional debate about the issue has been extremely small. Sources of evidence remain confined to the memoirs or anecdotes of former ministers, plus a small number of more verified accounts of contemporary decisions uncovered by political journalists. The growth of unattributable leaking of Cabinet proceedings by dissatisfied members (and by the PM's own staffs on his or her behalf) has slightly increased the volume of information available. But none of this evidence can easily be presented as systematic or comprehensive, and the reliability of almost all versions of events is contested by one side or another. 'Cabinet studies' of a more systematic kind thus usually turn out to be analyses only of the most directly observable phenomena (such as how long ministers stay in one job before moving on).

Cabinet government is the oldest model, reaching its peak of influence in Ivor Jennings's massive historical account published in 1949. The Prime Ministerial power thesis was set out piecemeal at various points in this century, but perhaps in its most concentrated fashion in the late 1950s, culminating in John Mackintosh's *The British Cabinet*, first published in 1962. Further work in the late 1970s began to explore alternatives to the sterile polarised alternatives of the 1950s and 1960s debates. James Callaghan's decision to launch a 'Great Debate' on education in 1977, by making the first Prime Ministerial speech about the issue in forty years, highlighted the extent to which Premiers never get involved in large areas of domestic policy-making. The segmented decision model is widely accepted as oral folklore among political scientists, but has yet to be given systematic statement. The bureaucratic co-ordination model is a relatively recent spin-off from the long-running left-wing view of the civil service as a conservative power-bloc obstructing attempts at radical change (see section below on the civil service). Its most developed statement is Brian Sedgemore's *The Secret Constitution* (1980) where it is used to explain the limited ability of Tony Benn as Energy Secretary to impose his own priorities on his department.

* * * * * *

TOPIC 7: THE CIVIL SERVICE

Key question: Does the civil service role in government decision-making give any particular slant to the kinds of policies adopted?

Public administration view. The British civil service is a unique and successful solution to the problem of how lay politicians can control highly complex and specialised areas of policy-making. A layer of 'generalist' administrators are interposed between specialist or technical staffs and ministers. Their function is to pre-process information and advice so that ministers can make informed decisions between options; to co-ordinate policy and manage relations with the public and Parliament; and to provide an important element of continuity between different administrations by virtue of their perman-ence and impartiality. Limited movement between depart-ments, and recruitment to a class of positions on the basis of general educational qualifications, both foster non-sectarian, public-interest-orientated values. Civil service anonymity preserves their impartiality. Lifelong career paths within the service foster its independence from outside influences, and extensively socialise those who rise to senior ranks into its professional values and methods of working.

Power-bloc model. The civil service is an important conservative veto group in UK politics. It is predominantly (and increas-ingly since the late 1960s) recruited from Oxbridge, with disproportionate numbers of upper-middle-class and public school entrants, a social profile that becomes even more skewed at senior levels. It is an immensely secretive group, with a strong internal value consensus of a centrist conservative kind, highly developed methods of defending its own interests, and excellent Whitehall information networks running across departmental boundaries. Civil servants use their control of administration and expertise to 'shut out' radical ministers from influencing policy in ways unfavourable for their longer-term plans, and to damp down changes in final policy that result from electoral victories for either party. Since Conservative governments typically have less wish to change the *status quo*, however, civil service obstruction and policy influence is clearly most adverse for Labour governments.

Bureaucratic over-supply model. Bureaucracies differ from firms because instead of supplying separate units of output to customers at a unit-price, they supply the legislature with a whole block of output in return for a certain overall level of budget. Thus only those inside the bureaucracy know what an agency's cost curves are really like. Bureaucrats exploit this monopoly of information about their operations to advance their personal self-interest as much as possible. All civil servants are better off in periods when the budget is growing – since demand for their services will increase, the opportunities for promotion expand, and 'fringe benefits' can be hidden away in annual budget rises. Agencies will therefore continuously seek to expand their budgets, even when the social value of extra public services they provide is less than the costs of producing these services. This over-supply of government outputs will be limited only by the need for agencies not to actively reduce social welfare. But a government bureau may still supply up to twice the socially optimal level of outputs – (the level that would be supplied by private firms under market competition).

* * * * * *

The public administration view is the conventional wisdom on the civil service. Although the modern civil service was only fully defined in the early years of this century, this sort of analysis has a longer background of development, crystallising the key features of an ideal of administration under representative government described by John Stuart Mill, for example. The public administration view dominates textbook discussions of the civil service, as well as being strongly endorsed by civil servants themselves and by most senior party politicians of the post-war period. Its survival as the orthodox account, despite criticisms of Whitehall practices made by the Fulton Report (1968) and the English Committee (1977), is a tribute to the civil service's ability to command the loyalties of those who study it or work with it in government. The main areas of controversy within the public administration view centre on whether there is a case for having greater specialised recruitment and training for senior managerial positions, rather than relying primarily on 'generalists' trained 'on the job' as at present; whether the civil service is too orientated towards servicing ministers' political and policy requirements, and insufficiently concerned with the efficient management of the public sector as a whole; and whether or not there is a case for reducing the pervasive secrecy of British government's operations. Brown and Steel (1979) provide a typically uncritical statement of the orthodoxy.

The power-bloc model also has a long history, having been powerfully expressed by Harold Laski in the inter-war period (as part of a wider attack on the anti-Labour bias he perceived in British constitutional arrangements at this time). Following the generally co-operative relations between the 1945–51 Labour government and Whitehall, the view became less fashionable, especially since the 1950s and early 1960s seemed to indicate a slow but persistent opening-up of civil service ranks to non-Oxbridge candidates. Labour's markedly less successful attempts to promote changes in the 1964–70 period, plus the progressive re-establishment of Oxbridge predomin- ance and the non-implementation of the Fulton report's reform proposals, all prompted a rehabilitation of the power- bloc model. Ralph Miliband's 1969 book, *The State in Capitalist Society*, gave it central prominence in an essentially sociologi- cal argument that the class origins and socialisation of people in senior civil service positions play a key role in undermining attempts by working-class parties to alter the fundamental operations of capitalist societies. Critical revelations about civil service manipulations made by Labour ex-ministers, notably in Richard Crossman's diaries (1979), provided better evidence for the model than hitherto, a pattern repeated after the demise of the 1974–9 Labour government. But the standard of debate between exponents of the orthodox view and left critics like Miliband and Crossman has remained generally very poor, primarily because both sides rely almost solely on competitively rehearsing practitioner opinions and assorted anecdotes. No systematic research that could offer compelling support for either position has yet been undertaken in the contemporary period, largely because access to documents or even to informed personnel is unlikely to be feasible under existing arrangements. Exponents of the power-bloc model claim, however, that the overwhelming mass of historical evidence accumulating for periods outside the 'closed' thirty-year period is favourable for their case – although again a systematic reanalysis using this data has not yet been attempted. A very readable version of the debate between the power-bloc model and mainstream views is provided by Crowther-Hunt and Kellner's *The Civil Servants* (1980).

The bureaucratic over-supply model is the most recent and the most theoretically based account of civil-service operations. Its key source is the economic (or 'rational man') model of bureaucracy developed in the early 1970s by the American economist William Niskanen, and set out briefly in his book *Bureaucracy: Servant or Master?* (1973) and quite clearly in P. M. Jackson's *The Political Economy of Bureaucracy* (1982, ch. 5). While other rational-man models have been taken up by a wide range of writers (for example, in analysing voting behaviour), the economic model of bureaucracy has been promoted largely by exponents of 'new right' ideologies, such as the Institute of Economic Affairs in Britain. Very little empirical work has been done on the model, although its exponents can call on a rather small literature dealing with instances of 'waste' in the civil service for a store of anecdotes to set against the public-administration orthodoxy: for example, Leslie Chapman's book, *Your Disobedient Servant* (1979) documents instances of apparently unnecessary spending. But the bureaucratic over-supply model only became widely known in the early 1980s as Thatcher's government embarked upon a prolonged battle with Whitehall ministries in an attempt to cut back public-spending programmes

* * * * * *

Topic 8: Quasi-governmental Agencies

Key question: Why have an increasing number of executive functions at national or regional level been administered by quasi-governmental agencies?

Administrative accountability model
This is the 'mainstream' public administration view and has two elements.

(i) Public corporations are far and away the most important governmental bodies. They differ from central departments in being only indirectly answerable to Parliament via their supervising ministry, and in retaining day-to-day control of their own commercial operations. The appointment of corporation boards by ministers, plus control of investment programmes, a veto over pricing decisions, and government-set financial targets, suffice to maintain accountability. Operating in commercial markets keeps corporations efficient and responsive to consumer demands.

(ii) A wide range of one-off governmental bodies 'tailor-made' for particular tasks have also been set up. These are typically controlled by appointments to their executive committees and via funding – but few generalisations can be made. They exist for diverse purposes – e.g., to distance government from detailed policy implementation, to create an intermediary body in sensitive policy areas, to involve professions or major interest groups in policy implementation, to provide more flexible forms of administration, or simply to 'massage' civil-service manpower figures downwards.

Inter-governmental model. Policy-making in advanced industrial states has become increasingly large-scale and complex. The growth of quasi-governmental agencies (QGAs) helps to combat decision difficulties by:

(i) 'Factorising' administration so that different decision functions are allocated to different agencies. For example, in the civilian nuclear-power policy area one agency develops reactor technology, another acts as contractor in building nuclear-power stations, yet another places orders for new reactors, and still others supply nuclear fuels, inspect reactor safety and set permissible radiation levels for reactor operation. Complex policy-making is undertaken via interactions between separate agencies, each with a specific role and certain resources but also dependent on the others' co-operation. Decisions emerge from a structure of inter-governmental relations, rather than being centrally made by some unattainable process of perfectly rational policy-planning.

(ii) Allowing the extensive professionalisation of policy-making. QGAs controlled by professional staffs are set up to handle single-issue policy areas where the decisions involved are too technical to be determined by a conventional political process (e.g., civilian nuclear energy) or where personal services tailored to individual needs are required (e.g., health-care provision). Here a generalist civil service controlled by elected politicians controls only overall funding while detailed policy implementation rests with professionals. The public interest is safeguarded because no one elite controls more than a single policy area, and because professional staffs regulate their actions in line with an internal ethic of respect for the public interest (as a quid pro quo for their greater work autonomy).

The dual state thesis. The state apparatus in capitalist societies is pressured in contradictory ways, both to foster business profitability (the accumulation function), and to maintain social stability and an impression of impartiality in its dealings with different social classes (the legitimation function). These pressures are managed primarily by allocating different functions to different state institutions. Local government and politically visible areas of central government are used for consumption issues that are not of fundamental importance for owners of capital. On these issues it does not matter as much if radical or working-class parties gain control of the policy area via electoral successes. But more fundamental policy areas of direct concern for business must be insulated from this risk. Setting up national or regional quasi-governmental agencies (QGAs) removes key production issues from direct political control, makes these issues difficult for the public to organise around, and allows business (and less often the trade unions) to be integrated into a close pattern of corporatist relations (see above). QGAs plus corporatist policy-making are able to generate inititatives and undertake planning that the conventional civil service (or any other line bureaucracy) would find very difficult to cope with. QGAs are consequently often used in policy areas (such as nuclear energy) where the state is engaged in promoting its own new solutions to social problems.

* * * * * *

Most textbooks on British politics contrive to suggest that the civil service plays the predominant role in administering government policies in the UK. The public administration literature in particular has gone on concentrating the vast bulk of its attention on central government departments, portraying them as 'line' bureaucracies where there is a clear channel of authority down a single hierarchic organisation, from ministers and permanent secretaries at the top of the pyramid to staff at the grass roots whose job is to implement policy on the ground. The main exceptions to this pattern have obviously been the local government services – which are separately explained in the local democracy model (see below) – and the nationalised industries. Public corporations are the only kind of quasi-governmental agency that have been analysed at all in the post-war conventional literature. Even then, most attention has focused on the now rather dated conception of the public corporation defined by Herbert Morrison in the 1940s, rather than on the actual working practices of state industries and firms and their increasingly complex relations with central departments. In the late 1970s the existence of a variety of quasi-governmental agencies (misleadingly described as Quangos) became a source of political controversy due to complaints about the scope of ministerial patronage made by Tory backbenchers. At the same time, an extensive American literature on the 'contract state' and 'government by other means' began to be noticed in the academic literature. A. Barker (ed.), *Quangos in Britain* (1982) sums up the mainstream reaction to these stimuli. Some preliminary mapping of QGAs has been undertaken plus case studies of the policy roles. But progress to date on systematising this knowledge has been slow.

But the explosion of QGAs has been seen in more dramatic terms by some neo-pluralist writers, such as Charles Lindblom in his major work, *Politics and Markets* (1977). He sees the organisational fragmentation of policy-making as a major response to the sheer difficulties of trying to undertake integrated or comprehensive planning of the increasingly difficult decisions handled by advanced industrialised states. Various political scientists have pointed out that in the UK at present central government has devolved policy implementation either to QGAs or to local authorities. Civil service manpower is still quite large at 11 per cent of all public sector workers, but over two-thirds of these people work in just three policy areas – defence establishments (excluding the armed forces); tax collection; and the payment of state benefits or pensions. There are of course still a few remnants of 'line administration' in central departments, such as the prison service. But on the whole, if we take out the three special areas mentioned above (where there are good strategic or financial-control reasons for central government to hang on to policy implementation), the picture is now one of 'non-executant central departments'. Whitehall departments draw up legislation, advise ministers, and monitor other agencies' work, moving money around between QGAs and local government in response to changing needs and priorities, but always at several stages remove from operational administration. Inter-governmental relations hence become of critical significance for policy development. And while the growth of QGAs has allowed the civil service to continue operating in its amateur–generalist tradition by devolving tasks requiring professional and technical expertise to other bodies, there has been a consequent diffusion of power out of the Whitehall bureaucracy and into the hands of specialised policy elites in each issue area. Although this view is now quite widely held and discussed, it has not yet been summarily described in direct relation to UK government.

The dual state thesis offers a general theory of the distribution of government functions between different sorts of institutions, rather than a specific account of QGAs alone. The thesis is a reaction against the failure of radical accounts in the late 1970s to offer an account of state operations that matched the complexity of the internal differences and conflicts between diverse government agencies. Its argument, as expressed by Cawson and Saunders (1983), draws heavily on the corporatist literature. Empirical work applying the model to particular QGAs or policy areas in still sparse but this approach seems to provide a promising basis for future research.

* * * * *

Topic 9: Local Government and Urban Politics

Key question: What do local political institutions contribute to the system of representative government in Britain?

Local democracy model. Elected local authorities add a valuable extra dimension to representative government. Citizens gain a useful channel for complaints via their local councillors, and party competition in local elections ensures that they can control overall local authority policy-making in the same way as at national elections. Decentralisation of responsibilities to local government allows variations in policy preferences across communities to find expression within a framework set by national majority rule. It helps prevent the overloading of central government and makes constructive use of local knowledge and expertise. Council politics provides a valuable training ground for people subsequently recruited into national politics, and acts as an annual organising focus in the work of local party branches. It also helps educate citizens in general in the detailed workings of democracy applied to immediately visible issues. Control of many councils by the party in opposition at Westminster helps stabilise policy change on locally administered policy issues, dispersing considerable influence to opponents of government policy changes and often delaying or frustrating implementation of Westminster initiatives. These constraints typically force central government to try and work in partnership with local authorities, rather than simply imposing Westminster policies via new legislation which councils have to accept. 'Partnership' relations produce many points of access to urban policy-making, both nationally and locally.

Insulated local elites view. Local party competition does not help to create significant citizen control over local policy-making because:

(i) Citizens vote on national lines (for or against the Westminster government) at local elections. A local party with unpopular policies may be returned because of its national standing, while a council implementing popular local policies may none the less be thrown out because of their party's poor national standing. Local elites know that this occurs and hence have little incentive to anticipate citizens' reactions to their local policy decisions. Even if they do read local election results as signals of local policies' popularity the result will be irrational, since up to 90 per cent of the swing at local elections is accounted for by national factors.

(ii) Because major party support draws on different social groups, and these groups live in different areas, a nationally balanced two-party system may co-exist with extensive one-party control at a local level. At the most important tier of local government a large majority of British citizens live in 'safe' areas for one party, where even violent swings of party support will never produce changes of council control.

(iii) Local government administration is carried out by professional staffs who orientate themselves more towards their national-level associations and journals than to local needs or ideas.

Local state model. The apparent independence of local authorities is illusory. Councils are integrated into the basic operations of the capitalist state, so that their policies can never diverge radically from central state requirements. Local authorities are allowed to administer only policies concerned with consumption issues (e.g., education, public transport or council housing). Policies that involve business interests more directly are concentrated in central government or quasi-governmental agencies. 'Local democracy' absorbs citizen protests in less important issues and provides an ideological 'front organisation' which helps to disguise the real nature of the capitalist state.

* * * * *

Local politics in Britain remained very much a cinderella area of political science until the 1970s. There was no counterpart to the vigorous American community-power debate of the 1950s and 1960s. The British conventional wisdom was that UK local authorities were much less exposed to external 'community' influences than US city governments. Thus institutional or public-administration accounts of council politics could capture the more limited local political scene in this country. The first large-scale research investigations of local policy-making began in the early 1970s, when a stress on local party competition and on 'partnership' patterns of central–local relations were added as new elements in the orthodox view espousing the value of local democracy. Studies such as Ken

Newton's *Second City Politics* (1976) noted the problems caused by national voting in local elections, but concluded that since local political elites behave as if they will be held electorally responsible for their policies, party competition still provides a genuine control over their activities. In addition Newton argued that there is a vigorous local interest-group process which has been underestimated in the earlier literature.

In the later 1970s, however, urban politics were transformed into one of the most fast-changing areas of political science, partly by a new range of radical political-economy approaches imported from France and partly by a rapid growth of urban-policy studies exploiting the easier access for systematic research available at the local level. The policy studies have typically discovered a rather narrow process of policy-making, with the key linkages being those between local elites and central government, rather than local electoral competition. The view of local elites as being insulated from citizen control by nationally orientated voting, one-party control and the professionalism of council staffs has been most clearly set out in Dunleavy, *Urban Political Analysis* (1980, especially ch. 5).

Radical approaches have diversified into a number of variants, including approaches focusing on consumption services whether or not they are administered by local government, applications of the dual state thesis (see above) to local politics, and the local state model set out here. First expressed by Cockburn's *The Local State* (1977), the model views local authorities as no more than extensions of a single, ultimately repressive state apparatus. Its popularity has receded in the 1980s when left-wing Labour councils have come to be seen even on the Marxist left as a valuable institutional foothold for the defence of working-class interests.

* * * * * *

Topic 10: The Growth of Government

Key question: Why did the scope of government activities grow rapidly up to the mid-1970s and slow down thereafter?

Pluralist view. The growth of government activities up to the mid-1970s reflects:

(i) the progressive extension of full 'citizenship' in social and economic terms to all sections of the community, responding, after a lag, to the earlier extension of the franchise. Public opinion pressures expressed in party competition underlay virtually all additions to the welfare state and the growth of a mixed economy. These changes have substantially equalised social conditions, redistributing income towards the weakest social groups.

(ii) changes in the demographic composition of the population: e.g., increased numbers of schoolchildren and later of elderly people. Once a welfare-state framework was established in the 1940s, these demographic shifts triggered rapid growth first in education, and later in the health and personal social services. Conceivably, different demographic trends in the 1980s and 1990s will produce lower government activity even if the current policy framework is not changed.

(iii) the reduced fiscal pressures on government in a period of economic growth.

The new right model. The growth of state intervention in the economy and other social arrangements indicates a chronic pathology in a pluralist political system. Party competitive elections contribute to this instability by bidding up voters' expectations to unrealistic levels, and by encouraging manipulations of economic policy for party advantage in election years. The interest group process may lead to log-rolling, where packages of policies appealing to different intense minorities are put together and will command a majority of votes, even if each policy considered on its own would be rejected by voters. Bureaucratic pressures for budget maximisation similarly push up the level of state activity. State growth has primarily benefited the public sector middle class, rather than achieved any real redistribution of income. Finally, the inefficiencies of public sector provision mean that initially quite small interventions may trigger progressively greater state involvement, to try and combat the market with distortions and mis-allocations of resources triggered by government-absorbing functions best left to market processes.

Neo-Marxist view. The growth of state intervention was a

response to the historically specific conditions of post-war economic growth. Keynesian crisis-management strategies seemed to offer a way of combining interventions favourable to business interests with measures to promote social stability and a blurring of social class divisions. Many costs of production were transferred from businesses directly to state expenditures; increases in the 'social wage' helped to keep down pressure for wage increases; and business activities became progressively more underwritten by state subsidies, initially in high-technology areas but later in a quite general way. State growth is politically self-stabilising, however, as public/private sector conflicts fragment social class alignments. It also generates fiscal contradictions as the tax burdens imposed by rising state expenditures begin to restrict private profit accumulation and demand for marketed goods and services. Since the mid-1970s both these pressures have held back the further growth of public expenditure, with a consequent worsening of the legitimation problems as welfare services are eroded.

*   *   *   *   *

For pluralist writers changes in the post-war role of the state in Britain have been seen as the culmination of a much longer process of social reform originating in the nineteenth century with early extensions of the franchise, and continuing into the mid-twentieth century as the social implications of universal suffrage finally fed through into the creation of the welfare state. But for a long time the new scale of government activity was masked from a political science viewpoint by other post-war changes. The run-down of Britain's military capabilities from great-power status to that of a large European nation state, combined with de-colonisation throughout the 1950s, created an immense amount of slack in the political system. Overall public-expenditure levels remained static during that decade, while Whitehall offices and seats at the Cabinet table were vacated in line with the decline of the British Empire. It was only during the 1960s and early 1970s that the pressure of possible 'governmental overload' began to be detected both in declining levels of policy co-ordination and in the traumatic attempts to screen out less important issues from Cabinet.

These were largely unsuccessful in the super-ministry reform period culminating in the Heath government's shake-ups of Whitehall, local government and the NHS; but much more permanent changes were made via the growth of a sizeable quasi-governmental sector below Whitehall departments. D. Ashford, *Policy and Politics in Britain* (1981) suggests that the growth of government can be understood in terms of two types of consensus – among voters in general and among political and other elites – and the ways in which they have evolved first in response to post-war affluence and latterly to the increased difficulties of economic management in an age of chronic stagflation or recession.

The new right take a robustly critical view. For them governmental growth is a serious pathology threatening not only fiscal stability but freedom itself. Although this view was articulated early in the post-war period by Hayek and others, it remained very much a normative position rather than a detailed empirical analysis of actual trends. The growth of rational-man models of politics attracted economists into the field during the late 1960s and 1970s and many of their accounts of elections, interest groups and bureaucracies focus on the conditions under which policy stability or instability will be created. Again, Tullock's *The Vote Motive* (1975) provides a useful survey of this wide-ranging view which has leapt to prominence since its adoption as the working philosophy of the new Tory right wing.

Neo-marxist accounts of increased state intervention form part of a wider rethink of Marxist political science as a whole which took place during the mid 1970s, largely in response to innovations in the French, German and American literatures. Prior to this, conventional or orthodox Marxism had tended to dismiss state growth in advanced industrial societies as of minor importance for their fundamentally oppressive nature. But newer variants take seriously the scale of changes introduced into liberal democracies' operations by the extended state. They offer a functionalist account of these changes, arguing not that they are minor, but that they were positively beneficial for owners of capital, either in terms of direct subsidies and benefits, or indirectly in terms of the creation of a 'class compromise' between some sections of the workforce and corporate capital. There are now numerous rather different versions of the basic neo-Marxist approach. A readable but rather orthodox Marxist view is provided by the Conference of Socialist Economists', *Struggle over the State* (1981), while a more difficult but very short statement of a much less conventional neo-Marxist perspective is provided by Offe and Ronge, 'Theses on the Theory of the State' (1975).

* * * * * *

The Major Theoretical Positions

Like most academic disciplines, political science shows a pattern of uneven development across different empirical topics. But underlying the variations in the type of debate and the volume of work conducted on different issues, there are some broad-ranging and long-running disputes between major theoretical positions. One of the better known of these is that between pluralists and Marxists, which continues to define a focal point for numerous controversies on large-scale issues. But there have also been important developments on each side of this debate. Marxist approaches to politics have fragmented into at least three distinct strands, disagreeing with each other about the extent to which political processes are determined by economic processes, and about the mechanisms by which the state apparatus in capitalist societies comes to adopt policies that foster business profitability and dominance. However, much of this debate remains at a theoretical level and has not been directly applied to the analysis of British politics. For this reason, and because I have summarised the outlines of these disputes within Marxism elsewhere (Dunleavy, 1981a), I shall only hint at these variations in my description of Marxist views here.

On the liberal side of the dispute there have also been important changes, however, which have been rather more directly translated into accounts of British politics. The rather complacent tone of classical pluralism, which tended to claim in the 1950s and 1960s that 'everything is for the best in the best of all possible worlds', has begun to be sharpened up. In the reformulated versions of classical pluralism in the early 1980s there is less attempt than there was to explain away lapses from liberal democratic ideals, and a greater readiness to criticise and to advocate reforms of anomalies and deficiencies in political processes. In part this has been a response to an obvious worsening of the social stability and economic prosperity of British society since the 1960s, for which pluralists seek political explanations. It is also in part a response to two newer liberal positions which criticise the institutions of classical pluralism from different perspectives. On the one hand, the new right argue that pluralist procedures de-stabilise British society by fostering the growth of the state, eroding market forces, and moving away from an attachment to constitutional-legal modes of problem-solving towards simple interest bargaining in a way that reduces the authority and the competence of government. They call, in consequence, for a return to older, more restrictive conceptions of the role of government. On the other hand, neo-pluralists argue that an advanced technological society cannot be run without an extended role for the state and without moving towards ever more sophisticated types of policy-making machinery, many of them far removed from the fairly simple models of representative government.

Perhaps the best way to round off this review of current thinking in British political science is to briefly discuss how each of these four approaches brings together or integrates the various topic views or models outlined above. Of course, as Table 13.1 indicates, there are some topics on which particular overall approaches have no distinctive view. And there are several topics where approaches adopt mixed views, or where the same model of a specific topic is integrated into divergent overall approaches. None the less, as I hope the discussion below makes clear, a consideration of overall approaches can reduce the apparent complexity of the specific topic views.

REFORMULATED PLURALISM

The reformulation of classical pluralism into a more critical and reformist view began in the later 1970s, perhaps responding to many of the same dissatisfactions that in practical party

TABLE 13.1 *Overall views of British politics*

Topic	View adopted by				
	Reformulated pluralism	New right view	Neo-pluralist approach	Marxist views	
1. Electoral behaviour	Mixed party identification/issue voting model	Issue voting model		Mixed party identification/structural model	
2. Party competition	Responsible party model	Adversary politics model		Responsible party model	
3. Interest group process	Pluralist model (but more critical)	Logic of collective action model	Corporatist view (liberal variant)	Corporatist view (radical variant)	
4. Mass media	Public opinion control model	Public opinion control model (for press alone)	Dominant values model (weak version)	Dominant values model (strong version)	
5. Parliament	Transformative model	[Normatively espoused legal model]	Westminster model (generalised variant)	[Separate view: Commons as sustaining ideology of 'Parliamentarianism']	
6. Cabinet government	Segmented decision model	Bureaucratic over-supply model	[Separate view: central executive power diffused out]	Bureaucratic co-ordination model	
7. Civil service	Public administration model			Power-bloc model	
8. Quasi-governmental agencies	Public accountability model	Critical variant of public accountability model	Inter-governmental relations model	Dual state model	
9. Local government	Local democracy model	[Separate view]	Insulated local elite model (weak version)	Insulated local elite or local state models	

politics led up to the formation of the SDP and the apparent revival of centrist politics in the early 1980s. The approach remains pluralist because of three characteristics: its emphasis on the existence of a deep level of societal consensus underlying the manifest conflicts of political life; its argument that government in a liberal democracy is essentially neutral in its dealings with different social groups; and its stress on party competition as a key mechanism by which citizens control leaders (Saunders, 1982, p. 14). But the reformulation of pluralism is much more attached to 'one person one vote' procedures, using them as a critical touchstone against which to assess existing practices.

The approach takes a mixed or variable view of citizens' voting behaviour, typically using an amalgam of the party identification and issue voting models to explain the continuities and changes in voting patterns over the last decade (McLean, 1982, chs 1, 2, 4). This is combined with an adversary politics model of party competition in which the over-polarisation of the major parties relative to the electorate is blamed on the plurality voting system (which protects the main parties from voter discontents), and on the very limited and imperfect forms of intra-party democracy (which allow the views of small groups of 'extreme' activists to prevail over the more 'moderate' views of the major parties' grass-roots members). The adoption of proportional representation in some form, plus 'one person one vote' systems of intra-party democracy are seen as key changes necessary to make party competition work successfully again (Bogdanor, 1981). This critical stance also partly reflects an opposition to the role of 'power brokers' within the parties, especially the dominant position of trades-union leaders in the Labour Party's federal structure. In its reformulated version, pluralism has incorporated some elements of the logic-of-collective-action model into its view of interest groups – so that extraneous factors generating inequalities between different types of interest groups are now acknowledged.

But the pluralist view of other institutions remains more optimistic. The public-opinion-control model is seen as still offering a satisfactory explanation of the mass media's performance, although the trend for newspaper ownership to pass from specialised news companies to large multi-nationals who run papers as a small sideline to their mainstream operations has generated some concern. Parliament is seen as operating in a more transformative way than hitherto, and therefore to some extent anticipating the sort of changes that would be likely to follow a change of electoral system. On the whole, pluralist writers still defend the idea that cabinet government plays an important role in the British executive, although their current position probably lies closer to the segmented decision view than to the older Cabinet-government ideal. This positive stance continues to hold in relation to the civil service, where the public administration view remains dominant. But in its reformulated version pluralism is now more critical of 'excessive' government secrecy and of administrative restrictive practices that deprive citizens of useful means of controlling the bureaucracy (such as the inadequate UK public audit procedures). Similarly pluralists subscribe to the public accountability model of quasi-governmental agencies, but are concerned to streamline and clarify the lines of accountability between these bodies and Parliament, and to see clearer limits on the operations of ministerial patronage when appointing these agencies' boards. At the local government level reformulated pluralism advocates the same changes in electoral systems as at the national level, while still vigorously defending local democracy (despite current imperfections in party competition) against the encroachment of central government controls (Bogdanor, 1980, ch. 2).

Finally, the reformulated pluralist view of state growth adds onto the basic model described in Topic 10 a more critical account of the adverse impacts of state growth in 'overloading' government institutions, and perhaps in getting the state involved in too many interdependency relations with external social groups (King, 1975). In the worsened economic situation, this approach sees a need for government both to retain a level of intervention that can continue to sustain societal consensus, and to be rather more selective than in the past in taking on new responsibilites.

THE NEW RIGHT

The new right are sharply differentiated from both mainstream pluralism and from the traditional Tory far-right in Britain by their consistent reliance on rational-choice models imported from economics to describe political processes. The much older Tory right are overtly inegalitarian, reject welfare or utility maximisation as a legitimate goal of government, and are at times openly contemptuous of democracy (Scruton, 1980). But the new right claim to have a consistent market liberal approach to politics. And unlike pluralism, their central image of the UK political system is as a series of imperfect markets with one inherent flaw, a built-in tendency towards uncontrolled state growth.

The approach takes a clear-cut issue-voting view of electoral behaviour, linking this with a strong version of the adversary-politics model that is fiercely critical of the operations of the two-party system. The new right blame the barriers on new parties entering the competition for the tendency they perceive for existing parties to bid-up voters' expectations to 'unrealistic' levels (Brittan, 1975a). The major parties are also able to pack their manifestos with promises to deliver private goods to different minority groups, secure in the knowledge that the very imperfect nature of party competition will ensure that majority dissatisfaction with many of these commitments can never surface in voting patterns. Similarly the new right use the logic of collective-action model of interest group formation to criticise concentrations of power in major lobbies. They argue that groups such as the trades unions, which operate in both economic and political 'markets', tend to reduce market efficiency, introducing rigidities (for example, a union minimum wage-rate) and preventing adjustments that would take place under purer market conditions (Brittan, 1975b). The new right also strongly endorse the 'free press' model of media operations but are very critical of the other part of the public-control view, namely public service broadcasting. They argue that restrictive state regulation has been one of the key forces keeping down the number of radio and TV outlets, and that broadcasting would operate better in a deregulated market framework on the same principles as the free press.

The key new right view of political institutions is their claim that bureaucracies are always budget-maximising in their operations, and that this has been a central motor of the crippling growth of the state in post-war liberal democracies.

This leads them to search for any institutional form that can impose some sort of 'market discipline' on civil service expansionism. The new right are consequently very critical of the *de facto* reduction of Parliamentary powers and anxious to see legislative scrutiny of budgets and expenditure re-established at a high level: hence they make a normative call for the restoration of a legal model of Parliamentary powers. They have no distinctive view of the controversy over Cabinet government. But they have strong views about the proliferation of quasi-governmental agencies without effective Parliamentary control, calling for stronger public-accountability requirements, and for functions better handled by private firms to be 'hived off' out of the state sector altogether. Local government is seen as a positive force to the extent that people can exert a market control over local policies by moving between areas of the country to find a mix of local taxes and services that appeals to them. But since Britain has the fewest and largest local authorities for a country with its size of population of any Western country, and since central government provides much of the funds for local services, the extent to which British local authorities are forced to compete with each other to attract residents and businesses is probably much lower than elsewhere.

The basic problem for new right analysis is that Britain's constitution makes some of their key reform proposals (which were developed in the USA) very difficult to apply here. For example, it is impossible in the UK to entrench in the constitution a requirement that state expenditures be kept below a certain proportion of GNP, for such a rule could be changed at will by any Commons majority. Similarly the idea of setting time-limits to the existence of central government ministries that would be embedded in Parliamentary statutes setting up particular policy programmes (so-called 'sunset legislation'), founders in the UK because the organisation of government departments is set by crown prerogative powers without reference to Parliament. Hence the approach seems to be driven back from a desire to curtail state growth by constitutional expedients into simply hoping that the 'right' political party keeps on winning general elections.

NEO-PLURALISM

Neo-pluralist theory has responded to the limitations and imperfections of classical pluralism in a diametrically opposed way to the new right. It combats evidence of inadequacies in conventional democratic controls over state activity by looking for the new kinds of control systems to sustain the public interest in policy formulation. And it combats the new right's pessimism by denying that state intervention is an aberration or a distortion of government policies by private interests. Rather, neo-pluralists argue that state intervention in advanced industrialised societies is an essential element in undertaking the complex task of societal guidance towards rationally planned goals (Galbraith, 1969).

Neo-pluralists say relatively little about input politics. They are sceptical of the issue voting model of electoral behaviour, without really endorsing party identification accounts either. Citizens try to decide policy questions on their merits, but within options presented to them by political parties, major interest groups, large corporations, and the mass media (Lindblom, 1977). Neo-pluralists also see a considerable measure of background convergence between the major parties' programmes; whatever their rhetoric might suggest, both Conservative and Labour remain committed to extensive state guidance of social development. Both parties confront the same policy problems at a macro level, and while their solutions remain distinct and appeal to different values, their rival strategies tend to move broadly in step. This is partly because liberal corporatism (the integration of major economic peak associations into the achievement of state policy goals) has tended to grow over time. Of course, this change away from older forms of representative government can be interrupted by a government seeking to dispense with the apparatus of interest mediation which corporatism provides, as the Thatcher administration did since 1979. But the costs of such efforts will be great. For example, controlling wage inflation without resort to an incomes policy negotiated with the trade unions may be possible if a government pursues a policy of artificially creating a recession to scare union leaders and their members into submission. But the evidence from British experience in the early 1980s suggests that the rise in unemployment needed for this strategy to work may be very large and very hard to control or* halt once it is set in motion. In the long run, neo-pluralists argue that it is unlikely such drastic non-corporatist strategies can continue to command electoral support. Neo-pluralist writers acknowledge a certain amount of truth in the dominant-values model of mass media operation. In particular they recognise that business does have some ability to mould people's preferences. But they argue that it is naive to expect equal consideration to be extended to all viewpoints in any society, and that the relative prominence of some values in Western democracies does not preclude the existence of a substantial pluralism of political positions and ideas.

Neo-pluralists are sceptical of the scope for increasing the legislature's role in policy-making. Parliament and Cabinet are institutions of finite capacity; unlike bureaucratic state agencies their membership is fixed, and it is not feasible to significantly expand their ability to process issues in detail. If the range of government policies increases (as it has done consistently since the early 1960s), then to avoid chronic overload their attention has to be focused more on strategic policy questions, leaving the detailed formulation of policy increasingly unscrutinised. But if detailed policy control has seeped away from representative institutions, this does not mean that it has accrued to the civil service, especially not one constituted on the idosyncratic 'generalist' model beloved by Whitehall. Neo-pluralists argue, instead, that the whole central machinery of government has seen power trickle away into a penumbra of quasi-governmental agencies and sub-national governments. Hence the inter-governmental-relations model of QGAs plays a major role in their overall picture of government. Of course, central control over these bodies remains crucial to their operations – indeed in some areas (such as financial control) central state discipline over subordinate bodies and local authorities has been tightened up, especially under the Thatcher government. But central control has coarsened, focusing now almost solely on crude fiscal measures such as cash limits or attempts to dictate spending-patterns for local authorities. In the short term, and in one sense, these attempts are definitionally effective. But in the longer term they will become exposed to adverse reactions from subordiante bodies and to internal contradictions, as general rules applied to very diverse subordinate agencies generate increasing numbers of anomalies and paradoxes (see Chapter 5).

Finally, neo-pluralists argue that it is very unlikely that state intervention in the economy or in social engineering will decrease in the future. Priorities within the extended state may be reassessed, and there may be a period of stasis in the overall expansion of government. But we should expect progress in designing planning and policy-making technologies to continue and to facilitate new developments in government activities (Etzioni, 1977).

MARXIST APPROACHES

Marxist approaches have continued to develop and diversify rapidly in response to the apparently sharp deterioration in Britain's economic performance and social cohesiveness. It is impossible to do justice here to the many sophisticated variants on this spectrum of views, so I shall concentrate on trying to indicate where a conventional Marxist view and more recent reinterpretations (neo-Marxist views) diverge.

Conventional Marxists remain more attached to the party identification model of voting behaviour than almost any other group of political scientists. In the 1960s they successfully fought off claims that the class de-alignment of voting represented the 'embourgeoisement' of the working class or the 'withering away' of class inequalities (Westergaard, 1970). In the current recession such views seem even more implausible, and conventional Marxists simply rebut evidence of issue voting or voter disaffection from the main parties, by appealing to the mobilisation of bias against a class view of politics, especially in the mass media. Newer approaches are prepared to acknowledge, however, that the decline of class influences on political alignment cannot just be ignored, and for them the structural model of voting may become more attractive in explaining why manual workers, for example, have voted less distinctly in successive elections. Most Marxists endorse a responsible party model of party competition, in which the emphasis is laid on the necessity for Labour to adopt a very clear radical programme and a more democratic constitution, if they are to persuade less easily mobilised groups that it will be worthwhile to turn out and vote for socialist policies. The key problem confronting left political movements generally in getting their viewpoint across to the mass of people is the acute 'dominant values' bias in the mass media, and this has attracted increasing attention from Marxist writers. The growth of corporatism in interest group–government relations is also seen as creating major difficulties. This has led to extensive co-optation of consensual practices by an illiberal, almost authoritarian, approach to key problems.

But it is perhaps on institutional questions where conventional Marxists and more recent variants diverge most. Most conventional Marxist writers argue that Parliament remains important only as a key institution perpetuating the myth of democratic control over government (Miliband, 1982, ch. 2). They put forward a consistent picture of the state apparatus as peopled by upper class or upper-middle class figures, with conservative values, opposed to radical change, and consistently exploiting their grip on the levers of power to frustrate any left electoral majority (Miliband, 1969). Thus they emphasise that the central executive is co-ordinated by the bureaucracy more than the Cabinet, that the civil service is a power-bloc with distinct interests of its own, and that local authorities are a 'local state' inescapably locked into realising policies that further capitalist interests. Neo-Marxist views, in contrast, argue that the particular form of institutions, their detailed workings or the sort of personnel who control them make very little difference to policy outcomes. State agencies are not directly pressured by owners of capital so much as structurally constrained by the logic of their position to go on pursuing policies that foster capital accumulation and legitimate current social arrangements. In managing tensions between these twin imperatives, however, the design of state institutions can be more important. Hence the dual state model of the distribution of functions between central departments, quasi-governmental agencies and local authorities is important for these writers, especially in suggesting that corporatist politics will prevail on issues of crucial importance for capitalist state functions, while more pluralist patterns will be found only on less important issues.

All Marxist writers agree that the British state confronts a serious crisis or series of crises in the 1980s. By crisis they do not mean (as pluralist critics often suppose) 'a point of inevitable deterioration or collapse'. Rather, a crisis denotes a stage of an illness in which the patient's condition either begins to degenerate rapidly or begins to decisively recover, reaching some new level of stability (at least for a time) (Habermas, 1976, ch. 1). But there is considerable disagreement about whether the nature of the British crisis is primarily economic (as more conventional Marxists maintain) or additionally involves rather separate and equally serious political and ideological crises (as neo-Marxists suggest).

Guide to Further Reading

Where works are already given in the Bibliography we have provided author and date only.

Chapter 1   The Resurgence of Ideology

The general issues raised in this chapter are discussed at different levels of abstraction in: Habermas, (1976) – this is the most comprehensive, but also the most abstract, of works dealing with the crisis in the role of the state in Western society; A. Wolfe, *The Limits of Legitamcy*, (Collier-Macmillan, 1977) – Wolfe takes the line of Habermas but the thesis is more fully developed and linked to a large amount of empirical material; Middlemas (1979) – a work by a historian on the development of the state in modern Britain and the deep historical roots of comparatism; R. Rose and G. Peters, *Can Government go Bankrupt?* (Macmillan, 1978) – an interesting volume that deals in some detail with the claims that the modern state is subject to too many demands. M. Oakeshott, *Rationalism in Politics* (Methuen, 1962) – is the most distinguished work by a modern Conservative thinker. Oakeshott is discussed at some length by Gilmour (1978). S. Brittan, 'Hayek, the New Right and the Crisis of Social Democracy', *Encounter* (1980) is the most incisive and thoughtful contribution to the place of neo-liberal economic ideas in modern British politics; H. Drucker, *Doctrine and Ethos in the Labour Party* (Allen & Unwin, 1979) – a useful corrective to the view that an account of a political party in terms of its ideology and doctrines can be exhaustive; B. Crick, *In Defence of Politics*, 2nd edn (Penguin, 1982) – this is a useful idiosyncratic view of the relationship between politics and different modes of political thought. The new edition has an additional chapter which sheds some light on aspects of the Labour Party that are discussed in this chapter.

Chapter 2 Voting and the Electorate

The readings mentioned in Chapter 13, Topic 1, provide references for items relevant to the different theoretical positions in this field, but in addition, the following books are useful. Iain McLean, *Dealing in Votes* (Martin Robertson, 1982, chs 1–4), provides an entertaining introduction to British and American voting behaviour and outlines clearly a number of problems and approaches. There was a strange dearth of book-length discussions of elections in the 1970s, only belatedly and partially filled by the expensive and technical volume by Crewe and Sarlvik (1983). By contrast, the 1983 election has produced a veritable flood of studies. Dunleavy and Husbands (1984) provides a wide-ranging discussion of the pre-election run-up, the election campaign and media coverage, a survey analysis of social and issue influences on voting, and a discussion of the electoral geography of the 1983 results. Rose and MacAllister (1984) concentrate on how the different nations in the UK voted in 1983. Curtice, Heath *et al.* (1984/5) analyse the results of the largest post-election survey.

Chapter 3 Parties and Parliament

Finer (1975) is the most challenging recent work about the party system. There has been no systematic analysis of this thesis, but Alan R. Ball, *British Political Parties: The Emergence of a Modern Party System* (Macmillan, 1981) disagrees with Finer; Finer (1980) gives a more rounded summary of the debate; Beer (1982) forsakes responsible party government in *Britain Against Itself*. Philip Norton (1981) *The Commons in Perspective* is the most interesting book about parliament for some time. Up-to-date information about changes in parliament and parliamentary procedure can most accessibly be found in the journal *Parliamentary Affairs*. The argument that parliament is (nearly) an irrelevance to the government of modern Britain is argued in a sustained way by Richardson and Jordan (1979).

There is much less of value to read on the Conservative Party than on Labour, but Philip Norton, *Conservative Dissidents* (Temple Smith, 1978) is good, albeit from a strongly anti-Heath point of view. The flavour of the anti-egalitarian Tory right can be gained from Scruton (1980). The humanitarian Tory view is best stated by K. Middlemas,

'Unemployment: the Past and Future of a Political Problem', *The Political Quarterly*, vol. 51, no. 4 (October–December 1980).

The odour of the Labour Party in the 1970s can best be gleaned from Richard Ingram's *Goldenballs* (Coronet, 1979) – don't start reading it late at night. Alan Warde, *Consensus and Beyond* (Manchester University Press, 1982) fails to discuss recent controversies but is admirable on the background to them. An insight to this debate can be gleaned from Martin Jacques and Francis Mulhern, *The Forward March of Labour Halted?* (Verso, 1981). Trotskyist politics gives rise to much paranoid writing, but an example of a Trot campaign, which also gives an idea of Scottish politics at its mid-1970s euphoric peak is, H. Drucker, *Breakaway: The Scottish Labour Party* (Edinburgh Student Publications Board, 1978).

The shrewdest book on the SDP is a novel written twenty years ago by Michael Frayn, *On the Outskirts* (Collins, 1964); and the best review of the numerous books by the party's leaders and about the party is contained in Brian Barry's review in *Political Quarterly*, vol. 53, no. 3 (July–September 1982).

Chapter 4   Government at the Centre

There is obviously an enormous amount of literature on British central government and the themes touched on in this chapter. The points made about the general and constitutional background are developed further in Beloff and Peele (1980), and in Norton (1982). On the central political institutions of cabinet and prime minister perhaps the best introduction is still Mackintosh (1962). On the narrower questions of administrative efficiency and the civil service, Crowther-Hunt and Kellner (1980) is an excellent introduction, which may be supplemented by G. K. Fry, *The Administrative Revolution in Whitehall* (Croom Helm, 1981), and John Garrett, *Managing the Civil Service* (Heinemann, 1980). An unusual and useful collection of essays on the impact of cuts is Hood and Wright (1981).

Personal memoirs provide a rich source of further information about the way British government operates in practice. *The Crossman Diaries* (1979) is now something of a classic. Pliatzky (1982) is useful for its insights into public expenditure and for Pliatzky's own views on the role of the civil service. Barnett (1982) complements the civil service viewpoint with racier political fare.

Undergraduates who wish to keep up with current developments in British politics are bound to rely heavily on journals. Of especial help in this field are *Parliamentary Affairs*, *Public Administration* and *Public Law*, although the more general journals, *Political Studies* and the *British Journal of Political Science*, also contain some relevant articles.

Official and parliamentary papers may be essential reading from time to time. The *Report of the Fulton Committee* (Cmnd 3638) (HMSO, 1968) is a useful document both for its recommendations and for the understanding of the assumptions behind attempts to reform the Civil Service. Thereafter the *Eleventh Report from the Expenditure Committee*, 1976–77, and *The Civil Service: Government Observations on the Eleventh Report from the Expenditure Committee* (1978) are helpful indicators of the movement of opinion about the organisation of the civil service prior to Thatcher's administration. Two reports from the Treasury and Civil Service Committee are also highly relevant: *The Future of the Civil Service Department* (1980–1 Session), and *Efficiency and Effectiveness in the Civil Service* (1981–2 Session). The government's observations on the latter report are to be found in *Efficiency and Effectiveness in the Civil Service: Government Observations on the Third Report from the Treasury and Civil Service Committee* (Cmnd 9616) (HMSO 1982). On internal management see *Financial Management in Govenment Departments* (Cmnd 9058) (HMSO, 1983).

Chapter 5   Beyond Whitehall

The field of inter-governmental relations beyond Whitehall is not well studied in Britain at present, so that it is more than usually difficult to suggest further reading at a reasonably introductory level. There are many books on local or urban politics, public corporations, etc., but we have concentrated on just a few references that take further the themes of our chapter. However, one survey of agencies beyond central government is useful: R. A. W. Rhodes and E. Page, 'The "Other Governments" of Britain', in I. Budge (ed.), *Political Processes in British Society* (Longman, 1983). An up-to-date account of QGAs is provided by Barker (1982) – the chapters by Nevil Johnson and Christopher Hood are especially useful as introductions; be warned, however! – the book further adds to the confusion over terms by describing QGAs as 'governmental bodies'. Central–local relations are well explored in Rhodes (1981). Some of the theoretical issues involved are discussed by P. J. Dunleavy, 'Social and Political Theory and the Issues in Central Relations', in G. Jones (ed), *New Approaches to the Study of Central–Local Government Relationships* (Gower, 1980).

Chapter 6   Economic Policy

F. Blackaby (ed.), *De-industrialisation* (Heinemann, 1979) is a collection of articles on the definition and measurement of Britain's industrial decline. Brittan (1977) reprints some of Brittan's commentaries in the

Financial Times, together with some longer pieces on aspects of economic policy in the 1970s; written from a monetarist standpoint. B. Gould *et al.*, *Monetarism or Prosperity* (Macmillan, 1981) provides a critical view of monetarism and advocates major changes in Britain's foreign economic policy in order to achieve prosperity. Hood and Wright (eds) (1981) is a collection of articles on the crisis of public expenditure in the 1970s and the new mechanisms of control.

B. Jordan, *Mass Unemployment* (Martin Robertson, 1981) – this book deals with the causes and the theories of unemployment and the political strategies for overcoming it, and is written from a Marxist standpoint. W. Keegan and R. Pennant-Rea, *Who runs the economy?* (Temple Smith 1979) – written by two financial journalists this book explores the policy-making process and the impact of parties, civil servants, the financial markets, industry and the trade unions upon policy.

Chapter 7   Social Policy

Barnett (1982) – an unusually frank book by a British ex-Cabinet Minister that makes the Crossman diaries look discreet. Bosanquet and Townsend (1980) gives the background on the Callaghan administration. Dunleavy (1981b) gives a full story of the high-rise housing fiasco together with much else.

Field (1981) gives the best picture of the 'fiscal' and 'occupational' welfare states.

C. Jencks, *Inequality* (New York, Basic Books, 1972) – this 'reassessment of the effect of family and schooling in America' remains afloat after ten years of academic gunnery. Le Grand (1982) has altered the debate. Pliatzky (1982) is an informative account by the Treasury civil servant who was in charge of public spending during the IMF crisis; particularly revealing in conjunction with Barnett's account. Royal Commission on the Distribution of Income and Wealth (RCDIW), Report no. 8, *Fifth Report on the Standing Reference*, Cmnd 7679 (HMSO, 1979) contains indispensable data on recent changes in income distribution. Titmuss (1976) – this essay, first published in 1956, set concepts that have dominated all subsequent debate.

Chapter 8   Foreign and Defence Policy

Capitanchik (1977) is a brief survey of public attitudes towards defence issues over a twenty-year period, in a good, though inevitably uneven, collection of essays. *The Economist*, 'Britain's Foreign Office', pp. 25–9 (27 November 1982) is a very well informed account of the differences between the FCO and the Prime Minister's Office in recent times.

The Falklands Campaign: The Lessons, Cmnd 8758 (HMSO, December 1982) This is the official view. Hobkirk (1976) is a collection of specialist essays, published for the National Defence College. House of Commons, Defence Committee (1982) *The Handling of Press and Public Information During the Falklands Conflict* is an absorbing report on a relatively minor, but controversial aspect of the Falklands campaign. Nailor, (1973) – an essay about the structures and linkage of foreign and defence policy, in a collection of pieces that, in its day, broke new ground as far as detail and analysis were concerned. *The Times*, 29 November 1982, pp. 15–17, contained an unusually well-prepared brief on current issues in defence policy and the East–West balance. And for further reading: Burrows and Edwards (1982); Flynn (1981); Hagan (1982); Taylor (1978).

Chapter 9 The Police

The peculiar autonomy of policing within British politics is reflected in the absence of an extensive literature on the subject and of any really thorough bibliography. The most extensive bibliography that is at all readily available is *The Police of England and Wales: a bibliography 1829–1979*, which is available from the librarian of the Police Staff College, Bramshill. However, as its title implies, it does not cover Scotland and Ireland and is incomplete in other respects.

Indispensable basic publications on police are the annual reports of Her Majesty's Chief Inspectors of Constabulary for England and Wales and for Scotland (HMSO). The annual report of the Commissioner of Police for the Metropolis (HMSO) completes the basic picture. Each individual chief constable produces an annual report to the local police authority. These reports are difficult to obtain, though local libraries should hold local reports. However, though indispensable, these reports are uninformative about many important issues, such as finance. On this subject, the yearly *Police Statistics*, published by the Chartered Institute for Public Finance and Accountancy, are essential. The Police Complaints Board produces an annual report which is published by HMSO, and which is rather more thoughtful than the ritualised uncontroversiality of the HMI reports. The standard modern history of the police is T. A. Critchely, *A History of Police in England and Wales*, 2nd edn (Constable, 1978); as befits a work by the former head of the Home Office Police

Department, it offers the Whitehall eyeview of policing, but it is thorough and bleakly thoughtful. The true social history of policing has yet to be written.

Two good starting-points for the law-and-order debate of the 1970s and the place of the police within it are Stuart Hall, *et al.*, *Policing the crisis*, (Macmillan, 1978), which offers a broad neo-marxist account of the Heath era; and Ben Whitaker, *The Police in Society* (Methuen, 1979), a rambling but well-researched account of the liberal dilemmas of modern police. Simon Holdaway (ed.), *The British Police* (Edward Arnold, 1979) is an important collection of essays that may be more useful to the student.

The attitudes of police officers and their approach to the job are brilliantly revealed in James McClure, *Spike Island* (Pan, 1981), an account of policing inner-city Liverpool. Peter Manning's *Police Work* (MIT Press, 1979) offers a more structured approach and is an essential starting-point for police sociology. J. Mervyn Jones, *Organisational Aspects of Police Behaviour* (Gower, 1980), exposes the myth and reality of the beat patrol. Robert Reiner, *The Blue-coated Worker* (Cambridge University Press, 1978) offers fascinating material on ordinary officers' views but is primarily the key text on the Police Federation.

There are few books by service police officers, but there is a host of police memoirs. Of contemporary interest is Robert Mark, *In the Office of Constable* (Fontana, 1979), the autobiography of the most important policeman of the 1970s; an extremely opinionated book. John Alderson has not yet offered an autobiography. His *Policing Freedom* (Macdonald & Evans, 1980) is a somewhat laborious but enormously important attempt to set out an alternative perspective for modern policing. On 'community policing', the key works are Evelyn Schaffer, *Community Policing* (Croom Helm, 1980) – much better than the introduction by David McNee might imply; Colin Moore and John Brown, *Community versus Crime* (Bedford Square Press, 1981), an account of the Exeter project; and Brown's *Policing by Multi-Racial Consent* (Bedford Square Press, 1982).

Police–black relations are more thoroughly covered in the literature than many other aspects. Derek Humphry, *Police Power and Black People* (Panther, 1972), was pioneering. Martin Kettle and Lucy Hodges, *Uprising: the Police, the People and the Riots in Britain's Cities* (Pan, 1982) is more up-to-date. The pamphlet literature on police and race is extensive. See, in particular, the work of the Runnymede Trust and of the Institute of Race Relations.

The politicisation of the modern police force is dealt with by Reiner (above) and, especially, by Tony Bunyan, *The History and Practice of the Political Police* (Quartet, 1976). Two other important follow-ups to

Bunyan, are Peter Hain (ed.), Humphry and Brian Rose-Smith, *Policing the Police, Vol 1* (John Calder, 1979) on complaints and the terrorism laws; and Hain (ed.), Martin Kettle, Duncan Campbell and Joanna Rollo, *Policing the Police, Vol 2* (John Calder, 1981) on politics, computerisation and the Special Patrol Group. Ackroyd, Margolis, Rosenhead and Shallice, *The Technology of Political Control* (Pluto, 1981) is the key text on police technology and weaponry. Paul Gordon, *Policing Scotland* (Scottish Council for Civil Liberties, 1981) extends these analyses to Scotland, which most writers normally ignore; Robert Baldwin and Richard Kinsey, *Police Powers and Politics* (Quartet, 1982), on the criminal procedure debate, is a notable exception.

The periodical literature is thin. The force periodicals are *Police Review* (weekly), an in-house magazine; *Police* (monthly) the mouthpiece of the Federation, which should not be assumed to speak for ordinary police; *Police Journal* (quarterly), a mixture of the interesting and the appalling; *Police Studies* (quarterly), which takes itself very seriously and has many contributions from the USA. *State Research Bulletin* (every two months, currently suspended) was a trail-blazing and influential critical survey of policing.

Chapter 10   Trade Unions and the Government

The general overview, which is mainly factual but, when analytical, quite good, is Barnes and Reid (1980). For a most detailed look at government–union relations see Holmes (1982) – the chapters on the Industrial Relations Act and the 1973–4 miners' dispute ought to be read in conjunction with Chapter 10 of this book. Barnett (1982) captures the mood of policy-making 1974–9 and is very perceptive on the change in government–union relations which ends in the 'winter of discontent'. For an alternative view to Barnett's, David Coates's Marxist study, *Labour in Power?* (Longman, 1980) put that case as best as it can be put.

Chapter 11   Two New Protest Groups: The Peace and Women's Movements

The British women's liberation movement has not been widely studied by academics, and there is no one academic book exclusively devoted to the subject. The journal *Feminist Review* has carried regular articles, as have such publications as *Spare Rib*. Vicky Randal's *Women and Politics* (Macmillan, 1982) contains a particularly lucid and readable account of developments up to 1981, and also provides an extensive bibliography of feminist, academic and feminist–academic sources. For those with a more specialist interest, David Bouchier's *Idealism and Revolution* (Edward Arnold, 1978) outlines ideological developments in the British and American movements in the late 1960s and early 1970s.

Although several texts are available on the early years of CND, there are as yet no academic books that concentrate on the growth of the peace movement since 1979. On the early CND, the most useful source is R. Taylor and C. Pritchard, *The Protest Makers* (Pergamon, 1980). This gives a detailed account of the disarmament movement between 1958 and 1965; it also uses survey evidence to trace the subsequent development through the 1960s and 1970s of the attitudes and loyalties of early CND activists. For more contemporary information, one may turn to books from within the movement; although polemical in tone, they offer useful insights into questions of strategy and tactics. One such is M. H. Ryle, *The Politics of Nuclear Disarmament* (Pluto Press, 1981), which offers a stimulating argument on the role of CND in contemporary British politics.

Chapter 12　Northern Ireland

Books on Northern Ireland have maintained an uneasy relationship with the political violence: before 1968 there were no more than three political textbooks covering the Province, now there are more than 200. A good general introduction, because it is concise and written for outsiders, is Paul Arthur, *The Government and Politics of Northern Ireland* (Longman, 1983). A more detailed and up-to-date administrative account is W. D. Birrell and A. Murie, *Policy and Government in Northern Ireland: Lessons of Devolution* (Gill & Macmillan, 1980). One neglected aspect of the problem has been Protestant reaction to the 'troubles'. An American historian, D. W. Miller, has written a fascinating account of 'conditional loyalism' entitled *Queen's Rebels* (Gill & Macmillan, 1978). An equally fascinating account comes from a Marxist triumverate, P. V. Bew, B. Gibbon and H. Patterson, *The State in Northern Ireland 1921–72* (Manchester University Press, 1979). Finally, a speculative book of essays on possible constitutional initiatives is D. Rae (ed.), *Political Co-operation in Divided Societies* (Gill & Macmillan, 1982).

Further developments can be followed in *Fortnight* – which appears once a month and is published in Belfast.

Bibliography

Ackroyd, C., Margolis, K., Rosenhead, J., Shallice, T. (1977) *The Technology of Political Control*, Harmondsworth, Penguin.

Alexander, A. (1982) *Local Government since Reorganisation*, London, Allen & Unwin.

Alt, J. (1982) 'The Case of the Silk Stocking Socialists and the Calculating Children of the Middle Class', *British Journal of Political Science*, vol. 12.

Arthur, P. (1983) *Government and Politics of Northern Ireland*, 2nd edn, London, Longman.

Ashford, D. (1981) *Politics and Policy in Britain*, Oxford, Blackwell.

Baker, B. (1981) *The Far Left: An Exposé of the Extreme Left in Britain*, London, Weidenfeld & Nicolson.

Barker, A. (ed.) (1982) *Quangos in Britain*, London, Macmillan.

Barnes, D. and Reid, E. (1980) *Governments and Trade Unions: The British Experience 1964–79*, London, Heinemann.

Barnett, J. (1982) *Inside the Treasury*, London, André Deutsch.

Beattie, A. (1979) 'Macmillan's Mantle: the Conservative Party in the 1970s', in *Political Quarterly*, vol. 50, no. 3, July–September.

Beer, S. (1982) *Britain Against Itself*, London, Faber & Faber.

Behn, R. (1983) 'Fundamentals of Cut-back Management', in Zeckhauser, R. S. and Leebaert, D. (eds), *What Role for Government*, Durham, Duke University Press.

Behrens, R. (1979) *The Conservative Party from Heath to Thatcher*, Farnham, Saxon House.

Beloff, M. and Peele, G. (1980) *The Government of the United Kingdom: Political Authority in a Changing Society*, London, Weidenfeld & Nicolson.

Benn, T. (1979) *Arguments for Socialism*, Harmondsworth, Penguin.

Benn, T. (1980) 'The Case for a Constitutional Premiership', in *Parliamentary Affairs*, vol. xxxiii, no. 1 (Winter).

Benn, T. (1982) *Arguments for Democracy*, Harmondsworth, Penguin.

Berrill, Sir K. (1980) The Stamp Memorial Lecture, 2 December.

Bogdanor, V. (1981) *The People and the Party System*, Cambridge University Press.

Bosanquet, N. (1982) 'Living with Cash Limits: The Case of the National Health Service', *Public Money*, September.

Bosanquet, N. and Townsend, P. (eds) (1980) *Labour and Equality*, London, Heinemann.

Bradley, I. (1981) *Breaking the Mould? The Birth and Prospects of the Social Democratic Party*, Oxford, Martin Robertson.

Brittan, S. (1971) *Government and the Market Economy*, London, Institute of Economic Affairs.

Brittan, S. (1975) 'The Economic Contradictions of Democracy', in *British Journal of Political Science*.

Brittan, S. (1976) *Participation without Politics*, London, Institute of Economic Affairs.

Brittan, S. (1977) *The Economic Consequences of Democracy*, London, Temple Smith.

Brittan, S. and Lilley, P. (1977) *The Delusion of Incomes Policy*, London, Temple Smith.

Brown, R. and Steel, D. (1979) *The Administrative Process in Britain*, London, Methuen.

Buchanan, J. M. (1960) *Fiscal Theory and Political Economy*, Berkeley, University of California Press.

Burrows, B. and Edwards, G. (1982) *The Defence of Western Europe*, London, Butterworth.

Butler, D. and Sloman, A. (1979) *British Political Facts*, London, Macmillan.

Butler, D. and Stokes, D. (1969) *Political Change in Britain*, London, Macmillan (2nd edn 1974).

Byrne, P. and Lovenduski, J. (1978) 'Sex Equality and the Law', in *British Journal of Law and Society* (Winter).

Capitanchik, D. (1977) 'Public Opinion and Popular Attitudes towards Defence', in Bayliss, J. (ed.), *British Defence Policy in a Changing World*, London, Croom Helm.

Castle, B. (1980) *The Castle Diaries 1974–76*, London, Weidenfeld & Nicolson.

Cawson, A. (1982) *Corporatism and Welfare*, London, Heinemann.

Cawson, A. and Saunders, P. (1983) 'Corporatism, Competitive Politics and Class Struggle', in R. King (ed.), *Capital and Politics*, London, Routledge & Kegan Paul.

Chapman, L. (1979) *Your Disobedient Servant*, Harmondsworth, Penguin.

Cockburn, C. (1977) *The Local State*, London, Pluto Press.

Conference of Socialist Economists (1981) *Struggle over the State*, London, CSE.

Cooper, N. and Stewart, J. (1982) 'Local Authority Budgets 1982–83', in *Public Finance and Accountancy*, 17–21 June.

Coote, A. (1978) 'The Tories' Strange Affair with Women', in *New Statesman*, 13 October.

Coote, A. and Kellner, P. (1980) 'Powerlessness and How to Fight It', in *New Statesman*, 7 November.

Cosgrave, P. (1978) *Margaret Thatcher*, London, Hutchinson.

Coultas, V. (1981) 'Feminists Must Face the Future', in *Feminist Review*, no. 7.

Crewe, I. (1983) 'The Disturbing Truth Behind Labour's Rout', and 'How Labour was Trounced All Round', *The Guardian*, 13 and 14 June, 1983.

Crewe, I., Sarlvik, B., Alt, J. (1977) 'Partisan Dealignment in Britain 1964–74', in *British Journal of Political Science*, vol. 7.

Crosland, C. A. R. (1956) *The Future of Socialism*, London, Cape.

Crosland, C. A. R. (1963) *The New Socialism*, Melbourne University Press.

Crosland, C. A. R. (1974) 'A Social Democratic Britain', in *Socialism Now*, London, Cape.

Crossman, R. H. S. (1979) *The Crossman Dairies*, ed. Anthony Howard, London, Methuen.

Crowther-Hunt, Lord, and Kellner, P. (1980) *The Civil Servants: An Enquiry into Britain's Ruling Class*, London, Macdonald.

Curran, J. and Seaton, J. (1981) *Power Without Responsibility: The Press and Broadcasting in Britain*, London, Fontana.

Curtice, J. and Steed, M. (1982) 'Electoral Choice and the Production of Government', *British Journal of Political Science*, vol. 12.

Downs, A. (1957) *An Economic Theory of Democracy*, New York, Harper & Row.

Drucker, H. M. and Brown, G. (1980) *The Politics of Nationalism and Devolution*, Longman, London.

Duke, V. and Edgell, P. (1981) 'Public Expenditure Cuts in Britain and Local Authority Mediation' (Paper to the PSA Urban Politics Group, Birmingham University, December).

Duke, V. and Edgell, P. (forthcoming) 'Public Expenditure Cuts in Britain and Consumption Sectoral Cleavages', *International Journal of Urban and Regional Research*.

Dunleavy, P. (1979) 'The Urban Basis of Political Alignment', in *British Journal of Political Science*, no. 9.

Dunleavy, P. (1980a) 'The Political Implications of Sectoral Cleavages and the Growth of State Employment', in *Political Studies* (two parts).

Dunleavy, P. (1980b) *Urban Political Analysis*, London, Macmillan.

Dunleavy, P. (1981a) 'Alternative Theories of Liberal Democratic Politics: the Pluralist–Marxist Debate in the 1980s', in D. Potter (ed.), *Society and the Social Sciences*, London, Routledge & Kegan Paul.

Dunleavy, P. (1981b) *The Politics of Mass Housing in Britain, 1945–75*, Oxford, Clarendon Press.

Dunleavy, P. and Husbands, C. (1984) *British Democracy at the Crossroads,* London, Allen & Unwin.

Economist, The (1982) 'Britain's Foreign Office', 27 November, pp. 25–9.

Eltis, W. and Bacon, R. (1978) *Britain's Economic Problem: Too Few Producers,* London, Macmillan.

Epstein, L. (1980) 'What happened to the British party model', in *American Political Science Review,* vol. LXXIV, no. 1, March.

Etzioni, A. (1977) 'Societal overload', in *Political Science Quarterly,* 92.

Eurobarometer, (1979) *European Men and Women in 1978,* Brussels, Commission of the European Communities.

Field, F. (1981) *Inequality in Britain: Freedom, Welfare and the State,* London, Fontana.

Finer, S. E., Berrington, H. D., Bartholomew, B. J. (1961) *Backbench Opinion in the House of Commons 1955–9,* Oxford University Press.

Finer, S. E. (ed.) (1975) *Adversary Politics and Electoral Reform,* London, Anthony Wigram.

Finer, S. E. (1980) *The Changing British Party System, 1945–79,* Washington, DC, American Enterprise Institute.

Fisk, R. (1975) *The Point of No Return,* London, Andre Deutsch.

Flackes, W. D. (1980) *Northern Ireland: A Political Directory, 1968–79;* Dublin, Gill Macmillan.

Flynn, G. (ed.) (1982) *The Internal Fabric of Western Europe,* London, Butterworth.

Galbraith, J. K. (1969) *The New Industrial State,* Harmondsworth, Penguin.

Gilmour, I. (1978) *Inside Right: A Study of Conservatism,* London, Quartet Books.

Glasgow University Media Group (1976) *Bad News,* London, Routledge & Kegan Paul.

Glasgow University Media Group (1980) *More Bad News,* London, Routledge & Kegan Paul.

Glasgow University Media Group (1982) *Really Bad News,* Writers' and Readers' Publishing Co-op.

Grimond, J. (1979) *Memoirs,* London, Heinemann.

Grimond, J. (1978) *The Common Welfare,* London, Heinemann.

Habermas, J. (1976) *Legitimation Crisis,* London, Heinemann.

Hagan, L. S. (ed.) (1982) *The Crisis of Western Security,* London, Croom Helm.

Hayek, F. A. (1944) *The Road to Serfdom,* London, Routledge & Kegan Paul.

Hayek, F. A. (1957) *The Constitution of Liberty,* London, Routledge & Kegan Paul.

Hayek, F. A. (1976) *Law, Legislation and Liberty,* London, Routledge & Kegan Paul.

Haywood, S. and Hunter, D. J. (1982) 'Consultative Processes in Health Policy in the United Kingdom', in *Public Administration*, vol. 60, no. 2, Summer.

Heclo, H. and Wildavsky, A. (1981) *The Private Government of Public Money*, 2nd edn, London, Macmillan.

Heffer, E. (1973) *The Class Struggle in Parliament*, London, Gollancz.

Hennessy, P. (1981) 'Prime Minister Resists a Spirit of Openness about Government', *The Times*, 10 February.

Her Majesty's Government, (1982) *The Falklands Campaign: The Lessons*, HMSO, Cmnd 8758.

Himmelweit, H., Humphreys, P., Jaeger, A., and Katz, M. (1981) *How Voters Decide*, London, Academic Press.

Hirsch, F. (1976) *The Social Limits to Growth*, London, Routledge & Kegan Paul.

Hobkirk, M. (1976) 'Defence Organisation and Defence Policy-Making in the UK and USA', in Martin, L. W. (ed.) *The Management of Defence*, London, Macmillan.

Holmes, M. (1982) *Political Pressure and Economic Policy: British Government 1970–74*, London, Butterworth.

Hood, C. and Wright, M. (eds) (1981) *Big Government in Hard Times*, Oxford, Martin Robertson.

House of Commons, Defence Committee (1982) 1982–83 Session, First Report, *The Handling of Press and Public Information During the Falklands Conflict* (HC17/1) 8 December.

Huntington, S. (1982) *American Politics: The Promise of Disharmony*, Harvard University Press.

Jackson, P. M. (1982) *The Political Economy of Bureaucracy*, Banbury, Phillip Allen.

Jencks, C. (1970) *Education Vouchers*, Cambridge Centre for the Study of Public Policy.

Jenkin, P. (1982) Interview in *Marxism Today*, December.

Jennings, Sir I. (1979) *Cabinet Government*, Cambridge University Press.

Jones, J. (1977) *The Human Face of Labour: the 1977 Richard Dimbleby Lecture*, London, BBC Publications.

Joseph, Sir K. (1975) *Why Britain Needs a Social Market Economy*, London, Centre for Policy Studies.

Joseph, Sir K. (1975) *Reversing the Trend*, London, Centre for Policy Studies.

Joseph, Sir K. (1976) *Stranded in the Middle Ground*, London, Centre for Policy Studies.

Joseph, Sir K. (1978) *Equality*, London, J. Murray.

Kavanagh, D. (1982) 'Still the Workers' Party? Changing Social Trends in Elite Recruitment and Electoral Support', in Kavanagh, D., *The Politics of the Labour Party*, London, George Allen & Unwin.

King, A. (1975) 'Overload: Problems of Governing in the 1970s', in *Political Studies*, 23.

Kogan, D. and Kogan, M. (1982) *The Battle for the Labour Party*, London, Fontana.

Layfield, F. (1976) *Report of the Committee of Inquiry into Local Government Finance*, London, HMSO, Cmnd 6453.

Le Grand, J. (1982) *The Strategy of Equality*, London, Allen & Unwin.

Lee, M. (1981) 'Whitehall and Retrenchment', in C. Head and M. Wright (eds), *Big Government in Hard Times*, Laver, Martin Robertson.

Lindblom, C. (1977) *Politics and Markets*, New York, Basic Books.

Luard, E. (1979) *Socialism without the State*, London, Macmillan.

Mackintosh, J. (1962) *The British Cabinet*, London, Methuen.

McKenzie, R. (1963) *British Political Parties*, rev. edn, London, Heinemann.

McLean, I. (1982) *Dealing in Votes*, London, Martin Robertson.

Marquand, D. (1982) *Introduction to J. P. Mackintosh on Parliament and Social Democracy*, London, Longman.

Michie, A. and Hoggart, S. (1978) *The Pact: the Inside Story of the Lib–Lab Government, 1977–78*, London, Quartet Books.

Middlemas, K. (1979) *Politics in Industrial Society*, London, André Deutsch.

Miliband, R. (1969) *The State in Capitalist Society*, London, Weidenfeld & Nicolson.

Miliband, R. (1982) *Capitalist Democracy in Britain*, Oxford University Press.

Miller, W. L. (1977) *Electoral Dynamics in Britain since 1918*, London, Macmillan.

Miller, W. L. (1978) 'Social Class and Party Choice in England', *British Journal of Political Science*, vol. 8.

Miller, W. L. (1981) *The End of British Politics: Scots and English Political Behaviour in the Seventies*, Oxford University Press.

Minkin, L. (1980) *The Labour Party Conference*, Manchester University Press.

Moran, M. (1977) *The Politics of Industrial Relations*, London, Macmillan.

MORI Poll (1979) *Index to International Public Opinion*, Oxford.

MORI Poll (1980) *New Statesman*, 7 November.

Nailor, P. (1973) 'Defence Policy and Foreign Policy', in Boardman, R. and Groom, A. J. R. (eds), *The Management of Britain's External Relations*, London, Macmillan.

National Economic Development Office, (1976) *A Study of the UK Nationalised Industries*, London, HMSO.

Newman, O. (1981) *The Challenge of Corporatism*, London, Macmillan.

Newton, K. (1976) *Second City Politics*, Oxford University Press.

Niskanen, W. (1973) *Bureaucracy: Servant or Master?*, London, Institute of Economic Affairs.

Norton, P. (1981) *The Commons in Perspective*, Oxford, Martin Robertson.

Norton, P. (1982) *The Constitution in Flux*, Oxford, Martin Robertson.

Offe, C. and Ronge, V. (1975) 'Theses on the Theory of the State', in *New German Critique*.

Olson, M. (1965) *The Logic of Collective Action*, Harvard University Press.

Owen, D. (1981) *Face the Future*, Oxford University Press.

Pattison, A. (1982) 'Resistance on Reform: the politics of comprehensive education, 1965–82, with special reference to Conservative-controlled Local Education Authorities', Open University PhD.

Peele, G. (1978) 'The Developing Constitution', in Ramsden, J. and Cook, C., *Trends in British Government since 1945*, London, Macmillan.

Penniman, H. R. (ed.) (1981) *Britain at the Polls, 1979*, American Enterprise Institute.

Pliatzky, Sir L. (1982) *Getting and Spending*, Oxford, Blackwell.

Rawls, J. (1972) *A Theory of Justice*, Oxford University Press.

Rhodes, R. A. W. (1981) *Control and Power in Central–Local Relations*, Farnborough, Gower.

Richardson, J. and Jordan, A. (1979) *Governing Under Pressure*, London, Martin Robertson.

Riddell, P. (1983) *The Thatcher Government*, Oxford, Martin Robertson.

Rose, R. (1969) 'Parties, Factions and Tendencies', in *Political Studies*, vol. xvii.

Rose, R. (1974a) *The Problem of Party Government*, London, Macmillan.

Rose, R. (1974b) 'Britain: Simple Abstractions and Complex Realities', in Rose, R. (ed.), *Electoral Behaviour*, New York, Free Press.

Rose, R. (1981) *Do Parties Make a Difference?*, London, Macmillan.

Royal Commission on the Distribution of Income and Wealth (1979) Report no. 8, *Fifth Report on the Standing Reference*, London, HMSO, Cmnd 7679.

Rush, M. (1979) 'The Members of Parliament', in Walkland, S. A., *The House of Commons in the Twentieth Century*, Oxford, Clarendon Press.

Russel, T. (1978) *The Tory Party: Its Policies, Divisions and Future*, Harmondsworth, Penguin.

Saunders, P. (1982) 'The relevance of Weberian Sociology for urban political analysis', in Kirby, A. and Pinch, S. (eds), *Public Provision and Urban Politics*, University of Reading, Dept of Geography.

Schwartz, J. E. (1980) 'Exploring a New Role in Policy-making: the British House of Commons in the 1970s', *American Political Science Review*, vol. 74, pp. 23–37.

Scott, H. (1954) *Scotland Yard*, London, André Deutsch.

Scruton, R. (1980) *The Meaning of Conservatism*, London, Macmillan.

Sedgemore, B. (1980) *The Secret Constitution*, London, Hodder & Stoughton.

Seldon, A. (1978) *Charge*, London Institute of Economic Affairs.

Seyd, P. (1980) 'Factionalism in the 1970s', in Layton-Henry, Z. (ed.), *Conservative Party Politics*, Macmillan.

Seymour-Ure, C. (1982) 'The SDP and the Media', in *The Political Quarterly*, vol. 53, no. 4, October–December.

Shell, D. (1981) 'The British Constitution in 1980', in *Parliamentary Affairs*, vol. xxxiv, no. 2 (Spring).

Smith, T. (1979) *The Politics of the Corporate Economy*, Oxford, Martin Robertson.

Stephenson, H. (1980) *Mrs Thatcher's First Year*, London, J. Norman.

Stephenson, H. (1982) *Claret and Chips: The Rise of the SDP*, London, Michael Joseph.

Tawney, R. H. (1931) *Equality*, London, Allen & Unwin.

Taylor, R. (1982) 'The Trade Union "problem" since 1960', in B. Pimlott and C. Cook, *Trade Unions in British Politics*, London, Longman.

Taylor, R. and Pritchard, C. (1980) *The Protest Makers*, Oxford, Pergamon Press.

Taylor, T. (ed.) (1978) *Approaches and Theory in International Relations*, London, Longman.

Thompson, E. P. and Smith, D. (1980) *Protest and Survive*, Harmondsworth, Penguin.

Titmuss, R. M. (1976) 'The Social Division of Welfare', in Smith, B. A. (ed.), *Essays on 'The Welfare State'*, London, Allen & Unwin.

Tullock, G., (1975) *The Vote Motive*, London, Institute of Economic Affairs.

Utley, T. E. (1975) *The Lessons of Ulster*, London, Dent.

Waldegrave, N. (1978) *The Binding of Leviathan*, London, Hamish Hamilton.

Walker, A. (ed.) (1982) *Public Expenditure and Social Policy*, London, Heinemann.

Wass, Sir D. (1984) 'Government and the Governed', The Reith Lecturer.

Westergaard, J. (1970) 'The Rediscovery of the Cash Nexus', *Socialist Register*.

Whiteley, P. (1982) 'The Decline of Labour's Local Party Membership and Electoral Base, 1945–79', in Kavanagh, D. *The Politics of the Labour Party*, London, Allen & Unwin.

Whiteley, P. and Gordon, I. (1980) 'Middle Class, Militant and Male', in *New Statesman*, 6 January.

Williams, S. (1980) *Politics is for People*, Harmondsworth, Penguin.

Young, Hugo (1976) *The Crossman Affair*, London, Hamilton/Cape.

Index